SOUTH PASADENA
A CENTENNIAL HISTORY

SOUTH
PASADENA

A
CENTENNIAL
HISTORY

BY JANE APOSTOL

SOUTH PASADENA PUBLIC LIBRARY

1888-1988

FOREWORD

THE HISTORY OF SOUTHERN CALIFORNIA has seen many a small community devoured by a large tax-hungry neighbor. One sturdy survivor is the town whose first century is chronicled in this history. Situated dangerously between Los Angeles and Pasadena, the three and a half square miles of South Pasadena (which some wish had been named San Pasqual from the original rancho) has managed to maintain its territorial integrity.

How did this happen? Because of the energy, faith and devotion of its citizens through their own government, plus the efforts of ad hoc groups which rallied to threats by selfish interests from within and without. This book is a heartwarming tribute to selfless individuals from the earliest times to the present age. It is also the story of grass-roots democracy at work. There has never been a time when communal living did not cause controversy. South Pasadena is no exception. Whether over saloons or freeways or relocation of the civic center, disagreement sometimes reached passionate heights until brought down by reasoned debate and compromise.

My reading of the manuscript was on the intellectual level of admiration for a story well organized and engagingly told, and also on another level of nostalgia for that faraway time from 1910 to 1930 when my brothers and I and our parents lived successively on Bank Street, Camden Court, Marengo Avenue, and Bonita Drive. By the end of those residences only my mother, one brother and I were left. And now only I.

From this history I learned that the street of our third residence was named for the Rancho Marengo of Joseph Lancaster Brent, until 1856 a part of the old Rancho San Pasqual. By chance I was the editor a few years ago of a memoir of General Brent's late grandson and my friend, Joseph Duncan Kenner Brent. Thus do our lives pass amidst unseen connections, revealed eventually by historical research such as that pursued by this book's author.

The sense of early times permeates her pages. The details are also present, very few of which I can add to as when I note the town's first "speed cops," Archie Cooper and Frank Higgins, also rode Indian cycles, or that the schools were closed the day Mary Pickford came to town on location in *Pollyanna*. Absent however is any account of the Halloween night when the Pacific Electric tracks on Fair Oaks were soaped so that the Pasadena Short Line could not make it up and over the hill. Residents of later times too will have their memories stirred by the historian who has delved deeply into the local archives.

Those twenty years on the sunny slope of the Raymond Hill, between the dove-haunted Monterey Hills and the green groves of what became San Marino, were idyllic. Loving parents, friends (a few of whom I still have), tolerant teachers, and one yea-saying librarian were lasting influences in my life. And of them all, dear old Nellie Keith, the city's librarian from 1895 to 1930, was the one who unknowingly determined my ultimate course.

In that time the little town lived happily hemmed in by the bigger cities, it alone possessing the qualities of both town and country. The worst problems lay to the north and south where expansion and growth brought their troubles with them. Our town inevitably felt the threat of those contiguous areas. Resistance and adaptation were the reasons for survival. Today South Pasadena exists as a classic model of what the good life in a small city can be.

LAWRENCE CLARK POWELL
Tucson, Arizona

CONTENTS

ILLUSTRATIONS

South Pasadena photographer T. D. Keith took this picture of the city in 1893. The large building to the north is the Raymond Hotel, and the mansion near the bottom of the photograph is Wynyate. Near the center of the picture (from left to right) are the Opera House Building, South Pasadena Hotel, Center Street School, and Methodist Church. The north-south street farthest to the right is present-day Fremont Avenue. *Courtesy of Huntington Library.*

PREFACE

It seems most appropriate that the South Pasadena Public Library should publish a centennial history of the city. The library can trace its roots back more than a hundred years—to 1886, when local bibliophiles organized a Social and Literary Society. Many of the members were also active in the South Pasadena Lyceum, founded in 1889 to open a free reading room and circulating library. Devoted volunteers kept the reading room in operation until 1895, when the South Pasadena City Council established a tax-supported public library.

Recent years have seen an upsurge of interest in local history. Long aware of the need for a book on South Pasadena, the library decided to publish a history of the city as its contribution to the 1988 centennial. Much of the research for the book was done at the South Pasadena library, whose special resources include photographic archives, city directories dating back to 1893, and microfilm copies of local newspapers published from 1893 to the present.

I extend warm thanks to City Librarian Jean Jones and to her predecessor, Mary Helen Wayne, for their enthusiastic support and valuable assistance. I also wish to thank library archivist Amy Kinard and her fellow librarians, Edythe Goodwin, Louise Mills, and Sherry Stauffer, who have been unfailingly helpful. My thanks go also to staff members Susi Shank Bechguenturian, Kathy Fielding, Laura Reeves, and Sumi Shibata for their many courtesies.

Research for the book was also carried on at the Huntington Library in San Marino. It was a privilege to work with its superb collection and to consult its staff. I owe thanks in particular to Alan Jutzi, Brita Mack, and Susan Naulty of the Rare Books Department, and to Virginia Rust of the Manuscripts Department.

Many people in the community have shared with me their expert knowledge of South Pasadena. City Clerk Ruby Kerr, Fire Chief Gene E. Murry, Police Chief William Reese, and Water Operations Foreman Ronald E. Stowe kindly answered questions related to their special fields. Betty Cowan, Robert Edgar, Jim Greulich, Mary Ida Phair, Vicki Steinmeyer, and Granville Thurman graciously provided information about the public schools.

I learned much about the early history of South Pasadena from talking with Myrtle Coots, John Dewar, Priscilla Roth Feigen, Walter and Natalie Garmshausen, Edward F. Roth, and Neva Smith. I profited also from conversations with Lois Boardman, Jane Brewer, Mary Bryce, Shirley Clark, Ted Colliau, Ricki DeKramer, Ysabel Fetterman, Jack Gillette, Barbara Greer, Christy Hedges, Laura Hudson, Janet Irish, Marion Marsh, Eunice Miyatake, Helen Otake, June Rogers, Whitney Smith, and Frank and Margaret Stoney. I am grateful to them all.

Edwin H. Carpenter, Dorothy Cohen, and Jane Dietrich read the original manuscript and helped improve it with their editorial advice. I deeply appreciate their many valuable suggestions.

Writing (and rewriting) the text was made much easier because Don Delson unlocked for me the mysteries of the word processor. His help is gratefully acknowledged.

Vance Gerry designed the dust jacket, Miriam Campbell prepared several of the maps that illustrate the text, and Sara Swan helped with artwork. My warm thanks to all three, and also to Don Morgan of Type Works and to Carl Niemack of Typecraft, friends of good printing.

City Manager John Bernardi and the South Pasadena City Council approved a generous loan to the library to help with publication costs. The Friends of the South Pasadena Public Library granted funds to copy historic photographs for the book. I am pleased to acknowledge the help advanced by the city and by the Friends.

I greatly appreciate the efforts of the Centennial Book Committee, and I thank its dedicated members: Tom Apostol, Karyn Ard, Harold and Dorothy Bauer, Gene Burrill, Dick Galbraith, Constantine Gertmenian, Jean Jones, Ben Lizardi, Ted Shaw, Anne Snyder, Mrs. Milton H. Sperling, Bob Stauffer, Philip and Sally Swan, Margaret Wallace, Mary Helen Wayne, and Gerry Williams.

Special thanks go to two longtime friends of the South Pasadena Public Library: Lawrence Clark Powell, who wrote the foreword, and Ward Ritchie, who designed the book.

Above all, I express heartfelt thanks to my husband for the myriad ways in which he helped. To paraphrase an immortal bard, I dedicate this book to Tom, with he knows what and he knows why.

JANE APOSTOL

Part I

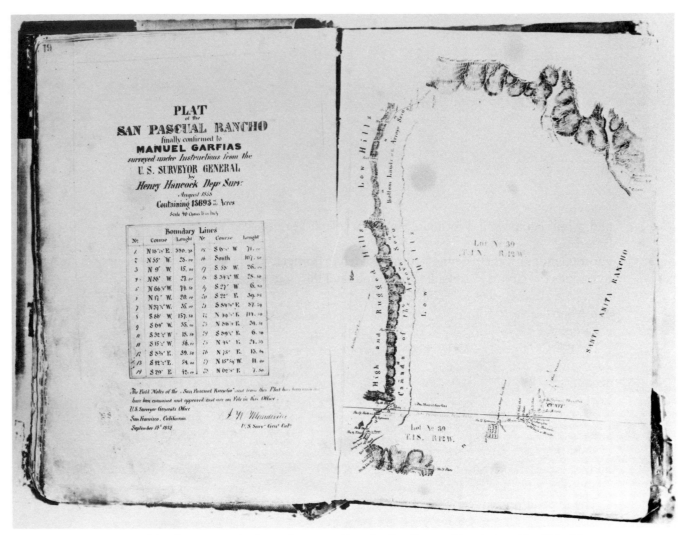

Manuel Garfias received a formal grant to Rancho San Pasqual in 1843 and had his title confirmed by a United States patent in 1863. Parts of modern-day Altadena, Pasadena, South Pasadena, and San Marino lie within the boundaries of Rancho San Pasqual. *Courtesy of Huntington Library.*

I

PASTORAL PRELUDE: 1769-1873

I am just agonizing to buy the whole thing.

DANIEL M. BERRY

SMALL, PROUD, AND INDEPENDENT, the city of South Pasadena has battled for a hundred years to preserve its status as a distinct—and distinctive—community. Less than three and a half square miles in area, South Pasadena lies between the far larger city of Pasadena, of which it was once a part, and the metropolis of Los Angeles. Three natural landmarks help define South Pasadena's borders. Raymond Hill, to the north, overlooks the city of Pasadena. The Monterey Hills, in the southwest, straddle South Pasadena's border with Los Angeles. The dry watercourse of the Arroyo Seco, arising in the San Gabriel Mountains and extending to the Los Angeles River, traces the western boundary of the city.

Described almost a century ago as "a winding, romantic strip of wild-wood," the Arroyo Seco links the city of today with the early history of the area. The first written accounts of the Arroyo go back to 1769, when the colonizing expedition of Gaspar de Portolá crossed what we know as the San Gabriel Valley. Several members of the company kept diaries that noted the hospitality of the Indians and the beauty of the landscape. The writers described wooded canyons, pleasant streams, and a profusion of wild grapes, blackberries, and roses. They also described a series of jolting earthquakes experienced during a week-long march from the Santa Ana River—Rio de los Temblores—to the vicinity of Los Angeles.

The expedition was marching north from San Diego to establish a presidio and mission on the Bay of Monterey, which Sebastian Vizcaíno had discovered in 1602. Portolá reached the San Gabriel River on July 30, 1769, and the next day camped near the place where Mission San Gabriel Arcángel was founded two years later. On August 1 the men dined on antelope and celebrated the holy day of Nuestra Señora de los Angeles de Porciúncula. On August 2 they saw the spacious watercourse of the Arroyo Seco, dry at that time of year but showing evidence that it overflowed its banks in the rainy season. The men camped by a beautiful tree-lined river they called the Porciúncula—and which we call the Los Angeles—and were welcomed by Indians from Yangna, a little village located in the area where Los Angeles City Hall stands today. Franciscan missionary Juan Crespí took note of the delightful setting, the fertile land, and other advantages for a future settlement. Twelve years later, the pueblo of Los Angeles was founded next to the brush huts of Yangna.

Although Portolá reached Monterey on his first expedition, he did not recognize it as the harbor described by Vizcaíno more than a century and a half earlier. Continuing northward, the company discovered the giant redwoods and San Francisco Bay before turning back to San Diego. Hiram A. Reid, Pasadena's pioneer historian, believed that

South Pasadena newspaperman George W. Glover stands by the great Cathedral Oak, which grew on the banks of the Arroyo Seco until 1952. A simple monument now marks the site. *Courtesy of Huntington Library.*

the return journey brought the expedition across the Arroyo Seco at flood tide and over land that is now South Pasadena. Directions and distances noted in the diaries, however, suggest it was the Los Angeles River, rather than the Arroyo, which the expedition crossed.

In April 1770 Portolá again marched to Monterey. Local tradition holds that he went through South Pasadena and worshipped under a great oak on the east bank of the Arroyo. The tree survived until 1952 and then was taken down. Marking its site is the Cathedral Oak Monument, on Arroyo Drive just south of Hermosa Street. There is no clear evidence that Portolá ever saw the Cathedral Oak, but he did travel across the San Gabriel Valley on three occasions. The name of South Pasadena's Monterey Road recalls the Sacred Expedition of Portolá and the founding of Mission San Carlos Borromeo in Monterey in 1770.

Mission San Gabriel Arcángel, fourth in the chain of missions, was founded on September 8, 1771. The Indians falling under its jurisdiction became known as Gabrielinos. They were a Shoshonean-speaking people, in the same linguistic family as the Hopis of Arizona and the Comanches of the Great Plains. Anthropologist A. L. Kroeber described the Gabrielinos as the wealthiest and most thoughtful Shoshoneans in California, with much influence on other tribes. He estimated the Gabrielinos numbered about five thousand in 1770. A few hundred of their descendants live in Los Angeles County today.

Portolá encountered Gabrielinos on the coastal plains extending from present-day El Toro to the vicinity of Topanga, whose Indian name was Topangna: the place where mountains run out into the sea. The names of Tujunga, Cahuenga, and Cucamonga also recall ancient Gabrielino villages.

In the Pasadena area, Gabrielinos lived on the banks of the Arroyo, where springs flowed year round, and alongside a brook just east of Raymond Hill. The village of Sonangna flourished where San Marino High School is today, and Aleupkingna was located somewhere on the present site of the Los Angeles State and County Arboretum in Arcadia. These and other local settlements took advantage of a great underground reservoir whose waters were held in check by the Raymond dike, or fault line, curving from the Arroyo Seco to Monrovia.

Much of our knowledge about the Gabrielinos comes from a series of letters published in the *Los Angeles Star* in 1852. Written by Scottish settler Hugo Reid of Rancho Santa Anita, whose wife Victoria was an Indian, they describe the Gabrielino way of life and its disappearance under mission rule.

With the coming of the Spanish, Gabrielinos were displaced from their native villages and gathered into the mission community. The land where they had hunted game and gathered acorns, nuts, and berries now was used by the mission for orchards and vineyards and for pasturing sheep and cattle. The Indians had to learn a new religion and new skills aimed at making them good Christian subjects of the king of Spain. "Thus there was destroyed a balanced and integrated scheme of living," Bernice Eastman Johnston says in her sympathetic book *California's Gabrielino Indians*, "but no white man of the time, and few of any other era, would have considered this as worthy of a moment's regret."

Gabrielinos labored at some fifty mission enterprises, such as baking bread, making

5

Four generations of Gabrielino Indians posed with South Pasadenan Horatio Nelson Rust at San Gabriel in 1883. The implements and baskets shown here were part of Rust's personal collection. *Courtesy of Huntington Library.*

bricks, tanning leather, and tending vineyards. They herded sheep along the Arroyo Seco and worked as lime burners in pits on the Arroyo. They also helped build and operate El Molino Viejo, California's first water-powered grist mill, now a San Marino landmark.

Spain planned to secularize the missions as soon as they had adequately prepared the Indians for pueblo life. With secularization, the missions would become ordinary parish churches, their lands released for other uses, and the Indians freed from supervision. Secularization finally occurred in 1834, by which time Mexico had won independence from Spain, and California was a Mexican province. Governor José Figueroa issued a proclamation ordering all the missions secularized between 1834 and 1836. Half the mission lands were to be distributed among the Indians, and the remaining property was to be placed in the care of lay administrators. Despite Figueroa's good intentions, few Indians received shares of land, and fewer still retained them. Most of the property once controlled by the missions was given away in huge land grants on which ranchos were established.

One Gabrielino who did receive mission land was Bartholomea of Comicrangna, the mission-educated woman better known as Victoria Reid. She brought her husband an impressive dowry—La Huerta de Cuati, 128 acres in what is now San Marino. Benjamin D. Wilson bought the property in 1854 and made it the nucleus of his Lake Vineyard Ranch. Both lake and vineyard are gone now, and Lacy Park covers the old lake bed.

West of Cuati and the adjoining Rancho Santa Anita was a tract of about fourteen thousand acres extending north to the San Gabriel Mountains, west to the Arroyo Seco, and south to the Monterey Hills. Most of Altadena, a large part of Pasadena, and portions of South Pasadena and San Marino lie within the boundaries of the tract, which the mission fathers called El Rincón de San Pascual. Later settlers changed the original Spanish name—and spelling—to Rancho San Pasqual.

In 1833, a month before Mexico decreed secularization and a full year before it became effective, Juan Mariné petitioned the governor for Rancho San Pasqual. Mariné was a native of Spain, a retired lieutenant of artillery, and a resident at Mission San Gabriel. He recently had married Doña Eulalia Pérez de Guillén, a devoted worker at the mission and the patron, friend, and teacher of Victoria Reid. Mariné received the grant to Rancho San Pasqual in 1835 but apparently did not build a house there or cultivate the land, as required by Mexican law to retain legal title. Mariné's heirs sold their interest in the ranch, one son bartering his rights for six horses and ten head of cattle. José Pérez (a relative of Doña Eulalia) and Enrique Sepúlveda next filed claim to the ranch and received a grant in September 1840. Both men built adobes on the east bank of the Arroyo, the first houses since Gabrielino days to be built in what is now South Pasadena.

Pérez died in 1841, Sepúlveda lost interest in the ranch and moved to Monterey, and Rancho San Pasqual was again available to claimants. The next owner was Manuel Garfias, a lieutenant colonel in the Mexican cavalry. He was granted the property on November 28, 1843, but did not settle there at once. He and his bride, the socially prominent Luisa Avila, made their first home in Los Angeles. Absorbed with town life, and then with the affairs of war, Garfias left the management of his new rancho to his

7

The buildings of Mission San Gabriel Arcángel date back to 1775, when the mission was moved to its present site. This photograph was taken around 1880. *Courtesy of Huntington Library*.

Adobe Flores, the oldest house in South Pasadena, served as temporary headquarters for the Mexican army in 1847. T. D. Keith photographed the adobe around 1890. *Courtesy of Huntington Library*.

capable mother-in-law, Doña Encarnación Sepúlveda de Avila, who stocked the property with horses and cattle and moved her foreman and vaqueros into the two adobes. Historian Reid calls Doña Encarnación the real founder of Rancho San Pasqual as a commercial enterprise.

The oldest house in South Pasadena is the adobe on Foothill Street, on the south slope of Raymond Hill. Early writers called it the Pérez adobe, but historians now believe it was built by Manuel Garfias some time between 1843 and 1846. A later owner, Clara Eliot Noyes, named the house El Adobe Flores, a reminder that for one night it served as headquarters for the Mexican general José María Flores.

In January 1847 Flores and his Californios skirmished with United States detachments outside Los Angeles, then withdrew to a campsite on Raymond Hill. On the evening of January 9, Flores met in the Raymond Hill adobe with Garfias, Andrés Pico, and other trusted advisors to draw up their plan of surrender to the United States. Four days later the opposing commanders, Andrés Pico and John Charles Frémont, signed the Treaty of Cahuenga, which ended the war between United States and Mexican forces in California.

After the war Garfias became a United States citizen and played a role in local politics. He served a term on the Los Angeles city council and was the first treasurer of the county. In 1852 Garfias built an impressive house on Rancho San Pasqual, not far from the Cathedral Oak and the spring in the Arroyo Seco that still bears his name. Benjamin S. Eaton, who lived in the Garfias house from December 1858 until the following July, described it as one of the finest country homes in Southern California. "It was a one-and-a-half story adobe building," he wrote, "with walls two feet thick, all nicely plastered inside and out, and had an ample corridor extending all around. It had board floors, and boasted of green blinds—a rare thing in those days." The rafters were cut from sycamore wood hauled from the west side of the Arroyo. In 1877 Eaton used some of the heavy timbers from the crumbling adobe for Hillcrest, the house he was building on Buena Vista Street in South Pasadena.

Garfias did not prosper as a cattle rancher, and in 1858 he borrowed $8,000 from Dr. John S. Griffin to help meet expenses. Unable to pay his debt at the end of the year, he decided to sacrifice the ranch. On January 15, 1859, he deeded the property to Benjamin D. Wilson, who was Griffin's business partner. Garfias spent the rest of his life in Mexico and served for a time as United States consul in Tepic and San Blas. His sons—Manuel E. Garfias, who became a general in the Mexican army, and Mariano José Garfias, who became a lawyer in Mexico City—were the first non-Indian children born in what is now South Pasadena.

In 1859 Griffin bought an undivided half-interest in Rancho San Pasqual, and over the next decade he and Wilson sold off more than half its acreage. The earliest sale in what is now South Pasadena was to attorney Joseph Lancaster Brent, who purchased about eight hundred acres from Wilson in 1859—most of the land from Rancho San Pasqual and the rest from an adjoining ranch. At the outbreak of the Civil War, Brent left California and joined the Confederate army, attaining the rank of brigadier general. He had named his ranch and its prominent hill Marengo to commemorate the famous battle between Napoleon and the Austrians in 1800. There is still a Marengo Avenue in South Pasadena—and a Brent Avenue as well—but the hill has been known

9

Manuel Garfias owned Rancho San Pasqual from 1843 until 1859, when he deeded the ranch to Benjamin D. Wilson. *Courtesy of California Historical Society/Ticor Title Insurance (Los Angeles).*

Daniel M. Berry recommended in 1873 that the California Colony of Indiana buy a portion of Rancho San Pasqual. "The Scenery is worth $10 per acre," he wrote back to Indiana, "and the climate is unsurpassed." *Courtesy of Huntington Library.*

as Raymond Hill since 1886, when Walter Raymond built a hotel there.

In 1870 David M. Raab, a German emigrant who had farmed for Wilson, bought about sixty acres (at two dollars an acre) west of the Marengo Ranch. The parcel lay within an area now bordered by Fremont and Meridian avenues and Buena Vista and Mission streets. Raab's Oak Hill Dairy was the first business in South Pasadena, and one of the first dairies in the country to use pasteurization.

On September 12, 1873, a visitor from Indiana looked at Rancho San Pasqual and wrote home the next day, "I am just agonizing to buy the whole thing but can't do it." The visitor was Daniel M. Berry, who was seeking land for the California Colony of Indiana. His enthusiasm for Rancho San Pasqual led to the founding of Pasadena four months later.

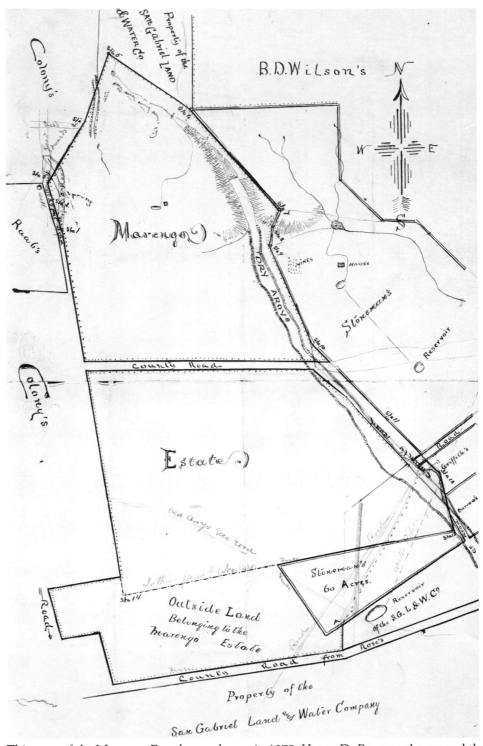

This map of the Marengo Ranch was drawn in 1875. Henry D. Bacon, who owned the property then, used it for raising stock and for growing citrus, grapes, and walnuts. *Courtesy of Huntington Library.*

CHRONOLOGY

1200

Possibly around 500 BC, ancestors of the Gabrielinos filter into California. By 1200 Gabrielino culture has taken the form noted by the Spanish during their explorations.

1769

Gaspar de Portolá leads an overland expedition from San Diego to Monterey.

Title to all land in California is vested in the King of Spain.

1771

Mission San Gabriel Arcángel is founded on September 8.

1816

Father José María de Zalvidea designs El Molino Viejo, which is built with Gabrielino labor.

1822

California becomes Mexican territory.

1834

Governor José Figueroa issues a proclamation on August 9 secularizing the missions.

1835

Governor Figueroa grants Rancho San Pasqual to Juan Mariné.

1840

Governor Juan Bautista Alvarado grants Rancho San Pasqual to José Pérez and Enrique Sepúlveda.

1843

Governor Manuel Micheltorena grants Rancho San Pasqual to Manuel Garfias on November 28.

1848

California is ceded to the United States by the Treaty of Guadalupe Hidalgo, signed on February 2.

1850

California joins the Union on September 9 and becomes the thirty-first state.

1851

Congress creates the Board of Land Commissioners to investigate private land titles in California.

In 1920 the Oneonta Park Chapter of the DAR placed a historic marker on the Adobe Flores. Pat Kelley and Jane Plumb, costumed as Spanish children, joined DAR members for the ceremony. *Courtesy of Oneonta Park Chapter, Daughters of the American Revolution.*

1852

The *Los Angeles Star* publishes Hugo Reid's "Letters on the Los Angeles County Indians."

1853

Manuel E. Garfias is the first non-Indian child born in what is now South Pasadena.

1854

Benjamin D. Wilson purchases La Huerta de Cuati.

On April 25 the United States Board of Land Commissioners confirms the Garfias claim to Rancho San Pasqual.

1859

Garfias deeds Rancho San Pasqual to Benjamin D. Wilson on January 15. Dr. John S. Griffin buys an undivided half-interest in the ranch on May 4.

Joseph Lancaster Brent buys a tract and names it the Marengo Ranch.

1863

A United States patent, issued on April 3, confirms the Garfias title to Rancho San Pasqual.

1870

David M. Raab buys a tract on which he establishes the Oak Hill Dairy, the first business in South Pasadena.

1873

Daniel Berry, agent for the California Colony of Indiana, visits Rancho San Pasqual.

T. D. Keith photographed Center Street School before the bell was placed in the tower in 1890. *Courtesy of Huntington Library.*

THE FOUNDING DECADES: 1873-1899

A church or school on every hill
And NO SALOON IN THE VALLEY.

HIRAM A. REID

"IN MAY 1873," wrote Hoosier doctor Thomas B. Elliott, "a few warm blooded and adventurous persons who could not endure the frigid cold of northern winters gathered at Indianapolis, Indiana, and formed a society for removal to some more equable climate." After considering Texas, Florida, and Louisiana, the group "unanimously resolved that Southern California was the spot uniting the blessings of the tropics without their heat, malaria or enervating influences." Elliott's brother-in-law, Daniel Berry, came West with orders to find fifty thousand acres of semitropical fruitland for members of the new California Colony of Indiana.

Immediately after his arrival in Los Angeles, Berry began looking for property that was "well timbered, well watered, and adapted for the culture of citrus fruit." The search took him to Rancho Santa Anita (too expensive), San Fernando (too little water), and Anaheim (too sandy and full of fleas). He then visited Rancho San Pasqual, which filled him with delight. His guide was Benjamin S. Eaton, brother-in-law of Dr. Griffin and owner of the Fair Oaks Ranch, which lay within the old Rancho San Pasqual boundaries. Eaton showed Berry the acreage Dr. Griffin hoped to sell and explained how it could be irrigated with spring waters from the Arroyo. He then showed off Fair Oaks, whose citrus trees and sixty thousand grapevines affirmed the productivity of the land.

Berry sent Elliott an exuberant report on Rancho San Pasqual. "The wood is plenty," he said, "the water delicious and cool, leaping out of the rocks on the side in little cascades. . . . Have promised to take two hundred acres for you and me. Wish we could take more. . . . It is right in line with all the best orange orchards and vineyards here and just as good, *with more water*." In a happy aside he added, "And then the climate and scenery are heavenly. I slept over there last night in the clear transpicuous air and awoke to the music of a thousand linnets and blackbirds in the evergreen oaks."

On September 18, 1873—less than a week after Berry wrote to Elliott— the New York investment firm of Jay Cooke and Company failed, bringing on the panic of 1873. Many Indianans now found it difficult to sell their homes and come West. Berry therefore organized a new buying syndicate with a remnant of the old Indiana Colony plus associates he had met in California. Representatives of the new group met in Los Angeles on November 11, 1873, and formed the San Gabriel Orange Grove Association. "Judge Eaton acts as President, and is just the man for it," Berry told Elliott. "He

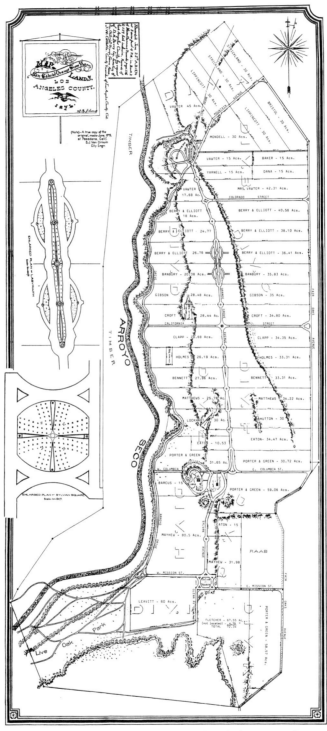

The San Gabriel Orange Grove Association subdivided a tract of 1,500 acres in 1874. Calvin Fletcher owned the parcels labeled "Mayhew." *Map redrawn by Miriam Campbell from a copy of the 1874 original.*

has a flourishing place on a former part of this ranch and will superintend free the water works, of which he knows more than any man I have seen." An irrigation ditch built for Wilson by Eaton in 1867 was the first attempt to bring water from Devil's Gate, in the Arroyo Seco, to Rancho San Pasqual.

Griffin was eager to sell his portion of the ranch, but first he and Wilson had to agree what that portion was and where it lay. After acrimonious debate, Griffin took about four thousand acres at the western boundary. On December 26, 1873, he deeded the land to Thomas F. Croft, vice-president of the San Gabriel Orange Grove Association, for a down payment of $6,250 on the purchase price of $25,000. Three days later, Croft transferred title to the association.

Subdividing began at once on the fifteen hundred acres that were nearest the water supply: from the Arroyo Seco east to Fair Oaks Avenue (renamed Fremont Avenue in South Pasadena), and from the vicinity of Monterey Road to about one mile north of Colorado Street (now Colorado Boulevard). A committee of three directed the first work on the new development. A. O. Porter served as chairman, Eaton supervised construction of waterworks, and Calvin Fletcher took charge of subdividing. He planned the tract so every stockholder would be assured of a good location and good land. Fletcher also took pains to preserve the beauty of the landscape. When he laid out Orange Grove Avenue, he left two great oak trees standing in the middle of the roadway to keep them safe "from private cupidity or stupidity."

On the morning of January 27, 1874, the colonists met on Orange Grove Avenue to choose the land they wanted. It was a lovely day, according to Eaton. The hills were green, and the earth was carpeted with flowers. After a picnic lunch, the people gathered on nearby Reservoir Hill. Daniel Berry called the roll, and the twenty-seven stockholders, or their proxies, indicated which lots they preferred. The committee members offered to choose last and to let those with the fewest number of shares go first. "In about twenty minutes the whole business was settled without a clash," Eaton reported, "and every man had secured *just what he wanted*. Everybody seemed happy and a general love feast ensued."

Calvin Fletcher invested in 180 acres south of Columbia Street, but he returned to Indiana to live. Andrew O. Porter, Perry M. Green, William J. Barcus, Ward Leavitt, and Benjamin S. Eaton also bought at the southern end of the colony, and all five built homes in what is now South Pasadena.

Within a few weeks after the colonists chose their land, Eaton was supervising work on an up-to-date water system. Instead of relying on the usual *zanja* or open ditch to bring in water, he had three miles of pipe laid from Devil's Gate in the Arroyo to a reservoir near the present intersection of Walnut Street and Orange Grove Avenue in Pasadena. Another pipeline, running along Orange Grove, carried water to the southern part of the colony.

For over a year the new community had no name. "Now what name can suggest beauty, fertility, [and] salubrity?" Berry wrote to Elliott. "Some long Indian word probably." Dr. Elliott asked a friend who had been a missionary to the Indians if he knew "some Indian word of pleasant sound which would serve as an appropriate and significant name for the new settlement." Elliott also mentioned a phrase used by Manuel Garfias to describe the location of his ranch house: *la llave del rancho*, the key

19

Andrew O. Porter, one of the directors of the San Gabriel Orange Grove Association, built just south of Columbia Street in 1875. The Porter house is a Cultural Heritage Landmark. *Courtesy of Bob's Photo Center.*

In 1882 George Glover, Sr., and his wife Mary Jane opened the Hermosa Vista Hotel, in which South Pasadena's first post office was located. A mailbox and a sign reading Hermosa Post Office can be seen on the verandah. *Courtesy of Security Pacific National Bank Photograph Collection/Los Angeles Public Library.*

of the ranch. Elliott's friend replied with four Indian phrases that he translated as: crown of the valley, key of the valley, peak of the valley, and hill of the valley. All incorporated a Chippewa word transcribed as Pâ-sâ-de-ná. The stockholders met on April 22, 1875. Rejecting Indianola, Granada, and San Pasqual as names for their town, they voted seventeen to four in favor of Pasadena.

By 1876 about forty families lived in Pasadena. They had a literary society, a hand-written newspaper (*The Reservoir*), and a scholar who carried the mail from Pasadena to Los Angeles. The mail carrier was Donald M. Graham, a lawyer who knew Greek, Latin, and Hebrew, and who became the first mayor of South Pasadena.

"Doctors, lawyers, mechanics, Colonels and Majors are plentiful," reported one Pasadena settler, "but they can all don blue overalls and turn the soil for their fruit trees as if 'to the manner born.' The largest orange orchard yet set out here has four hundred trees; every resident has an orchard of semi-tropical fruits often numbering ten or twelve varieties."

Unimproved land, with water, was selling for $75 to $150 an acre. The San Gabriel Orange Grove Association had only a few lots still for sale, but B. D. Wilson owned the large tract adjoining Pasadena on the east. After forming the Lake Vineyard Land and Water Association, he subdivided twenty-five hundred acres extending from Fair Oaks Avenue to a little beyond Wilson Avenue. A business center quickly developed in the vicinity of Fair Oaks and Colorado Street, with a post office, general store, butcher shop, and smithy. The colony's first schoolhouse was moved to the same area and placed on a five-acre lot donated by Wilson.

The schoolhouse originally stood on Orange Grove Avenue, just below California Street, by one of the great oak trees Fletcher had saved. It was a convenient location for colonists who had begun thinking of themselves as South Pasadenans. They were therefore annoyed to have the school moved several miles to the north. Reacting with spirit, they petitioned for a school district of their own. The County Board of Supervisors granted the request, and on March 5, 1878, classes began in Clinton B. Ripley's house on Columbia Hill, at the southwest corner of Columbia Street and Orange Grove Avenue.

South Pasadenans also petitioned for their own post office. On November 28, 1882, the Hermosa office was established in the Hermosa Vista, South Pasadena's first hotel, with Frank M. Glover as postmaster. "The name 'Hermosa' for their post office proved unsatisfactory to the people of that vicinity," according to Hiram Reid, "because it lost to them the prestige of the name 'Pasadena.' " In 1884 the post office changed its name to South Pasadena. By that time the post office building was at Columbia Street and Sylvan Avenue—a name later changed to Orange Grove Avenue, like its Pasadena counterpart.

In 1884 Pasadena began working to incorporate, but most South Pasadenans preferred to stay out of any city that was formed. As businessman O. R. Dougherty put it, "All we want is to be let alone. [We] have a post office, a school, and want to govern them ourselves, and don't want any outside interference." The County Board of Supervisors took such protests into consideration when drawing boundaries for the proposed new city. On June 19, 1886, Pasadena officially incorporated, with Columbia Street dividing it from South Pasadena.

Horatio Nelson Rust, who owned one of the first nurseries in South Pasadena, built this house in 1882, at what is now the southwest corner of Fremont Avenue and Monterey Road. *Courtesy of Priscilla Roth Feigen and Edward F. Roth.*

This house was built at Columbia Street and Orange Grove Avenue during the boom of the eighties. Thaddeus S. C. Lowe lived here from 1903 to 1908. G. A. Gertmenian bought the house in 1918 and was photographed with his son Harold a few years later. *Courtesy of Constantine Gertmenian.*

BRING THIS CATALOGUE TO THE SALE.

The Most Picturesque Spot in the County.

Only 20 Minutes' Ride from Los Angeles.

GRAND PEREMPTORY

CREDIT SALE AT AUCTION

OF THE

LINCOLN PARK TRACT,

PASADENA,

By BEN E. WARD,

Real Estate and General Auctioneer,

OFFICE: OLD CHIEF OF POLICE OFFICE, 31 N. SPRING ST., LOS ANGELES.

—o‡o—

Don't Forget the Day and Date—

SATURDAY, APRIL 24th, 1886.

TITLE PERFECT—Copy of Certificate with Every Lot.

THE ABOVE IS A SPECIMEN OF THE OAKS WITH WHICH THE PARK IS COVERED.

The Pasadena Brass Band will furnish the **music.**

A Fine Lunch will be served under the grand old oaks, Free of charge.

Every lot to be sold without reserve. Stop paying rent, buy a lot and become your own landlord.

TERMS OF SALE—$25 on fall of the hammer; half cash; balance on or before one year, at 10 per cent. per annum.

FOR CATALOGUES and further information, call on BEN E. WARD, the Auctioneer, 31 N. Spring Street, L. A.; WARD BROS., Pasadena; GEO. WILSON, on the tract; PIERCE BROS., East Los Angeles.

FINE SPRING WATER WITH EVERY LOT.

Pasadena and South Pasadena were still one community at the time of this auction of land along the Arroyo Seco. *Courtesy of Huntington Library.*

The Raymond opened in South Pasadena in 1886. "It is not necessary that one should say the Raymond *Hotel*," said a contemporary guide book. "There is but one Notre Dame, but one Acropolis, but one Colossus, and so there is but one 'Raymond' when South California is mentioned." *Courtesy of Huntington Library.*

Like most towns in the San Gabriel Valley, South Pasadena was covered with orchards and vineyards that were beginning to yield to subdivisions. In the spring of 1885, O. R. Dougherty opened the first real estate office in town and offered lots for sale along Meridian Avenue. His South Pasadena Land Office was strategically located at Mission Street and Sylvan Avenue, on the stage route between Los Angeles and Pasadena. Donald M. Graham drove the first Pasadena stage—a second-hand buggy he called "The Great Moral Hack," explaining that, unlike most stage drivers, he was not profane.

There were two general routes between Los Angeles and South Pasadena. One went through the Arroyo and was impassable in the rainy season. The other route, known as the adobe road and roughly parallel to the present Huntington Drive, was soft, muddy, and full of ruts in the winter. Travelers rejoiced when the Los Angeles and San Gabriel Valley Railroad began passenger service on September 16, 1885. South Pasadena was now linked by rail to Pasadena and Los Angeles, and a business district grew around the new depot at Meridian Avenue and Center Street.

In 1885 a school opened on Center Street, in the developing downtown area. (Both street and school were renamed El Centro in 1908 to avoid confusion with a Center Street in Pasadena.) George W. Wilson, the first teacher at Center Street School, taught only a year before he caught "boom fever" and left to sell real estate.

Residential development flourished in South Pasadena, with "villa lots" advertised as only a twenty-minute ride from Los Angeles. The Malabar Tract, between Mission Street and Monterey Road, predicted it would become a favorite place for suburban living as it was convenient to the railroad and offered "the advantages of a city with the healthfulness, lovely scenery, and low taxation of a country property." Lincoln Park, a tract in the area of Monterey Road and Pasadena Avenue, claimed a dual advantage: proximity to the railroad and to the proposed Grand Boulevard along the Arroyo Seco from East Los Angeles to Pasadena. It advertised sublime views and a health-giving atmosphere: "No Fog! No Wind! Sunshine the Prevailing Element."

Not everyone was enchanted by the real estate boom. Writing in the *South Pasadena Bell* in 1888, editor John Sharp deplored the number of abandoned orchards and vineyards. "The prayer of our people," he said, "should be 'Good Lord, deliver us from too much boom,' and where land becomes 'too valuable to raise crops upon,' the owners, as a matter of local pride, should at least keep the land well tilled, even if for no other reason than to keep up the beauty of the landscape."

Advantages of scenery, climate, and a railroad brought South Pasadena a great tourist hotel in 1886. It was built especially for clients of Raymond & Whitcomb, a Boston travel agency offering package tours to Southern California during the winter months. On a visit to Pasadena in 1883, Walter Raymond found no luxury hotel in the area and decided to build his own. For its location he chose Bacon Hill (once called Marengo Hill, and soon to be known as Raymond Hill). This was a tract of fifty-five acres on the old Marengo Ranch, at the northeast corner of South Pasadena.

To obtain a level building site, workers had to blast thirty-four feet from the hill-top—an effort requiring a thousand kegs of black powder and a ton of dynamite. Other workers set up a brickyard on the premises. Using local clay, they fired more than a million bricks for the foundation walls and chimneys. Emmons Raymond—one

Wynyate—Welsh for vineyard—stands on a hill that once looked over grapevines and apricot and peach trees. The photograph was taken soon after the completion of Wynyate in 1887. The left-hand figure on the stairs is owner Donald M. Graham, first mayor of South Pasadena. Wynyate is a Cultural Heritage Landmark and on the National Register of Historic Places. *Courtesy of Huntington Library.*

of the forty original stockholders of the Santa Fe—came to his son's financial rescue when construction costs proved far higher than expected.

The two-hundred-room Raymond Hotel opened with a grand ball on November 17, 1886. Fifteen hundred guests attended the opening, described by one reporter as the most notable and brilliant event that had yet occurred in Southern California. Many guests arrived by train, for the Los Angeles and San Gabriel Valley Railroad skirted Raymond Hill and had a depot behind the hotel. After the Santa Fe took over the little railroad in January 1887, tour groups had direct service from the East Coast to the Raymond.

In 1886 the Santa Fe and the Southern Pacific railroads fought a bitter rate war that contributed to a land boom in Southern California. As each line undercut the other, emigrants seized the opportunity to come West at bargain rates. In 1885 the fare from Kansas City to Los Angeles was ninety dollars. By 1886 it had dropped to five dollars, and on the afternoon of March 6 it reached the record low of one dollar. Although prices rose immediately, they stayed at a reasonable level, and for about a year it cost less than twenty-five dollars to come from the Midwest to Southern California.

At the beginning of the rate war, emigrants came to California by the hundreds, and then by the thousands. Many bought land, and the price of real estate steadily increased. Finally, as the price of a ticket plummeted and word spread of fortunes to be made in real estate, emigrants and boomers stampeded to Los Angeles.

South Pasadena shared in the general ferment and prosperity. At least thirty developers filed tract maps in 1887, when the boom was at its peak, and as many as a hundred buildings went up in town. Probably the most splendid was Wynyate, the hilltop mansion of Donald M. Graham and his wife, author Margaret Collier Graham. The house is now on the National Register of Historic Places and admired as a triumph of Queen Anne architecture.

Before 1887 South Pasadena had few businesses except for two hotels on the outskirts, two general stores, and one real estate office. By the end of the year, real estate offices had multiplied, and a meat market, a barber shop, and a smithy had opened. During 1887 George Lightfoot's South Pasadena Hotel went up on Center Street, between Meridian and Diamond; and Donald M. Graham and his brother-in-law, Dr. Richard J. Mohr, let the contract for their brick Opera House Building on Center Street west of Meridian. Franklin H. Smith and John H. Jacobs built the fifty-room Hotel Marengo at the corner of Monterey Road and what is now Fremont Avenue, but the hotel burned down shortly after its grand opening.

In 1887 the Methodists dedicated the town's first church, a five-thousand-dollar building just a block away from the Center Street schoolhouse. The Nazarenes also built on Center Street, erecting a little chapel in 1897. The Presbyterians built on Columbia Street in 1888, and the Baptists built on Mission Street in 1891.

Most South Pasadenans agreed with the rousing sentiment expressed by Dr. Hiram Reid, who was a leader in the temperance movement:

"A church or school on every hill
And NO SALOON IN THE VALLEY."

When a beer garden opened at Mission Street and Sylvan Avenue, a delegation begged the owner to use the property "for a good and legitimate purpose," but he

27

The Graham & Mohr Opera House Building was built in 1888 and razed in 1939. The official bench mark for the city in 1889 (657.86 feet above sea level) was established at the top of the stone coping under the Opera House windows. *Photograph by H. J. Kenny; courtesy of Huntington Library.*

The Marengo Hotel had a grand opening in 1888 but burned down soon afterwards. *Courtesy of Huntington Library.*

South Pasadena's first downtown hotel, built in 1887 at Center Street and Meridian Avenue, had hot and cold running water, two bathrooms, and an elevator. *Courtesy of Huntington Library.*

ignored the request. Matters worsened in 1887 when saloons were forced out of Pasadena by that city's antisaloon ordinance, and the establishments relocated south of Columbia Street. Within a few months, according to Reid, South Pasadenans "found they must either incorporate so as to have police control over their territory, or else be blotched and cursed at every eligible corner by the diabolical traffic. And thus they were compelled by sheer necessity for self-protection to incur the expense and trouble of forming a city corporation."

At the election held on February 25, 1888, eighty-five people voted for incorporation, twenty-five against it. The city boundaries (attacked by some as "vague, inaccurate, and uncertain") were the same as those of the school district: the Arroyo Seco on the west, the Raymond brook and its outwash on the east, Columbia Street on the north, and the Los Angeles city limits on the south.

The winning candidates for the South Pasadena board of trustees (all getting between eighty-three and eighty-six votes) were Donald M. Graham, George W. Wilson, Adrian A. Burrows, David R. Risley, and William P. Hammond. (In later years the board of trustees became known as the city council, and the president as mayor.) Also elected in February were Ammon B. Cobb as marshal, John H. Jacobs as treasurer, and Charles C. Miles as clerk. In the next few months city officials were appointed: William S. Knott attorney, Franklin H. Smith recorder, or magistrate, Martin B. Selman deputy marshal, and Emanuel Peters fruit-pest inspector.

On March 2, 1888, South Pasadena was officially incorporated as a city of the sixth class—a general law city with a population not above 3,000. (South Pasadena claimed a population of slightly more than 500.) The trustees held their first meeting on March 8 in the Smith & Jacobs real estate office and chose Donald M. Graham as president. The first three ordinances fixed the time and place of meeting and set the bonds for city clerk, treasurer, and marshal. One of the first expenditures was fifteen dollars for the official seal, which is still in use today. The stylized tree in the design—perhaps intended as an oak—is shown in modern adaptations as an orange tree.

Reminiscing in 1909, Margaret Collier Graham recalled that the trustees met at Wynyate soon after their election to discuss an antisaloon ordinance. "Mr. Graham was not a prohibitionist," she wrote, "but he was opposed to saloons, and after the board adjourned he came to me in great amusement and said, 'It would have been well to remove the wine glasses and the whiskey bottle from the sideboard before meeting to organize a prohibition town.' "

On March 12, 1888, the trustees passed South Pasadena Ordinance 4, an exact copy of Pasadena's antisaloon law, which had been appealed to the California Supreme Court and found constitutional. The ordinance made it unlawful to establish or maintain "any tippling house, dramshop, cellar, saloon, bar, barroom, sample room, or other place where spirituous, vinous, malt, or mixed liquors are sold or given away; or any gambling room or other place of indecent or immoral character; or any slaughter house, powder house, or other place dangerous to the public health or safety of the inhabitants."

Before South Pasadena incorporated, saloons had sprung up on Columbia Street, Mission Street, Fair Oaks Avenue, and the road to Los Angeles that was called the old adobe road. South Pasadena eventually closed down all the saloons except those near

Ordinance No. 4.

An ordinance for purposes of police regulation, prohibiting places and things of immoral or indecent character, or dangerous to life or health.

The Board of Trustees of the City of South Pasadena do ordain as follows:

It shall be and is hereby made unlawful for any person or persons, either as owner, principal, agent, servant, or employe, to establish, open, keep, maintain, or carry on, or assist in carrying on within the corporate limits of the City of South Pasadena, any tippling house, dram shop, cellar, saloon, bar, bar-room, sample-room, or other place where spirituous, vinous, malt, or mixed liquors are sold or given away; or any gambling room or other place of indecent or immoral character; or any slaughter house, powder-house, or other place dangerous to the public health or safety of the inhabitants of said city; provided that the prohibitions of this ordinance shall not apply to the sale of liquors for medicinal purposes by a regularly licensed druggist upon the prescription of a physician entitled to practice medicine under the laws of the State of California; nor shall such prohibitions apply to the sale of such liquors for chemical or mechanical purposes.

In March 1888 the city council voted unanimously for an antisaloon ordinance. *Courtesy of South Pasadena Public Library.*

South Pasadena's first newspaper began publication in 1888. *Courtesy of Security Pacific National Bank Photograph Collection/Los Angeles Public Library.*

32

Los Angeles, which continued to defy the law. "To get rid of this offensive state of things," Reid explains, "it was thought necessary to have the city boundaries re-established, so as to exclude the incorrigible territory." A letter in the *Pasadena Star* suggests another reason for redrawing the boundaries: some people in the outlying area ("Arroyo Seco fellows and delinquents on the adobe road") refused to pay municipal taxes.

The city trustees called a special election for September 28, 1889, to vote on excluding the problem territory. Of the ninety-one people who voted, eighty-four favored exclusion. No one in the outlying area chose to remain part of South Pasadena. The California Secretary of State certified the results of the election, which established the city's boundaries essentially where they are today.

Another significant event of 1889 was the founding of the South Pasadena Lyceum, forerunner of the South Pasadena Public Library. Several people met on February 14, 1889, to establish a free reading room for the community. Fifty-six charter members paid a dollar each to buy books and periodicals, Graham and Mohr donated space in their splendid brick building on Center Street, and Jennie Collier served as volunteer librarian. The devoted efforts of Jennie Collier, her sister Margaret Collier Graham, and fund-raiser Howard Longley kept the free reading room operating until the city took it over in September 1895.

Not until 1893 did South Pasadena have a newspaper that survived more than a few months. The *South Pasadena Bell* published from February to December 1888. The *South Pasadena Citizen* had an even shorter span—July 30 to September 24, 1889. It was started solely to give official notice of the election to exclude from the city limits what Dr. Reid described as a "saloon-ridden settlement." Reid's prohibition paper, the *Pasadena Standard*, set type for the *Citizen*. The type forms were then carried to the Graham & Mohr Building, where O. R. Dougherty had set up a printing press in the council chambers.

In 1893 a group of South Pasadenans asked George W. Glover to start a local newspaper. They complained:

> If anything good and fine happened in South Pasadena, the Pasadena papers published the news as promptly as could be, and credited all the good things to Pasadena, with never an intimation that there was a difference between the two cities. But when . . . something occurred that possibly did not redound to the honor and glory of the town they published the news just as promptly, but South Pasadena got the full benefit of the publicity.

Glover began publishing the *South Pasadenan* on June 8, 1893. Although local merchants promised a subsidy of thirty-five dollars a month, they contributed less than half that amount, and Glover helped support the fledgling paper by peddling vegetables, eggs, and chickens.

Like much of Southern California, South Pasadena suffered from drought and depression in the nineties. The land boom had collapsed, and many houses and business establishments were empty. The South Pasadena Hotel was vacant except for the caretaker's apartment and a room Glover rented for his printing press. Business was so poor, he said, that "sometimes it was difficult to get a five-dollar bill changed, and still more difficult to get hold of one of the bills." In 1896 Glover suspended publication of the newspaper and went off to the gold rush town of Randsburg, where he established the town's first paper, the *Randsburg Miner*. It was 1902 before he resumed regular

Horsecars began operating between Raymond Station and downtown Pasadena in 1886. This car is headed west on Columbia Street. *Courtesy of South Pasadena Public Library*.

Electric trolleys linked South Pasadena to Pasadena and Los Angeles in 1895. The name on the car shows the company's intention to extend its line to Santa Monica. *Courtesy of Huntington Library*.

publication of the *South Pasadenan*. In January 1908 Glover sold the paper to B. F. Huntington, who renamed it the *Record*.

The last event Glover reported in 1896 was a move for disincorporation. It was led by people living along the Arroyo who complained that the city taxes they paid brought too few services in return. Two persuasive arguments for remaining an incorporated city were retention of the South Pasadena Public Library and the power to outlaw saloons. Although women had no vote, they campaigned vigorously against disincorporation and in favor of "a clean, moral, God-fearing community, organized to watch against sin and wickedness." Disincorporation lost by a vote of two to one.

With no local paper in 1898, South Pasadenans had to turn elsewhere for news of the Spanish-American War. If they happened to be in Los Angeles, they could hear the *Los Angeles Times* war whistle, which signaled the latest information. On May 1, 1898, the whistle blew three dots and a dash to proclaim Commodore George Dewey's victory at Manila.

South Pasadenans witnessed three headline events at the end of the century: the burning of the Raymond Hotel, arrival of the first electric streetcars, and the opening of the Cawston Ostrich Farm. The great Raymond Hotel caught fire on Easter Sunday 1895. Sparks from one of its twenty chimneys ignited the roof, and in less than an hour the hotel burned to the ground. Luckily, no one was injured. Rebuilt in 1901, the hotel was a South Pasadena landmark for another thirty years.

Southern California's first electric interurban line, the Pasadena and Los Angeles Electric Railway, linked South Pasadena with the two neighboring cities in May 1895. The trolley tracks in South Pasadena ran east along Mission Street from the Arroyo to Meridian Avenue, then turned in a northeast direction parallel to the Santa Fe tracks. The trolley cars, "finely upholstered and finished in mahogany," made the run every twenty minutes. "Thus made easy of access," said the illustrated monthly *Land of Sunshine*, "the charming valley of the Arroyo Seco will be built up densely along the way."

In 1895 the Santa Fe relocated its tracks in South Pasadena to eliminate a steep S-curve on Meridian Avenue. At the same time the old station was moved a short distance west, to a location near Center Street and Glendon Way. Two other railroads now had lines through South Pasadena: the Southern Pacific, which inaugurated service to Pasadena in June 1895 with a seaside excursion for students of Throop Polytechnic Institute; and the Terminal Railroad, which became the San Pedro, Los Angeles, and Salt Lake Railroad in 1901 and the Union Pacific in 1921.

In 1896 South Pasadena gained a world-famous tourist attraction—the Cawston Ostrich Farm, which opened on November 17 on a wooded plot bounded by Sycamore Avenue, Pasadena Avenue, and the Santa Fe railroad tracks. For twenty-five cents, visitors could stroll in a setting advertised as "free from any boisterous element and strictly first class." They could see nearly a hundred ostriches, from baby chicks to birds seven feet tall, and they could buy stylish feather boas, capes, muffs, and parasols. "Ostrich feathers are now as staple as diamonds," said one catalog. "They do not fluctuate in popularity like furs, and are constantly used." The farm conducted a tremendous mail-order business, and Edwin Cawston once boasted of receiving more mail than any other man in California.

Edwin Cawston described his South Pasadena ostrich farm as a semitropical park. To help irrigate the gardens, he installed a solar-heated steam engine that pumped 1,200 gallons of water a minute. *Courtesy of South Pasadena Public Library.*

36

Form No. 1.

THE WESTERN UNION TELEGRAPH COMPANY.
INCORPORATED
21,000 OFFICES IN AMERICA. CABLE SERVICE TO ALL THE WORLD.

This Company TRANSMITS and DELIVERS messages only on conditions limiting its liability, which have been assented to by the sender of the following message. Errors can be guarded against only by repeating a message back to the sending station for comparison, and the Company will not hold itself liable for errors or delays in transmission or delivery of Unrepeated Messages, beyond the amount of tolls paid thereon, nor in any case where the claim is not presented in writing within sixty days after the message is filed with the Company for transmission.
This is an UNREPEATED MESSAGE, and is delivered by request of the sender, under the conditions named above.

THOS. T. ECKERT, President and General Manager.

NUMBER   SENT BY   REC'D BY   CHECK

RECEIVED at 109 State Street, BOSTON, _____ 1895

Dated Echo Mountain Calif 14

To Walter Raymond Boston

It is with profound regret that I am now witnessing from Echo Mountain the destruction of your magnificent hotel on Raymond-hill from whose portals have gone forth the most prominent & desirable people in the United States and the world to settle among us. You have our sympathy in this loss and our encouragement for the new Raymond. T. S. C. Lowe

Courtesy of Security Pacific National Bank Photograph Collection/Los Angeles Public Library.

Only chimneys and the foundation remained after the Raymond burned down on Easter Sunday of 1895. *Courtesy of Huntington Library*.

A visitor to the Raymond Hotel in 1886 observed, "South Pasadena is not very large or pretty as yet but I know it must be, sooner or later." George W. Glover launched the first beautification campaign. Writing in the first issue of the *South Pasadenan*, he appealed for shade trees along the city streets. His campaign reached a triumphant conclusion on April 24, 1894, when a host of volunteers gathered at the South Pasadena Hotel and fanned out through the city to plant 800 eucalyptus trees and about 200 peppers.

The women of South Pasadena led the next city-beautiful campaign. On February 2, 1899, fifteen women gathered at the home of Ada J. Longley and formed the Woman's Improvement Association. Their first project was to beautify the rubbish-strewn lot around the Santa Fe depot. They leased the triangle of ground for a dollar a year and briskly set to work. In just a few weeks they cleared and leveled the land, piped in water, and gathered donations of flowers, trees, and shrubs. Washington's Birthday was planting day. Notices advised, "Free lunch in exchange for work. Men wanted." The men turned out in force and worked in a holiday atmosphere. By the end of the day South Pasadena had a new park. The women tended it until 1902, when the railroad took back the land for a lumberyard and other enterprises.

Over the years the club campaigned successfully for city parks, a street tree program, garbage collection, sanitary markets, and other public health measures. As one president modestly expressed it, the Woman's Improvement Association served as housekeeper for the community.

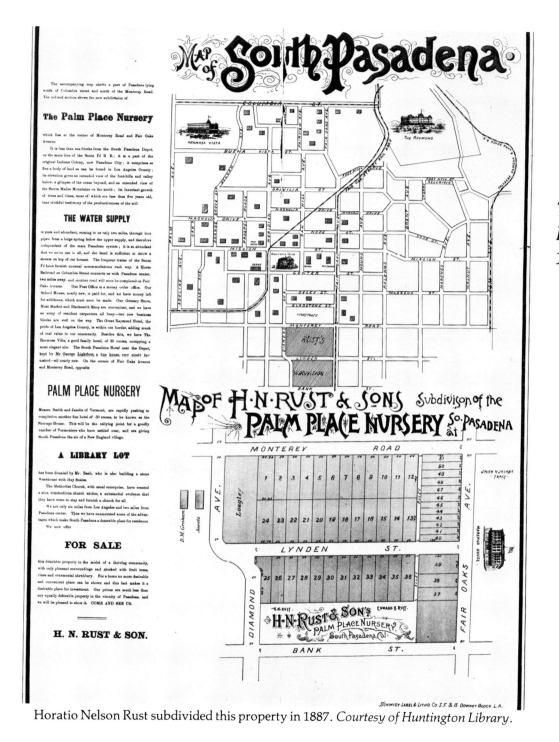

Horatio Nelson Rust subdivided this property in 1887. *Courtesy of Huntington Library.*

Benjamin S. Eaton supervised construction of a water system on Rancho San Pasqual. In this photograph, taken on Mount Wilson in 1892, Eaton is seated on the ground at the left. Harvard president Charles W. Eliot is in the middle of the second row, with Walter Raymond on his right and Thaddeus S. C. Lowe on his left. *Courtesy of Huntington Library.*

CHRONOLOGY

1873

Daniel M. Berry, agent for the California Colony of Indiana, visits Rancho San Pasqual. After the panic of 1873, Berry organizes a new buying syndicate, the San Gabriel Orange Grove Association.

Dr. John S. Griffin deeds 3962.35 acres to Thomas F. Croft, vice-president of the San Gabriel Orange Grove Association, for a purchase price of $25,000. Croft transfers title to the San Gabriel Orange Grove Association on December 29.

1874

Twenty-seven stockholders, or their proxies, meet on Orange Grove Avenue on January 27 to choose the acreage they want.

1875

The colonists name their settlement Pasadena.

1876

Benjamin D. Wilson subdivides his Lake Vineyard tract extending east from Fair Oaks Avenue in Pasadena.

A business center develops at Fair Oaks Avenue and Colorado Street.

1878

South Pasadena forms its own school district, and classes open in Clinton B. Ripley's home on Columbia Hill.

1879

P. M. Green is elected to the State Assembly, defeating the Democratic candidate by a vote of 109 to 6.

1880

On behalf of the San Gabriel Orange Grove Association, A. O. Porter and P. M. Green welcome President Rutherford B. Hayes to the Pasadena area.

1882

South Pasadena's first post office is established in the Hermosa Vista Hotel, with Frank M. Glover as postmaster.

1885

The Los Angeles & San Gabriel Valley Railroad begins passenger and freight service between Pasadena and Los Angeles.

O. R. Dougherty opens the South Pasadena Land Office, the first real estate office in town.

A school opens downtown on Center Street.

1886

Pasadena becomes an incorporated city on June 19.

The Raymond Hotel opens in South Pasadena.

A rate war between the Santa Fe and the Southern Pacific railroads brings thousands of emigrants to Southern California, and a land boom results.

1887

Pasadena passes an antisaloon ordinance.

The Santa Fe takes over the Los Angeles & San Gabriel Valley Railroad.

Lincoln Park School opens on a site near the Arroyo.

1888

The city's first newspaper, the *South Pasadena Bell*, begins publication.

South Pasadena becomes an incorporated city on March 2. Donald M. Graham serves as the first mayor. City trustees pass an antisaloon ordinance.

1889

David Collier, O. R. Dougherty, and Emanuel Peters are named to the first board of health.

The South Pasadena Lyceum opens a free reading room.

The city establishes its borders essentially where they are today.

1890

The United States Census records a population of 623 in South Pasadena.

The Los Angeles, Pasadena, and Glendale Railroad begins service through South Pasadena. In 1891 it is bought by the Terminal Railroad.

1893

The *South Pasadenan* begins publication.

The Raymond starts a hotel newsletter, the *Raymond Chit-Chat*.

1894

The Southern Pacific acquires the Ramona and Pasadena Railroad, which had built to the south city line of Pasadena near Raymond Station.

1895

The city establishes a free public library.

The Raymond Hotel burns to the ground.

The Santa Fe removes its tracks from Meridian Avenue to eliminate a steep S-curve.

The Pasadena and Los Angeles Railway Company builds an electric interurban line that links South Pasadena to Pasadena and Los Angeles.

The deputy assessor records 176 males in South Pasadena between the ages of eighteen and sixty. Thirty-eight of the men were born in other countries.

The Cawston Ostrich Farm opens on the Arroyo Seco.

A campaign for disincorporation loses at the polls.

George W. Glover suspends publication of the *South Pasadenan*.

1899

The Woman's Improvement Association organizes, and as its first project plants a park at the Santa Fe depot.

Some of the volunteers who planted shade trees in South Pasadena on April 24, 1894, had their pictures taken outside the newspaper office. The three men to the left of the doorway are William C. Brainerd, the first street superintendent; John H. Jacobs, the first city treasurer; and Alex Hinckley, for many years the city clerk. O. R. Dougherty, who opened the first real estate office in South Pasadena, is the third man from the right. *Courtesy of South Pasadena Public Library.*

First grade pupils at Center Street School posed with their teacher, Blanche Foster, in 1907. *Courtesy of South Pasadena Public Library.*

III

INTO THE TWENTIETH CENTURY: 1900-1909

*The city has been fortunate in its nearness to Los Angeles, the class of
people residing here, its educational advantages, and the purity of its
moral atmosphere. It has none of the objectionable elements; the
saloon and its train of lesser evils is entirely unknown, while the church,
the schools, and the library do their work of moral and
educational uplifting without restraint.*

SOUTH PASADENA BOARD OF TRADE, 1908

SOUTH PASADENA entered the twentieth century with a population of 1,001. The most
important building in town was the old Opera House Building, where no opera ever
played, but where the city offices and library were housed. Orange groves and barley
fields still covered large tracts of land, and the business center was minuscule. Located
on the north side of Mission Street by Meridian Avenue, it contained a post office and
half a dozen shops: a confectioner's, a combined cyclery and shoemaker's, a black-
smith shop, a general store, a grocery, and Adolph Garmshausen's South Pasadena
Bakery which advertised, "Drop a postal and our wagon will call promptly."

On New Year's Day of 1900, South Pasadenans joined some six hundred people
who rode across the new cycleway built by Pasadenan Horace Dobbins. "The foot
that works the pedal," he declared, "is the foot that moves the world." The elevated
wooden roadway went from near the Green Hotel in Pasadena to the foot of Raymond Hill and was high enough for a load of hay to be driven under it.

In 1901 South Pasadena once again boasted a great hotel. After the Raymond
burned down in 1895, Walter Raymond tried for six years to raise the money to
rebuild. Meanwhile, he let people use the hotel grounds as a park. For an admission
charge of ten cents, they could wander through the gardens or listen to band concerts.
Raymond's search for funds ended successfully when plumbing magnate R. T. Crane,
a frequent visitor to the old hotel, agreed to take a mortgage for $300,000. Sumner P.
Hunt and A. W. Eager designed the new Raymond, modifying plans drawn in 1896 by
architect T. W. Parkes.

On December 19, 1901, three-year-old Arthur Raymond pulled red and white rib-
bons attached to the great front doors, and the new hotel officially opened. It had a
columned verandah two hundred feet long and a dining room so large that young
Arthur later flew his model airplanes there. (Arthur Raymond went on to study aero-
nautical engineering and to become a vice-president of the Douglas Aircraft Company.
He helped design and develop such famous airplanes as the DC-3, the C-47, and
the DC-8.)

One popular feature of the new hotel was a nine-hole golf course with "greens"
made of sand mixed with oil. As at the first hotel, guests arriving by train were met at

45

The new Raymond opened on December 19, 1901. Built on the extended foundation of the old hotel, it had 275 rooms—many with private baths—and could accomodate 400 guests. A 1904 brochure described the Raymond as "the most superbly located hotel on the American continent, with every appointment perfect." *Courtesy of Huntington Library*.

Raymond Station by a tallyho. "They were charmed by this tradition," Arthur Raymond has said, "and expressed dismay when the old station was closed, forcing them to debark at the more distant depot in Pasadena and use an autobus."

George W. Glover revived the *South Pasadenan* in 1902 and assured his readers, "Politically the paper will remain steadfastly Republican." Writing in the issue for March 20, 1902, Glover observed with satisfaction that the town had wakened from a Rip van Winkle sleep and was advancing faster than any other part of Southern California.

"Watch us grow!" was the city slogan in 1902. There was talk of macadamized streets, a municipal water company, and a bridge over the Arroyo by the Cawston Ostrich Farm. Voters endorsed a $20,000 bond issue to enlarge the Center Street school, and the Pacific College of Osteopathy arranged to move into the long-vacant South Pasadena Hotel. The Raymond Villa Tract opened on two hundred acres south of the Raymond Hotel and proclaimed itself "the high class suburban property par excellence." With the upsurge in building, R. H. Seay started a lumberyard, the city's first.

The Raymond Villa subdivision advertised that no lot was more than a five-minute walk from the Pasadena Short Line, then under construction by the Pacific Electric Railway Company. The Short Line was an important link in a remarkable interurban network that eventually had more than a thousand miles of track joining cities and suburbs, the mountains and the sea.

Henry E. Huntington incorporated the Pacific Electric Railway Company in 1901. He had already acquired several interurban lines, and in 1902 he began construction of a high-speed trolley line from Los Angeles to Long Beach, another from Los Angeles to Monrovia, and a third from Los Angeles to downtown Pasadena. This was the Pasadena Short Line, which ran through South Pasadena along Fair Oaks Avenue.

The segment of the Short Line south of Columbia Street opened on November 9, 1902, with one trolley making half-hourly trips between the Raymond Hotel and the junction with the Alhambra Line. "The rolling hills through which the road passes are very pretty," wrote a Pasadena reporter. "There is no dust, and altogether the road is a delightful one."

Guests at the Raymond found it convenient to use the trolleys—or the Big Red Cars, as they were nicknamed. An elevator went from the hotel lobby to a pedestrian subway tunneled three hundred feet through Raymond Hill. Newspapers reported that the subway—a short walk from the trolley stop on Fair Oaks Avenue—was "carpeted with cork-lined matting and adorned at intervals with potted plants and fancy electric lights."

Before the Pacific Electric could complete the Short Line, it had to replace the Columbia Street Viaduct, an old wooden trestle spanning the tracks of the Santa Fe and Terminal railroads. Construction of a new bridge was delayed for months by a right-of-way dispute and by arguments as to how wide the bridge should be. Meanwhile, passengers going to and from Pasadena had to disembark at the foot of Raymond Hill, walk across the viaduct (which became known as the Bridge of Sighs), and change cars on the other side. The *Los Angeles Times* observed that the PE "had as much trouble getting across the little fifty-foot cut at Raymond Hill as Robinson

47

The Pacific Electric's Oneonta Park Station, at Huntington Drive and Fair Oaks Avenue, marked the junction of the Pasadena Short Line and the Monrovia Line. *Courtesy of Huntington Library.*

Crusoe had in getting away from his island." A bridge finally was built in 1903. Soon afterwards, the PE laid tracks across Mission Street in South Pasadena to join the Short Line to the old Main Line—the pioneering Los Angeles and Pasadena Railway acquired by Henry E. Huntington in 1899.

Walter Gillette, who built the first house on Fair Oaks Avenue (when it was still called Palermo), moved in shortly after the Pacific Electric began running through South Pasadena. "In those days," he recalled, "the Street Car Company was anxious for business; so all one had to do was to tell the conductor . . . that on the following Friday, or whatever day you intended to go to business again, that you would be at the corner nearest your house about 8:30, but if you were a little late, to wait."

A mission-style depot, at Huntington Drive and Fair Oaks Avenue, marked the junction of the Pasadena Short Line and the Monrovia Line. Huntington named the junction Oneonta after his birthplace in New York. In 1903 the Huntington Land and Improvement Company subdivided Oneonta Park, "not for the residences of million-aires . . . but for the well-to-do who aspire to what is artistic and who appreciate the opportunities here afforded for home building." Huntington insisted on large lots and ornamental trees. Many of the oaks, deodars, and Monterey pines were planted around 1905 under the direction of William Hertrich, then superintendent of Huntington's San Marino Ranch.

William R. Staats, one of Huntington's business associates, predicted of Oneonta Park: "Under the shadows of the wide-spreading oaks soon there will be the low East-Indian bungalow; on some elevated knoll, the Swiss chalet; where the oleanders and the magnolia bloom, quaint adobes will rear their walls. Gardens shall bloom here, rioting with roses and passion flowers; beauty shall prevail—and hundreds of home-seekers will be eager to seize upon this opportunity of finding such a resting place from the turmoil and stress of business life."

Oaklawn was another subdivision convenient to the Short Line. It lay south of Columbia Street, between Fremont and Fair Oaks avenues. Calling itself a private park among the oaks and orange trees, Oaklawn advised, "All the requirements of the most fastidious will here be found. Anyone wanting low-priced lots need not apply." Pasadena architects Charles and Henry Greene designed handsome portals for Oaklawn, a bridge to Fair Oaks Avenue, and a waiting station at the PE trolley stop.

A promotional booklet issued in 1905 remarked on "the large number of people of wealth and refinement" who were moving to South Pasadena. One of the new residents was retired lumber magnate P. G. Gates, who had built an imposing house at Monterey Road and Indiana Avenue. It boasted Steuben and Tiffany light fixtures, antique leaded glass windows, and such modern conveniences as an electric steam cabinet and a master vacuum cleaner. Five Gates brothers eventually built in South Pasadena. The family complex had a park, orchards, stables, tennis courts, and a billiard house, and even had its own fire station. In 1916 C. W. and P. G. Gates provided the funds for Gates Chemical Laboratory, now the oldest building on the Caltech campus.

Another prominent newcomer to the city was presidential widow Lucretia Garfield. "It goes without saying," George W. Glover wrote with some exasperation, "that the Pasadena papers will declare that she bought 'in Pasadena—just overlooking South

Pasadena' but it is in South Pasadena all the same." The Garfield house, on Buena Vista Street, is a Craftsman bungalow designed in 1904 by Charles and Henry Greene.

The first bank in the city opened in 1904 and held a reception in the new South Pasadena Bank building at Diamond Avenue and Center Street. The Woman's Improvement Association served punch, and a trio played music "of a higher class than the appreciation of the crowd warranted." Bank president G. W. E. Griffith gave a welcoming address, and vice-president Edwin Cawston made the first deposit—some four thousand dollars in receipts from the ostrich farm.

Another pleasant event that year was a Fourth of July picnic organized by women of the city. More than a hundred people lunched in the little park by the Santa Fe depot and listened to lively music played on the Graphophone of Ada and Leo Longley. Only one thing marred the occasion—the noise of passing railroad trains. Members of the Woman's Improvement Association were quick to point out the city's need for a quiet park and pledged their help in obtaining one.

In 1904 South Pasadena took a modest first step toward the formation of a high school. In September five students entered a ninth-grade class taught at the Center Street school by superintendent Noble Harter. The following year enrollment was up to thirty-two. For several years the students met in makeshift quarters, but in 1907 they had their own building and a six-acre campus bounded by Fremont and Diamond avenues and Rollin and Bank streets. The new high school opened on April 8, 1907, with a student body of sixty-five and a faculty of seven and with George C. Bush as principal.

The architects for the high school were South Pasadenan Norman Foote Marsh and his partner C. H. Russell. They were also the architects for California's new beachfront town of Venice. Marsh & Russell laid out the site plan for Venice and designed its first commercial buildings, including the arcaded Hotel St. Mark—now the Venice Center—on Windward Avenue. One of the unusual examples of Marsh's work in South Pasadena is the watering trough and wayside station that the Woman's Improvement Association gave the city in 1906. The Arroyo boulder structure—"for man and beast, with shade trees to cool it"—was built in the center of Meridian Avenue, just south of Mission. It stands opposite the simple frame building, now called the Meridian Iron Works, in which Aaron F. McReynolds ran a general store in the 1880s and 1890s.

One of South Pasadena's most colorful pioneers died in 1906. He was Horatio Nelson Rust: Yankee abolitionist and friend of John Brown, amateur archaeologist, Indian agent, nurseryman, and early subdivider. A fervent collector, Rust gathered 150 artifacts—mostly hammer stones, manos, and metates—when Buena Vista Street was graded in 1897. Rust took credit for naming two South Pasadena streets. When he arrived in 1882, he said, the Monterey road meant any of several trails running across his thirty-five acres. He plowed up what seemed to him the principal trail and established that as Monterey Road. In 1904 Rust successfully petitioned the city council to rename Fair Oaks Avenue for his friend John Charles Frémont. Thus the original Fair Oaks Avenue in South Pasadena became Fremont, and soon afterwards Palermo Avenue became what is now Fair Oaks.

Between 1906 and 1908 a number of commercial buildings went up along Mission

Horatio Nelson Rust displays a small part of his collection of Indian artifacts. Many items collected by Rust are now in the Logan Museum of Anthropology of Beloit College in Wisconsin. *Courtesy of Priscilla Roth Feigen and Edward F. Roth.*

South Pasadena architect Norman Foote Marsh designed numerous homes, schools, churches, and other buildings in the city. The firm of Marsh & Russell laid out the site plan for Venice, California. *Courtesy of South Pasadena Public Library.*

At the opening reception for the First National Bank in 1908, visitors were shown the vault filled with packages of twenty-dollar gold pieces. The staff members pictured here are (from left to right) Allie Coes, Herbert J. Vatcher, G. W. E. Griffith, Jonathan Dodge, and George W. Lawyer. *Courtesy of South Pasadena Public Library.*

Street, and the *South Pasadena Record* boasted, "Rapidly and surely the march of progress is wending its way from Fair Oaks west and from Meridian east." The first to build was Alexander R. Graham, who sought a measure of immortality by naming two buildings for himself. Early in 1906 he cleared a grove of eucalyptus trees at the southeast corner of Mission and Meridian and put up his concrete-block Alexander Building. Two years later he erected a brick structure next door and called it the A. R. Graham Building. At the other end of the block, the First National Bank (formerly the South Pasadena Bank) and the South Pasadena Savings Bank opened for business in a neoclassic building designed by Marsh & Russell.

Two new buildings went up on the north side of Mission Street, across from the elementary school. One was the Taylor Building (also designed by Marsh & Russell); and the other was the Herlihy Building, which had a public hall on the second floor and offered such varied entertainments as sleight of hand, minstrelsy, and dancing. General admission in 1908 was fifteen cents; dancing a quarter extra.

The series of new buildings inspired a kind of real estate round robin in 1908. The old South Pasadena Bank moved from Center Street to Mission Street; and Live Hardware, which had rented space in the old bank building, moved into the new Graham Building. The city offices then moved from the old Opera House Building into the vacated bank.

The public library also moved from the Opera House. In February 1908 it opened in a new six-room building at the southeast corner of Center Street and Diamond Avenue. A front-page story noted, "Few cities of our size can point with pride to such a building, so well equipped and so beautifully supplied with good, useful and wholesome books." Marsh & Russell designed the library, which was built with a gift of $12,000 from Andrew Carnegie.

Another front-page story in 1908 was the city council's decision to buy a fire truck, described in the article as "the new and up-to-date method of fighting fire." The truck was equipped with two chemical tanks and could be driven at forty-five miles an hour, guaranteed four times faster than the best team of horses. Just one year earlier, a citizens' committee predicted that South Pasadena could never afford a well-equipped fire department or a municipal water company. The city therefore would have to annex to Los Angeles or Pasadena. Annexation sentiment was strengthened by the recent passage of a Los Angeles bond issue to build an aqueduct from the Owens River, more than two hundred miles away. The *Los Angeles Times* proclaimed, "Titanic Project to Give City a River," and continued, "This new water supply, immense and unfailing, will make Los Angeles forge ahead by leaps and bounds and remove every specter of drought and doubt."

Water for South Pasadena was piped in by three private companies, each supplying a different part of town. None of the companies gave adequate service for an expanding population, and service to the western part of South Pasadena was especially poor. Water pressure was a problem throughout the city, especially when fighting fires. One practical suggestion was that people stop all sprinkling or irrigating from the time an alarm sounded until the fire-out signal.

An ordinance passed in October 1907 created a volunteer fire department in South Pasadena. Organization faltered, however, until 1909 when the new engine arrived

Into the Twentieth Century: 1900-1909

In 1908 South Pasadena ordered a fire truck, which was built by Auto-Vehicle of Los Angeles for $4,750. To start the engine, the truck was coasted down an inclined skidway. *Courtesy of Gene E. Murry.*

Motorcycle policemen Archie Cooper and Leslie J. Cooper were photographed around 1910 as they pretended to write a traffic ticket. Justice of the Peace J. B. Soper was in the rear seat of the Franklin automobile. *Photograph by H. J. Kenny; courtesy of South Pasadena Public Library.*

and N. G. Ledgerwood took over as fire marshal. He formed three volunteer companies, including one composed entirely of workers at the Model Grocery, where he was manager. If an alarm sounded in the daytime, the Model closed its doors while clerks and drivers ran to fight the fire.

The police department bought a bicycle for the chief in 1909. It also bought two motorcycles and launched a campaign against "automobile scorchers"—which meant anyone going more than fifteen miles an hour through town. In their first year of duty, the two motorcycle policemen arrested 166 speeders and collected $1,735 in fines, a sum almost equal to their combined salaries.

Reckless driving was one of the few serious problems faced by the police. As the newspaper observed in 1909, South Pasadena enjoyed an enviable moral and social environment, free from the saloon, the pool hall, and the evils of gambling. The ban on saloons dated from 1888, when the city incorporated. The ban on pool halls and billiard parlors was only a year old. The ordinance outlawing them was debated all the way to the United States Supreme Court and declared constitutional in 1912.

The pool hall ordinance specifically exempted hotels with more than twenty-five bedrooms, a concession to the Raymond. Nor were liquor laws enforced at the Raymond, which maintained a bar for its guests. The Hotel Capitola, which succeeded the osteopathic college in the old South Pasadena Hotel, was not so fortunate. In 1907 detectives acting for the prohibitionists had the Capitola proprietor arrested for having liquor on the premises. Like many others in town, Glover thought it unfair to wink at the transgressions of the majestic Raymond but to punish the little Capitola. He was further annoyed because "in a sense Hotel Capitola is of more benefit to South Pasadena than the Raymond. The Raymond does its business in Pasadena strictly, advertising itself as a Pasadena institution and getting its mail there, while Capitola advertises itself for what they both are—South Pasadena institutions."

One of the hotly debated issues of 1909 was whether South Pasadena should change its name to end the annoying misconception that it was part of Pasadena. Many people favored calling the city Oneonta. Others suggested Robleda, Calidena, Hermosita, or Poinsettia. The Cawston Ostrich Farm put an effective stop to any change at all by pointing out, "The prestige of South Pasadena has been established for years, and largely by the advertising of the Cawston Ostrich Farm. This advertising has circulated in every civilized country of the world, and in all the leading publications. . . . The name is good, and the city is prospering with it."

In October 1909 South Pasadena businessmen organized a Chamber of Commerce, with nurseryman Edward H. Rust as president. The Chamber must have delighted in the special booster issue of the *Record* published on December 16, 1909. Illustrated articles extolled South Pasadena's progress. In just five years it had grown from a village of 1,500 to a city of nearly 5,000, with a high school, a Carnegie library, a volunteer fire department, and a police department with two motorcycles. The streets were well lighted at night, and all but six miles of dedicated roadway had curbs and sidewalks. Although no streets had yet been paved, there was little or no mud to contend with because of good drainage. The *Record* claimed that every important line of business was represented in South Pasadena. Washburn Brothers advertised their combined real estate agency and automobile showroom, and the Model Grocery

55

boasted of its modern wagons and its fifteen horses, well-groomed and full of life. Most important of all, said the *Record*, South Pasadena had a special quality, "a moral and social environment that makes it peculiarly attractive as a place for raising children."

From 1910 to 1922 the post office was in the concrete-block Alexander Building on the south side of Mission Street. *Photograph by H. J. Kenny; courtesy of South Pasadena Public Library.*

In 1905 retired lumberman Don F. Gates built this house at 515 Monterey Road. Gates Place is named for the five Gates brothers who settled in South Pasadena at the turn of the century. *Courtesy of South Pasadena Review.*

President Theodore Roosevelt stayed at the Raymond Hotel in 1903 and joked that it was the first time he had come to California through the Panama Canal. Walter Raymond is the hatless man in the background. *Courtesy of Huntington Library*.

CHRONOLOGY

1900

The census records South Pasadena's population as 1,001.

1901

The new Raymond Hotel opens in December.

1902

The *South Pasadenan* resumes publication on March 20, the first issue since April 1900.

R. H. Seay opens the first lumberyard in South Pasadena.

In November the Big Red Cars of the Pacific Electric Railway make their first run through South Pasadena, going along Fair Oaks Avenue between Columbia Street and Huntington Drive.

A subdivision opens south of the Raymond Hotel, near the PE trolley line.

1903

The Pacific College of Osteopathy opens in the old South Pasadena Hotel.

President Theodore Roosevelt is a guest at the Raymond Hotel.

Subdivisions open at Oneonta Park and at Oaklawn.

1904

The South Pasadena Bank, first in the city, opens in a new brick building at Center Street and Diamond Avenue.

Professor Noble Harter teaches the first high school class: five students in the ninth grade.

1905

South Pasadena men organize a new civic group, the Progressive League, and elect Leo Longley president.

The Hotel Capitola opens in the old South Pasadena Hotel after the osteopathic college moves back to Los Angeles.

1906

The Woman's Improvement Association gives the city a wayside station and watering trough on Meridian Avenue.

A provisional committee sets up a YMCA program in the old Opera House Building on Center Street.

Business expands east along Mission Street toward Fair Oaks Avenue.

1907

The high school opens on a six-acre campus, with a student body of sixty-five and a faculty of seven, and with George C. Bush as principal. Five girls and one boy graduate in June.

The city authorizes a volunteer fire department and a fire marshal.

M. O. Eggleston establishes the first funeral home in town, and George W. Glover comments, "It is no longer necessary to go to Pasadena when you die."

The South Pasadena post office becomes a branch of the Los Angeles post office until 1918, then of the Pasadena post office until 1927.

1908

South Pasadena gets its first home delivery of mail.

Ordinance 262 makes billiard halls and poolrooms illegal except in hotels with more than twenty-five bedrooms.

Glover sells the *South Pasadenan*, which changes its name to the *Record*.

Center Street is renamed El Centro.

A gift of $12,000 from Andrew Carnegie finances a new library building.

1909

Mrs. E. E. Washburn's rose-covered carriage drawn by two Shetland ponies wins a banner and the fifteen-dollar first prize in the Tournament of Roses.

Fire marshal N. G. Ledgerwood organizes three companies of volunteers and accepts delivery of the city's first fire truck.

The Police Department buys two motorcycles and launches a campaign against speeders.

Clement A. Whiting, South Pasadena's first health officer, urges a ban on the common drinking cup in public places.

E. E. and L. L. Washburn open the city's first automobile showroom.

The city approves ten arc lights for the business district.

The Hotel Capitola is remodeled as the El Centro Apartments.

Businessmen organize a Chamber of Commerce, with nurseryman Edward H. Rust as president.

The Raymond Hill waiting station has served commuters for more than eighty years. Built in 1903, it was restored in 1978 and is now a Cultural Heritage Landmark. *Photograph by Ralph Tillema; courtesy of South Pasadena Cultural Heritage Commission.*

To symbolize its drawing power as a residential city, South Pasadena entered a floral magnet in the 1911 Tournament of Roses. Six black horses, with saddle blankets of dusty miller and red geraniums, pulled the wagon carrying the magnet. *Courtesy of Huntington Library*.

IV

PRIDE AND PATRIOTISM: 1910-1919

South Pasadena attracts and holds; come, you'll stay.

NELLIE WARNICK

E. E. BARDEN

SOUTH PASADENA began the decade and ended it with a patriotic flourish. In 1910, and again in 1919, the year's biggest community event was a Flag Day celebration. The Chamber of Commerce organized the program in 1910, scheduling it for Washington's Birthday. Flags waved throughout the city, and portraits of all the presidents hung along the six-mile route. The new fire truck headed a procession of decorated automobiles, carriages, and floats, which were accompanied by a military band and a fife and drum corps. The parade stopped briefly on Buena Vista Street while the band played outside Lucretia Garfield's home. When the celebration ended, the Chamber of Commerce saluted South Pasadena for its unity of spirit when any appeal was made to civic pride.

After years of boasting, "Not a dollar of bonded indebtedness!" the city held its first municipal bond election in 1910, to authorize funds for a bridge over the Arroyo Seco between Los Angeles and South Pasadena. The Lincoln Park League, whose members lived along the Arroyo, spearheaded the campaign for a bridge near the Cawston Ostrich Farm. The League had a valuable ally in R. W. Pridham, past mayor of South Pasadena and a new member of the County Board of Supervisors. Pridham helped negotiate an agreement by South Pasadena, Los Angeles, the county, and the Salt Lake Railroad to build a bridge and share the estimated cost of $128,000. On June 7, election day in South Pasadena, a megaphone man traveled through the city reminding people to go to the polls. Six hundred and twenty voters turned out, and all but thirty-three endorsed the city bond issue of $32,000.

South Pasadenans had fought to have a bridge; Angelenos fought to make it ornamental. They opposed the original plans calling for a long dirt fill at either end of the bridge and urged a more esthetic design that would not mar the beauty of the Arroyo. The supervisors eventually agreed to a six-span concrete bridge, with the added cost to be divided equally among the two cities, the county, and the railroad. The Cawston Ostrich Farm contributed $1,500 toward South Pasadena's share.

South Pasadena was jubilant at the prospect of increased traffic going through the city and helping revitalize the business district. Drivers shuddered, however, at the thought of South Pasadena streets, which were considered among the worst in the county. Oiling helped keep down the dust, but as an irate taxpayer wrote in 1902, "Pouring a lot of oil down on a road almost impassable (except at walking pace) does not make a fine boulevard. Neither does an eighty-foot strip of dirt." Soon afterwards the city bought a road grader and four mules to pull it. The city also experimented with oil tamping instead of surface oiling.

63

Mission Street was not paved until 1911. This view, taken in 1896, shows one of the Pasadena and Pacific Railroad's green trolley cars at Mission Street and Meridian Avenue. *Courtesy of South Pasadena Public Library.*

By 1910 there was enough traffic in town to warrant more permanent street improvements. Everyone agreed there must be a better way than hauling dirt on the streets in summer and having it wash away in winter rains. An editorial inquired, "Shall South Pasadena offer the travellers of Southern California chuck-holes, treacherous crossings, dust and mud when they cross the beautiful Arroyo Seco to enter the valley?" In December the city council approved asphalt paving for a two-mile stretch of Pasadena Avenue and Mission Street between the bridge site and Fair Oaks Avenue. The decision was hailed as the greatest step the city had taken in years.

Another decision was far less popular. The council ordered the city attorney to draw up an ordinance banning motion pictures, but nearly every businessman in town protested. The council yielded, but warned that it would not tolerate improper films that might demoralize or shock the public. Two men promptly installed a projector at 1118 Mission Street, and South Pasadena had its first motion picture show on September 1, 1910. That program has been forgotten, but *Uncle Tom's Cabin* was the feature when the South Pasadena Theater had its grand opening in October. "Other high class educational and historic motion pictures" were promised and the public was assured, "Nothing objectionable shown here."

In 1910 South Pasadenan Charles Beach Boothe received an impressive document making him, in effect, treasurer of a revolution. A successful businessman and financial counselor, Boothe was also a secret agent in an international conspiracy with the code name "Red Dragon." Its purpose was to finance Sun Yat-sen in his efforts to overthrow the Ch'ing Dynasty and establish a Republic of China. In return for their support, Boothe and other American backers expected free access to China's coal and mineral resources, the right to operate a central bank, a monopoly over coinage, and a ninety-nine-year concession to build and operate all railroads on mainland China. Sun was named provisional president of a Chinese republic in December 1911, but stepped aside after two months. Boothe died in 1913, eight years before Sun was elected president of a self-proclaimed national government at Canton. Not until 1966, when Stanford's Hoover Institution on War, Revolution and Peace acquired Boothe's papers, did South Pasadena learn that Sun may once have visited South Pasadena, and that the Boothe mansion at 1515 Garfield Avenue had once been financial headquarters for a revolution.

For California women, 1911 was a year of promise. Governor Hiram Johnson took office pledged to a number of reforms, including woman suffrage. It was a popular cause in South Pasadena. Almost a quarter of a century earlier, Margaret Collier Graham said of her neighbors in the Indiana Colony, "By the way, nearly all the women are women's rights women, and we have made an agreement to keep the subject before the literary society." They kept the subject before wider audiences as well. Margaret Vater Longley won national attention when elected vice-chairman of the state Populist convention in 1894. In 1896 she and her daughter-in-law, Ada Jackson Longley, helped organize the South Pasadena Woman Suffrage Campaign Committee to rally support behind a California voting rights amendment.

Between 1896 and 1910, California lawmakers showed little interest in votes for women. In 1911, however, a suffrage amendment was again placed on the ballot, and its supporters organized for battle. "We had little money and less political experience,"

65

said one woman, "but we had consecration of purpose." South Pasadenans formed a Suffrage Amendment Club and elected Ada Jackson Longley president. The club sponsored the first mass rally for women held in the city, and more than five hundred people attended. Grace Simons, another South Pasadena suffragist, became head of the Political Equality League (founded in 1910 by Pasadenan John H. Braly) and coordinated its campaign efforts. The League printed more than a million leaflets, mailed more than sixty thousand appeals, and in the last month of the campaign held as many as sixty meetings a week.

The election was held on October 10, 1911. For two days the outcome was in doubt. Suffragists followed the returns, said the *Woman's Journal*, first with despair, then with hope, and finally with jubilation. The amendment passed by about one vote per precinct. South Pasadena had a 45 percent turnout—330 voting for woman suffrage and 208 against. Supporters held a victory rally at El Centro School and joyously sang, "Glory, glory, hallelujah! The world is marching on!"

Within the next few years, a number of South Pasadenans blazed trails for other women. Mabel Walker Willebrandt, former principal of Lincoln Park School, became an assistant public defender in Los Angeles. Georgia P. Bullock served as referee in the Los Angeles police court, then as deputy district attorney and as municipal judge. She later became the first woman elected to the Superior Court in California. Dr. Lillian Whiting was the first woman president of the State Osteopathic Association; Florence Collins Porter, the first woman to be a presidential elector; and Alice Woertendyke, South Pasadena's first woman candidate for state legislature.

"Suffrage brings a great responsibility," said a patronizing gentleman in 1911, "and the ladies of this city are preparing themselves for that responsibility." He was speaking to a large public gathering called by the Woman's Improvement Association to discuss making the Arroyo Seco a great sunken garden. As early as 1894, George W. Glover suggested that cities bordering the Arroyo join in making a park from Los Angeles to the mountains. He envisioned winding roads, sparkling fountains, and roses climbing on old snags. Some of his ideas were echoed by the Arroyo Seco Parkway Association, organized in March 1912 with representatives from Pasadena, South Pasadena, Los Angeles, and Los Angeles County. Members discussed plans for a graceful boulevard winding through an ever-changing park. Theodore Roosevelt also expressed his enthusiasm for the Arroyo. After speaking at Occidental College in 1911, Roosevelt drove along the Arroyo Seco and observed, "This Arroyo would make one of the greatest parks in the world."

During the summer of 1912, the Woman's Improvement Association held a well-publicized picnic in the Arroyo—not within South Pasadena's borders, the women pointedly explained, for the city had no Arroyo park—but in Highland Park's Sycamore Grove. In a caravan of twenty-three automobiles, club members and their guests drove to the Arroyo Seco and triumphantly crossed the new bridge—the first people allowed to drive over it. After an excursion to view Devil's Gate and the canyon beyond, the group returned to picnic under the sycamores and listen to progress reports on city and county acquisition of parkland.

Not everyone in South Pasadena shared the women's enthusiasm for a park in the Arroyo. Some considered it a luxury, to be deferred until the city had a water com-

66

Ada J. Longley was active in the Woman's Improvement Association, the library, the campaign to build a high school, and the fight for woman suffrage. *Courtesy of South Pasadena Chapter #272, Order of the Eastern Star.*

By 1918 six dairies were operating in South Pasadena's Arroyo Seco. *Courtesy of Security Pacific National Bank Photograph Collection/Los Angeles Public Library.*

pany, sewers, and better fire protection. Indeed, it was not until 1922 that South Pasadena finally passed an Arroyo Seco bond issue and began acquiring land. Meanwhile, the Arroyo continued to be used by such varied interests as beekeepers, dairymen, a rock crushing company, and an evangelical church.

The most divisive question in South Pasadena between 1910 and 1913 was whether to annex to Los Angeles, which was eager to expand its boundaries. Those arguing for annexation claimed it would bring South Pasadena cheap light and power, access to a comprehensive sewer system, and a guaranteed share of Owens River water. Annexation sentiment was especially strong among people living near the Arroyo and those with business interests in Los Angeles. Supervisor R. W. Pridham was an influential spokesman for both groups. Another ally was the *South Pasadena Courier*, founded in 1913 by Walter Abbott.

The Chamber of Commerce opposed annexation. So did E. O. Wickizer, who became editor and publisher of the *Record* in 1910. Wickizer denounced annexation as a gobble-up scheme to enhance Los Angeles tax revenues and bonding capacity. He saw no reason to join Los Angeles and help pay for what he called a broken-down outfall sewer, an outrageously expensive aqueduct, and a harbor and municipal railway of as much benefit to South Pasadena "as the proverbial second tail to a cat." Furthermore, he warned, with annexation and the loss of home rule, South Pasadena might see Mission Street and Fair Oaks Avenue abandoned to "the open saloon, the vicious gambling hall, and the sinister poolroom."

As an alternative to annexing to Los Angeles, the Chamber of Commerce proposed that South Pasadena enter a "community of interests" with Pasadena and Alhambra. The three cities would remain independent but would cooperate in planning for such shared concerns as water, sewers, fire protection, and parks. The idea met with instant approval. Pasadena, South Pasadena, and Alhambra appointed a Tri-City Commission in 1911 and a Tri-City Sewer Board in 1915.

Meanwhile, other cities in the San Gabriel Valley expressed interest in working together more closely. In 1912 they formed the San Gabriel Valley Inter-City Commission, which included Pasadena, South Pasadena, and Alhambra as members. The group's rallying cry was, "United we prosper; divided we don't." Its ambitious twenty-four-point program included such varied goals as working for uniform city ordinances, boosting home business, and establishing a choir of a thousand voices.

On July 4, 1912, South Pasadena sponsored an inter-city celebration under the oaks at Garfield Park. Guests enjoyed a free barbecue and a musical program ranging from Handel and Haydn to the newly composed "Inter-City Quick Step." Headlines claimed that at least 4,000 people attended the picnic and at least 3,999 were satisfied.

Confident that South Pasadena could solve its problems without annexing to Los Angeles, the city council decided to press ahead with municipal improvements. In October 1913 it held a half-million-dollar bond election to vote money for sewers, a water company, and a modernized fire department. The water bonds fell just eighteen votes short of the necessary two-thirds majority; the other bonds passed easily. A second water bond election was held in November, two weeks after Los Angeles dedicated its new aqueduct, and water from the Owens River cascaded into the San Fernando Reservoir. Annexationists could not have hoped for more dramatic evidence

The Woman Suffrage Campaign Committee for South Pasadena (1896) and the Woman's Improvement Association (1899) were organized at the house built by Ada and Leo Longley in 1888. The house is now a Cultural Heritage Landmark. *Courtesy of South Pasadena Cultural Heritage Commission.*

The clubhouse at Fremont Avenue and Rollin Street was built in 1913 for the Woman's Improvement Association. Members changed the name of their group to the Woman's Club in 1924. *Photograph by H. J. Kenny; courtesy of South Pasadena Public Library.*

of the water available to Los Angeles and those communities that annexed to it. Once again the bonds for a South Pasadena water company were narrowly defeated. It was not until 1920 that water bonds finally passed, and then it was by an overwhelming ratio of six to one.

The bond election in October 1913 overshadowed the social event of the month, the dedication of a new clubhouse belonging to the Woman's Improvement Association. Ever since its founding in 1899, the club had met in temporary quarters—in the old Opera House, where members had to trundle their own chairs; in the Baptist Church, where the women were asked to help pay for a new carpet; and in the Masonic Hall, where their tea things were always being misplaced. In 1910 the club made a down payment on a lot at Fremont Avenue and Rollin Street, and architect Norman Foote Marsh donated plans for a building. Members proved ingenious fund-raisers. One year they raised five hundred dollars by going without new winter hats and contributing the price of a bonnet to the building fund. The Woman's Club of South Pasadena— successor to the Woman's Improvement Association—continues to meet in the clubhouse at Fremont and Rollin.

Near the clubhouse, and designed to harmonize with it, was a new substation of the Home Telephone and Telegraph Company. It offered direct service to Los Angeles without going through a long distance operator. The company promised phones to all who wanted them. Previously it could handle only a thousand subscribers in South Pasadena. Other residents used the rival Sunset Company, and some even subscribed to both services.

The city council had reluctantly allowed a motion picture theater to open in 1910. (Originally the South Pasadena Theater, it became the Gem in 1913—or as youngsters gleefully called it, the Germ.) Permitting theaters was one thing; permitting film companies was another. In 1913 the Lubin Company leased property on the Arroyo and began making a Western movie. Neighbors complained of having to put up with "the tail end of a circus." Ernest Sutton, who was then mayor, wrote in his autobiography:

> It seemed that along the Arroyo Seco a lot of people had come in and set up tents, built corrals and other unsightly structures and were riding roughshod over the district, shooting, whooping, making a great disturbance. The citizens living near said they were making motion pictures. We already know that over near the Cahuenga Pass a small settlement called Hollywood was having the same trouble, so the Council went down to investigate.

What it found was an Arroyo transformed to a Western scene: "saloons, hardware and grocery stores, hitching rack and all." The council took disapproving note of the tents and cook shanty, the covered wagons used for sleeping quarters, and the actors costumed as the rough characters of a frontier town. "An ordinance was passed," wrote Sutton, "forbidding this and other industries of like nature setting up shop in South Pasadena. We were threatened with a lawsuit, but in time the outfit pulled up stakes and left. Whether the town lost or gained by this action is only a matter of opinion."

Six years later the city welcomed a movie company. This time Mary Pickford was the star, Paul Powell—a South Pasadenan—was the director, and *Pollyanna* was the movie. Playing the title role, Miss Pickford alighted at the Santa Fe depot in an artificial rainstorm created by the South Pasadena Fire Department. An enthusiastic crowd watched America's Sweetheart being filmed. The Chamber of Commerce—equally enthusiastic—decided motion pictures had become educational and uplifting, and it recommended trying to attract studios to the city.

The *Record* carried a startling headline in 1913: "Plucky Woman Dons Man's Attire." The woman was Marie Caspari, who wore flannel trousers when taking part in South Pasadena's annual clean-up day. She told a reporter:

> I suppose that a great many persons will consider me immodest in appearing in men's clothing to do this work but I do not care. The idea of going out to work in dust, weeds and rubbish wearing long skirts that pick up germs with almost every movement of the body, does not appeal to me as sanitary. . . . When I start to do cleaning I always put on a pair of men's trousers, and when wearing them I do not feel in the least embarrassed. Why should I?

Another interesting headline in 1913 announced, "Local Passengers Take Aerial Trip." They were South Pasadena's two motorcycle policemen, Archie Cooper and Frank B. Higgins, who cruised eight hundred feet above the city in a dirigible designed and built by Roy Knabenshue, the first person to fly a dirigible in the United States. Knabenshue made a number of local flights in September 1913 to test a new control system and to see how he might balance his airship to carry a passenger load of twelve. A reassuring news story on the flights observed, "There is an utter lack of terror or even apprehension. Half the passengers Mr. Knabenshue has carried aloft are women, and not one of them has at any time during a trip expressed alarm, while on landing they have been unanimous and enthusiastic in their expressions of pleasure." The wooden hangar for the airship was on Marengo Avenue in Pasadena—or as the *Record* put it, just three hundred feet from South Pasadena's border.

Even a local drugstore made headlines in 1913. The owner, B. M. Weaver, invited George Lightonberg, "recognized dean of the soda water world," to create fancy drinks, sundaes, and fountain delicacies at Weaver's and to make ice sculptures in the drugstore window while a piano and violin provided background music. The newspaper reported that huge crowds packed the store, blockaded the sidewalk, and filled Mission Street from curb to curb.

Another news story in 1913 reported that South Pasadenans Harrye Forbes and her husband Armitage S. C. Forbes were placing replicas of mission bells along El Camino Real, the highway connecting the twenty-one missions between San Diego and Sonoma. Harrye Forbes—author of two books about the missions—designed the bells, which her husband manufactured.

In 1914 George M. Millard, "prince of bibliophiles," moved to South Pasadena from Chicago and set up a business in antiquarian books ("libraries formed or enriched") at his home on Huntington Drive. The poet Eugene Field once wrote of Millard, who made regular book-buying trips to Europe:

> All who have the means to buy,
> Ye who seek some rare old tome,
> Maniacs shrewd or imbecilic,
> Urban, pastoral or idyllic,
> Richly clad or dishabillic,
> Heed the summons bibliophilic:
> George Millard is home.

Paying twenty-five dollars for twenty-five minutes, passengers could fly over the San Gabriel Valley in Roy Knabenshue's dirigible. In the background is South Pasadena's Raymond Hotel. The aerodrome was located on Marengo Avenue in Pasadena. *Courtesy of Huntington Library.*

In 1914 the city hall moved into new quarters at Mission Street and Mound Avenue. Norman Foote Marsh designed the building, which housed the city offices, fire station, police station, and jail cells. *Courtesy of Security Pacific National Bank Photograph Collection/Los Angeles Public Library.*

A representative of the Seagrave Company stands with Fire Marshal Martin Wolf and fireman W. C. Trepp on the Seagrave engine purchased by South Pasadena in 1914. *Courtesy of Gene E. Murry.*

After Millard's death in 1918 his widow, Alice Parsons Millard, continued the business—first in South Pasadena and then in the famous Pasadena house designed for her by Frank Lloyd Wright.

The year 1914 was a time of civic improvement and civic pride. Bonds passed the previous year financed a sewer system, installation of fire hydrants, and the purchase of a Seagrave pumping engine, white with blue trim. The Seagrave remained in active service until 1931. Sold to a collector in 1946, it then embarked on a career in motion pictures.

At the end of 1914 South Pasadena dedicated its new city hall, at Mission Street and Mound Avenue. Not surprisingly, it was designed by Norman Foote Marsh, who already had a dozen buildings in town to his credit. The city hall not only housed the municipal offices, but also contained two jail cells, firemen's quarters, and a garage for the city's two fire engines. A special feature of the building was a discreetly located women's restroom, "a long-needed convenience for ladies passing through the city or transferring from one car line to another."

During the year, the Chamber of Commerce distributed two thousand picture postcards of South Pasadena and sponsored a contest for an official city slogan. One anonymous tourist suggested, "South Pasadena: the city of yelping dogs and crowing roosters." The Chamber chose instead two other entries and combined them to read, "South Pasadena attracts and holds; come, you'll stay." The slogan recalls South Pasadena's first New Year's float, entered in the Tournament of Roses in 1911. Designed by the high school art teacher, Ada Chase, it portrayed a great floral magnet, symbolizing South Pasadena's drawing power as a residential city.

European war news jolted the city in May 1915. One of its most prominent residents, Albert C. Bilicke, was among the 1,153 people drowned when a U-boat torpedoed the Cunard liner *Lusitania* off the coast of Ireland. Except for this tragedy, the war did not directly touch South Pasadena until February 1917, when the United States broke off diplomatic relations with Germany.

In the meantime, the city faced such mundane problems as tadpoles in the drinking water, reckless drivers on Raymond Hill (going twenty to forty miles an hour), and householders who saw no reason to pay for municipal garbage collection when they could burn or bury their kitchen scraps or feed them to the chickens.

In May 1915 South Pasadena turned on the new high-efficiency nitrogen lights installed on Fair Oaks Avenue and on Huntington Drive from Oneonta Station to Alhambra Road. The city boasted, "For the first time the people of Southern California will know what REAL street lights are." The community celebrated with a grand parade. The two fire trucks, decorated with American flags, joined four hundred private cars which drove from Raymond Hill to Oneonta Station along Fair Oaks Avenue. To prevent accidents, traffic officers stood at every streetcar crossing.

The city was heartened by increased building activity in 1916. Seventy-three houses went up, at an average cost of $3,100, compared with sixty-four houses in 1915 at an average cost of $1,900. There were several new bungalow courts and five new business buildings, including the Colonial Motion Picture Theater (top admission thirty cents for loges). In December 1916 the library broke ground for an addition that would almost double its floor space. By the time the new wing opened, the country was at war.

One South Pasadenan called into government service during the war was G. Harold Powell, who was asked to head the perishable foods division of the United States Food Administration. A distinguished horticulturist, Powell was well known for his writing and research on fruit storage and transportation. His study of blue mold in citrus led to improved techniques in picking, packing, and shipping of oranges and lemons. King Albert of Belgium recognized Powell's outstanding service in the Food Administration by awarding him the Cross of the Chevalier of the Order of the Crown.

South Pasadena responded with patriotic fervor to the declaration of war in April 1917. Within a few days the city organized a Home Guard with more than a hundred members. The high school introduced military training, and soon half the boys were drilling under the command of two students from Pasadena's Throop College of Technology.

Prompted by the Woman's Improvement Association, the city plowed up vacant lots for home gardens, and the Marengo Water Company offered free irrigation water from the fire hydrants. Nearly every family in town began raising vegetables. Children at the Boys' and Girls' Aid Society even grew sugar cane, which was crushed at a syrup mill on Palm Avenue. During summer vacations a score of high school boys answered the call to harvest crops in the San Joaquin Valley. They won praise for their diligence at work and their behavior in town.

In June 1917 the first volunteers left for the front, to join the ambulance corps. The Chamber of Commerce suggested that the city fly a flag with a star for each South Pasadenan in the service. When the banner was dedicated in March 1918, it displayed 190 stars. By the end of the war it held 315. Four gold stars commemorated those who had lost their lives. Among them was Marion Burns, the first boy to graduate from South Pasadena High School.

With most people wholeheartedly committed to the war, feeling against pacifism ran high. In October 1917 a small group of Christian Pacifists met in a private home on Huntington Drive. More than two hundred angry protesters broke up the meeting and drove its leaders out of town. An editorial noted approvingly, "Thanks to the stern determination of a large band of loyal citizens, South Pasadena is free from future danger of pacifist meetings. A cloud of shame would have rested on this fair city if drastic steps had not been taken, and taken promptly."

Following the example of the United States Congress, in 1918 South Pasadena passed an ordinance against seditious remarks. A few people were arrested, and several more kept under surveillance by zealous patriots. A five-man vigilance committee threatened to publish the names and excuses of "bond slackers" who refused to subscribe to the Liberty Loan drive. The threat probably was quite unnecessary. People gave with tremendous generosity, and their pledges twice surpassed the city quota by $200,000. People also gave generously to the Red Cross and worked long hours at such tasks as rolling bandages and knitting. An article on Red Cross contributors singled out for praise the Japanese residents of South Pasadena.

Shortly after one o'clock in the morning of November 11, 1918, South Pasadena received word of the Armistice. A fire engine with siren wailing drove up and down the main streets to herald the good news. Members of the Home Guard gathered at City Hall and sang, "We won't go home until morning." Cars dragging tin cans sped

A few days after the United States declared war on Germany, South Pasadena opened a Red Cross room with more than a hundred women workers. *Courtesy of Security Pacific National Bank Photograph Collection/Los Angeles Public Library.*

A Big Red Car is shown around 1920 on Mission Street just west of Fair Oaks Avenue. *Courtesy of South Pasadena Public Library.*

noisily through the city as passengers shouted, rang bells, and sounded horns.

On November 17 the churches sponsored a peace celebration on the high school campus. It was the first public gathering since October, when the terrible influenza epidemic reached South Pasadena. The schools, churches, library, and motion picture theater had closed down for eight weeks. Despite such precautions, the city had three hundred cases of flu and eleven deaths.

A special Flag Day celebration in June 1919 welcomed the veterans home. The day-long program included such pleasant diversions as a pie-eating contest and a street dance to the music of a twenty-piece band. Veterans were also welcomed back by the Rendezvous Club, a men's social club that the Home Guard had opened a few months earlier. In November, South Pasadena veterans met to organize American Legion Post No. 140. A month later they received the official charter and elected Walter I. Schoeffel as chairman.

Business began returning to normal in the spring of 1919, and the city launched a "Go Ahead Campaign" for improving roads, homes, and commercial buildings. One suggestion for boosting home sales was to paint the dark wood of craftsman bungalows a more cheerful color.

The newspaper ran a booster column in 1919 with impressive facts about South Pasadena. The city had, for example:

One men's club, one milliner's, one furniture store, one orange drink factory;

Two banks, two hardware stores, two greengrocers, two dry goods stores, two auto accessory stations, two feed and fuel dealers, two gas stove manufacturers, two restaurants, two public parks;

Three barber shops, three drug stores, three tailors, three women's clubs;

Four shoe repair shops;

Five miles of ornamental street lights (and thirty-five miles of improved streets, sixty miles of sidewalks);

Six public garages, six groceries, six real estate dealers;

Seven church organizations; and

Eight thousand thrifty, home-loving people.

The city also had one of the best-equipped high schools in the area, a public library with 17,000 volumes, and—of course—the world-famous Cawston Ostrich Farm and Raymond Hotel.

The ostrich farm lent an exotic note to South Pasadena. So did the Chinese vendors who came through town selling tea and ginger and lichee nuts. Balanced on each man's shoulders was a bamboo pole from which two great baskets were suspended. The vendors had long been a familiar sight in South Pasadena. A guest at the Raymond in 1886 described the vendors and their baskets, which in those days were filled with "dainty boxes, delicately carved woods, soft pale colors in crepe and silk and paper."

In 1909 the city had considered changing its name to something more distinctive. The Chamber of Commerce pursued the idea again in 1918 and 1919, complaining that people still believed South Pasadena was part of Pasadena. Residents proposed various alternatives, such as Raymond, Live Oaks, Deltadena, Liberty, and Lafayette. The *Pasadena Star-News* suggested the name of Beasley in honor of South Pasadena's new police chief, E. L. Beasley, who was also building inspector, city electrician, plumbing inspector, sewer inspector, custodian of city property, and city purchasing agent. (These various appointments netted Beasley a monthly salary of $125, plus an allotment of $25 for use of his automobile.) The campaign to rename South Pasadena fizzled once more but revived with greater enthusiasm in the late twenties and the thirties.

Employees of Chaffee's Basket Grocery, at 1012 Mission Street, posed in 1910 for H. J. Kenny, whose studio was a block away on El Centro. *Courtesy of South Pasadena Public Library.*

During South Pasadena's Flag Day celebration in 1910, a band played on Buena Vista Street, outside the home of presidential widow Lucretia Garfield. *Photograph by H. J. Kenny; courtesy of South Pasadena Public Library.*

Courtesy of Huntington Library.

CHRONOLOGY

1910

Census figures for South Pasadena show a population increase in ten years from 1,001 to 4,659—a rate of growth exceeded by only three cities in the state.

The Chamber of Commerce organizes a spectacular Flag Day celebration.

The city passes its first municipal bond issue, to pay for a bridge over the Arroyo Seco near the Cawston Ostrich Farm.

The South Pasadena Theater opens on Mission Street, and the city has its first motion picture show.

Marengo School opens in September.

A number of residents campaign for annexation of South Pasadena to Los Angeles.

The Pacific Electric lays two additional tracks on Huntington Drive.

Dr. Sun Yat-sen, plotting to establish a Republic of China, names South Pasadenan Charles Beach Boothe his sole foreign financial agent.

1911

The city enters its first float in Pasadena's Tournament of Roses and wins a silver cup.

The Suffrage Amendment Club, with Ada Longley as president, sponsors the city's first mass rally for women. By a vote of 330 to 208 South Pasadena endorses a constitutional amendment giving women the vote in California.

Pasadena, South Pasadena, and Alhambra form a Tri-City Commission for cooperation on mutual problems.

Former president Theodore Roosevelt suggests that the Arroyo Seco would make one of the world's great parks.

Huntington Hall, a ladies seminary, opens on Fremont Avenue. One building is a copy of an Elizabethan house, another of the Petit Trianon.

1912

The United States Supreme Court upholds South Pasadena's ordinance against pool halls.

Representatives from Pasadena, South Pasadena, Los Angeles, and Los Angeles County form the Arroyo Seco Parkway Association.

C. G. Bridgman organizes two Boy Scout patrols at El Centro School.

Members of the Woman's Improvement Association and their guests are the first to drive over the new bridge by the Cawston Ostrich Farm.

1913

South Pasadena votes bonds for sewers and a modernized fire department.

The city's two motorcycle policemen cruise over the city in Roy Knabenshue's dirigible.

The Woman's Improvement Association moves into its clubhouse at Fremont Avenue and Rollin Street.

The South Pasadena YMCA incorporates.

The Home Telephone and Telegraph Company builds a substation in South Pasadena and promises telephone service for all who want it.

Walter Abbott begins publication of the *South Pasadena Courier.*

Eleven-year-old Billy Axtman, "youngest newspaper publisher on the West Coast," writes, prints, and distributes a four-page newspaper, *The Leaflet.*

1914

The fire department, police department, and other government offices move into the new city hall building at Mission Street and Mound Avenue.

Fifteen charter members form the Oneonta Park Chapter, Daughters of the American Revolution.

A Merchants Association is organized as a Chamber of Commerce auxiliary.

1915

The fire department's new Seagrave pumping engine arrives.

The city installs nitrogen lights on Fair Oaks Avenue and along Huntington Drive.

South Pasadenan Albert C. Bilicke loses his life when the *Lusitania* is torpedoed.

1916

The library breaks ground for an addition.

1917

On April 6 the United States declares war on Germany.

South Pasadena organizes a Home Guard and introduces voluntary military training in the high school. During summer vacations, high school students help harvest crops in the San Joaquin Valley.

South Pasadena becomes the first city in Southern California to enact an ordinance against billboards.

E. O. Wickizer, publisher of the *South Pasadena Record,* acquires the *South Pasadena Courier.*

1918

The new city directory lists every automobile owner in town.

Following the example of Congress, South Pasadena passes an ordinance against seditious remarks.

The flu epidemic closes schools, churches, the library, and the motion picture theater for eight weeks in October and November.

The city celebrates the Armistice on November 11.

Business returns to normal, and the city launches a "Go-Ahead Campaign" to improve roads, homes, and commercial buildings.

A Flag Day celebration welcomes the veterans home.

American Legion Post No. 140 is organized in South Pasadena, with Walter I. Schoeffel as chairman.

The Chamber of Commerce suggests that South Pasadena adopt a new name.

Sun Yat-sen reportedly hid from political enemies for several weeks in 1910 in the Boothe house on Garfield Avenue. The sixteen-room mansion, built in 1906, was razed in 1972 when engineers advised that it was structurally unsafe. *Courtesy of South Pasadena Review.*

Courtesy of South Pasadena Public Library.

V

PROSPERITY AND GROWTH: 1920-1929

Ride with the Sun.

E. O. WICKIZER

SOME BOOSTERS CLAIMED that the early twenties heralded the dawn of a new era in South Pasadena. They referred especially to increased building activity but could have mentioned other evidence as well. The water bonds finally passed in 1920, and South Pasadena took the first steps toward forming a municipal water company. Teachers won a pay hike and now earned as much as $2,500 a year. In 1920 South Pasadena hired its first city manager, R. V. Orbison, luring him away from a job as city engineer in Pasadena. The city also purchased Garfield Park, which it had been leasing from the Southern Pacific Railroad. A beautiful spot with a stream and great oak trees, the park was only two blocks from the business center at Fair Oaks Avenue and Mission Street.

In 1921 Orange Grove Avenue was paved at last, an elementary school opened in Oneonta Park, and voters overwhelmingly endorsed a $12,000 bond issue for a combined war memorial and American Legion clubhouse. Legionnaires raised another $3,000 for the building, and the city donated a site at Fair Oaks Avenue and Oaklawn. Twenty thousand people watched Marshal Ferdinand Foch lay the cornerstone on December 4, 1921. French and American flags flew on Raymond Hill and in the newly named American Legion Park. Leon Dostert, a French war orphan living in South Pasadena, presented Marshal Foch with a bouquet of American Beauty roses paid for with the pennies of local schoolchildren. (Dostert had an interesting career after graduating from South Pasadena High School. He founded the Institute of Language and Linguistics at Georgetown University, served as General Dwight D. Eisenhower's interpreter in World War II, and helped create the simultaneous translation system used at the Nuremberg Trials and at the United Nations.)

The American Legion ceremony was not the only South Pasadena event to bring out crowds in 1921. More than a thousand people attended a springtime celebration held in the Arroyo Seco to bolster interest in an Arroyo park. The program featured birdcalls, a talk on wildflowers, and a Pageant of the Arroyo, with children costumed as bunnies, toads, lizards, and bees. Poet John Steven McGroarty made an eloquent appeal to preserve the beauty of the Arroyo. In 1922 voters passed a $100,000 bond issue to buy a hundred acres of the Arroyo Seco lying within the borders of South Pasadena.

South Pasadenans enjoyed two grand opening ceremonies in 1922. One was for the completed War Memorial Building, dedicated on Memorial Day by former Secretary of the Treasury William Gibbs McAdoo. The other was for the South Pasadena branch of the Security Trust & Savings Bank in its new quarters at Fair Oaks Avenue and Mission Street. More than two thousand people visited the branch and came

On December 4, 1921, Marshal Ferdinand Foch placed the cornerstone of South Pasadena's War Memorial Building and American Legion Clubhouse. The building, designed by Norman Foote Marsh, is a Cultural Heritage Landmark. *Courtesy of Security Pacific National Bank Photograph Collection/Los Angeles Public Library.*

The South Pasadena Garage and the Record Publishing Company shared this building at Fair Oaks Avenue and Hope Street until 1922, when the newspaper defied the city council and moved farther south on Fair Oaks. *Photograph by H. J. Kenny; courtesy of Huntington Library.*

away with a free illustrated booklet, *On Old Rancho San Pascual: The Story of South Pasadena*. Written by Laurance L. Hill, of the bank's publicity and advertising staff, the sprightly little booklet was the first publication devoted solely to the history of South Pasadena.

During the summer of 1922 the city began a year-long fight to enact a comprehensive zoning ordinance. Two measures passed by the council were overturned: one by the courts and one by referendum. Opponents claimed the measures would retard growth in the city and keep it from developing "as nature intended." In particular, they wanted more zoning for apartment houses and duplexes and more zoning for business on Fair Oaks Avenue. Before writing a third ordinance, the council held a public hearing and studied more than twelve hundred replies to a questionnaire it had sent to property owners. The new ordinance, passed in June 1923, made it easier to rezone for apartments and duplexes, and it extended the business district on Fair Oaks Avenue south to Monterey Road from the former boundary at El Centro Street.

A year before the zoning changed on Fair Oaks, a commercial building was already under construction there. E. O. Wickizer, publisher of the *Record* and the *Courier*, insisted he had a valid permit to build a newspaper plant in the block between Oxley Street and Monterey Road. He did indeed have a permit, but it had been issued to him by one city council and revoked a week later by a new council against which he had vigorously campaigned. Denying that the permit could be revoked, Wickizer proceeded with construction. He and his workmen were promptly arrested on a misdemeanor charge and threatened with further arrests each day that work continued. Wickizer obtained an injunction against the city, finished his building, then asked for an electrical inspection. When the city refused, Wickizer provided his own power by hooking up a Ford tractor to a generator. The Record Publishing Company thus became the first business in South Pasadena to have its own electrical plant—and the first business to locate on Fair Oaks Avenue south of El Centro Street.

Although much of South Pasadena was built up by 1920, there were still large areas undeveloped on Raymond Hill, in the Monterey Hills, and between Orange Grove Avenue and the Arroyo. Because of a tangle of legal and financial problems dating back to 1902, most of the Monterey Hills remained undeveloped for another forty years; but in 1924 one subdivision opened in the vicinity of Indiana Avenue and Monterey Road. This "tract of a thousand views" soon boasted a number of expensive homes, including copies of an Italian villa, a Spanish castle, and a medieval French chateau.

In 1924 work started on an elementary school in the northeast. The Board of Education had hoped to buy the Raymond golf course as a school site, but Walter Raymond protested that the board might as well ask to build in the hotel dining room. The board then chose a site of two and one-half acres near the Adobe Flores. While the school was being built, work also proceeded on a new city reservoir about a block above the school on Raymond Hill. On August 31, 1924, three days after the reservoir was filled, its walls gave way and five million gallons of water roared down the hill as far south as Huntington Drive. A five-foot wall of water smashed through the French doors at Las Flores School, leaving as much as two feet of mud in classrooms and hallways. Within five minutes the eastern part of the city was under one to two feet of water. It was fortunate that the break occurred at three o'clock on a Sunday morning, when few people were about. No one was injured, but damage amounted to some $50,000. Despite vehement objections, the city rebuilt the reservoir and it still remains in service.

At the same time that Las Flores School was under construction, the neighboring adobe was being carefully restored by its owner, Clara Eliot Noyes, and by architect Carleton M. Winslow. Mrs. Noyes, who bought the historic building in 1919, opened a tearoom in the adobe, and nearby she built four new adobes that became popular as artists' studios. South of the Adobe Flores she planted a cactus garden that is now owned by the city. The Adobe Flores, which appears on the National Register of Historic Places, was the first building in South Pasadena to be designated a Cultural Heritage Landmark.

A unique business in a landmark building opened in 1925—the Baranger Studios at Mission Street and Orange Grove Avenue. A. E. Baranger and his wife designed and built window displays for jewelers and opticians. In 1925 more than twelve hundred customers throughout the country subscribed to the Baranger service. Each month they received a new display: not only velvet-covered tables, trays, and stands, but animated figures such as cupids hammering away in the Cherubs' Wedding Ring Factory. "By the use of cunningly devised and beautiful miniature displays," the studios advertised, "a jeweler's window is given all the dramatic interest of a stage set in some gorgeous Broadway revue."

Klieg lights and Hollywood stars marked the opening of the Rialto Theatre on October 17, 1925. The initial program featured five vaudeville acts—many performers got their start at the Rialto—and the world premiere of a silent film comedy, *What Happened to Jones?* starring Reginald Denny and Laura LaPlante. The theater had a full stage and a mammoth Wurlitzer organ. Exuberant press releases also described overstuffed chairs in the loges, paintings of exquisite effect on the walls, and "draperies of the richest reds, blues, greens, yellows blended into restful mellowness under carefully shielded lights."

Baseball fans enjoyed a special treat in 1925 when the World Series came to Mission Street. The merchants rigged a platform on the Alexander Building, at the southeast corner of Meridian and Mission, and arranged for a play-by-play description of the Pirates-Redskins games. A telegrapher lent by the *Pasadena Star-News* got the latest word from the ball park, a scorekeeper chalked up the plays, and an announcer gave a running commentary. (The Pirates beat the Redskins, 4 to 3.)

Several events in 1926 affected local youngsters. The Boys' and Girls' Aid Society moved to Altadena in 1926 after thirty years in South Pasadena. In 1896 Olive Cleveland gave the Society two and one-half acres at Orange Grove Avenue and Mission Street, where in 1893 she had established the Free Will Children's Home. On the same property, in 1886, Edward Reinert operated a beer garden denounced by prohibitionists as "detrimental to the best social, moral, mental, and material interests of the people." Hiram Reid praised Olive Cleveland for converting a noxious property into "a place to *save* homeless boys instead of to *destroy* them." From 1893 until the present time, the site at Orange Grove and Mission has been devoted to young people. When the Boys' and Girls' Aid Society moved, the city used the property for Orange Grove Playground.

When the Garfield Avenue Reservoir broke in 1924, a five-foot wall of water slammed into the P. V. Schissler house on Hardison Place. *Courtesy of South Pasadena Water Division.*

The interior of the Rialto Theatre has changed very little since 1925. Once a showcase for vaudeville, the Rialto still has a full-size stage, a scenery loft, and dressing rooms for actors. *Courtesy of Security Pacific National Bank Photograph Collection/Los Angeles Public Library.*

These children lived in a house maintained by the Boys' and Girls' Aid Society on the present site of Orange Grove Playground. The metal pipe in the upper right-hand corner of the photograph was a fire escape chute that ran from the top floor to a sawdust pit. *Photograph by H. J. Kenny; courtesy of South Pasadena Public Library.*

A children's room—a long-cherished dream of city librarian Nellie Keith—opened in the library in 1926. The inviting room, with its own outside entrance, offered young readers a choice of three thousand books. The year 1926 also brought happy news to young campers: city permission for Boy Scouts, Campfire Girls, and the YMCA to build cabins on old dairy land in the Arroyo that South Pasadena had bought for its park system.

By 1927 most of the Arroyo Seco within South Pasadena had become city property. The people celebrated in April by planting some three hundred native trees in the park, alongside the little cascades and pools formed by Garfias Spring. Landscape architect Charles Gibbs Adams designed stone steps leading to the area. Adams had a lifelong love of the Arroyo. He had explored it as a boy at the turn of the century, when it was thickly wooded with sycamores, oaks, cottonwoods, and bays. Both the Arroyo and the Monterey Hills were a source of income for the youngster. He gathered mushrooms, watercress, and mustard greens to sell to hotel chefs in Pasadena; and he gathered toyon berries at Christmas time to sell to florists in Los Angeles. He also collected scorpions, centipedes, tarantulas, and even an occasional rattlesnake for the curio dealers in Los Angeles to preserve and sell to tourists. For many years Adams had a studio on the site of the old Garfias adobe, overlooking the Arroyo. Garden clubs and historical societies enjoyed meeting in his "outdoor living room," which was shaded by beautiful old pepper trees.

South Pasadena adopted a new slogan in 1927, borrowing it from the *Record*, which for several years had been advising, "Ride with the Sun," a boastful reminder that South Pasadenans who worked in Los Angeles commuted with the sun at their backs and no glare in their eyes. In 1927 the city flirted again with the thought of adopting a new name. "There's something about the prefix South," said a regretful editorial, "which is suggestive of an inferior section of the city of Pasadena." George W. Glover proposed Garfias as a name, but few others seemed interested, and once again the issue died.

South Pasadena's junior high school opened in 1928, on the east side of Fair Oaks Avenue between Oak and Rollin streets. Part of the site had long been used for the greenhouses and office of the Edward H. Rust Nursery. Rust and his father, Horatio Nelson Rust, had started a citrus nursery in 1884 with the seeds of oranges culled from Governor George Stoneman's Los Robles Ranch, in what is now San Marino, and from A. O. Porter's grove on Columbia Street. In two years the Rust Nursery had ten thousand young orange trees ready to be budded to the Washington navel and Eureka lemon. Many of the groves in South Pasadena and San Marino came from this stock. When Edward H. Rust bought out his father in 1892, he began growing ornamentals. His first large job was planting street trees in Oneonta Park. In 1915 he shipped palm trees to San Diego and San Francisco for their expositions celebrating the opening of the Panama Canal. Rust also had palm trees, oaks, and olives towed on barges to Catalina Island and planted there for William Wrigley, Jr.

Two days after the junior high school dedication in October 1928, South Pasadena dedicated a rebuilt El Centro School. Alice Nettleton Keith, who was in the first graduating class of 1892, presented the new school with a deodar and with historic photographs of El Centro taken by her father-in-law, Truman D. Keith.

South Pasadena's pioneer editor, George Wellman Glover, died in 1929, and his ashes were scattered under the trees of his home by the Arroyo. Glover was the founding editor of three newspapers: the *South Pasadenan*, the *Randsburg Miner*, and the *Roadrunner*, a short-lived paper published in Pasadena with his commentary on current news events. A fellow editor praised the *Roadrunner* for "clear, terse, sensible things said in virile, good American language."

The old *South Pasadenan*, which became the *Record* in 1908, took the name of *Foothill Review* in 1928. One of the social events reported that year was "a unique and remarkable dinner party" given at the Woman's Club by Mr. and Mrs. Keinosuke Kodani to celebrate their tenth wedding anniversary. After dinner the 150 guests enjoyed a special program of Japanese music and exhibition dancing. Most of the civic and social leaders of the town were present, along with classmates of young Takao Kodani. The Kodanis gave the party to express thanks to the Woman's Club, where they were employed, and to the city of South Pasadena for such privileges as a free education for their son. The *Foothill Review* described the evening in detail and observed, "One could not help but feel that such a happy event, founded on mutual respect and kindly spirit, would further international goodwill."

Most of the local news reported in 1929 was upbeat. The city discussed enlarging the library, and it purchased a building for the expanded police department. South Pasadena Masons decided to build a temple and collected more than $100,000 in pledges. A month after the stock market crash of October 29, the paper carried the optimistic statement of a San Marino engineer: "The country as a whole should suffer little or no ill effects from the Wall Street panic. . . . It is not whistling in the dark to say that the business outlook is good."

George W. Glover, founding editor of the *South Pasadenan*, declared in an early issue: "The *South Pasadenan* has lost two unpaid subscribers on the strength of its editorial demanding that people keep their chickens penned up, but it can't be helped. Nor will this paper by this or any other means be deterred from standing up for the right." *Courtesy of Huntington Library.*

*Prosperity
and Growth:
1920-1929*

For many years craftsmen designed and built animated window displays in the Baranger Studios on Mission Street. The building is now a Cultural Heritage Landmark. *Photograph by Tom Mossman.*

CHRONOLOGY

1920

The census records South Pasadena's population as 7,652—almost double the population of 1910.

R. V. Orbison becomes South Pasadena's first city manager.

Voters pass a $325,000 bond issue to finance a municipal water company.

The city buys Garfield Park, which it had been leasing from the Southern Pacific Railroad.

1921

Marshal Ferdinand Foch lays the cornerstone for a building designed to serve as municipal war memorial and American Legion clubhouse.

Orange Grove Avenue is paved after years of contention between property owners and the city.

Oneonta Elementary School opens on Fremont Avenue, south of Huntington Drive.

San Marino votes to join the South Pasadena High School District.

The first Girl Scout troop in South Pasadena is organized.

1922

Voters pass a $100,000 bond issue to acquire one hundred acres in the Arroyo Seco for a park.

William Gibbs McAdoo, Secretary of the Treasury during the war, dedicates the War Memorial Building.

Security Trust & Savings publishes *On Old Rancho San Pascual: The Story of South Pasadena.*

Oneonta Military Academy opens on Fremont Avenue, on the former campus of the Huntington Hall for Girls.

1923

Three groups organize in the city: the Oneonta Club, the South Pasadena Kiwanis Club, and the South Pasadena Realty Board.

General John J. Pershing plants a redwood tree at the War Memorial Building.

The city adopts a comprehensive zoning ordinance. One provision extends the business district on Fair Oaks Avenue south from El Centro Street to Monterey Road.

1924

The Garfield Avenue Reservoir breaks and floods the eastern part of the city.

Las Flores Elementary School opens on Raymond Hill.

Restoration begins on the historic Raymond Hill adobe, which a new owner has named the Adobe Flores.

The *South Pasadena Record* begins publishing a radio column "for the growing army of radio fans."

The Woman's Improvement Association changes its name to the Woman's Club of South Pasadena.

1925

The Rialto Theatre opens in a Moorish-style building on Fair Oaks Avenue.

1926

The city authorizes South Pasadena youth groups to establish camps on newly acquired parkland in the Arroyo Seco.

The South Pasadena Garden Club is founded by Charlotte M. Hoak and P. M. Grant.

The Boys' and Girls' Aid Society moves to Altadena after thirty years in South Pasadena.

A children's room opens in the South Pasadena Public Library.

1927

South Pasadena gives up the last city-owned horses and converts the municipal stables to a water department building.

Volunteers plant three hundred trees in the Arroyo, and the city dedicates two oaks to poet John Steven McGroarty, who had urged establishment of a park in the Arroyo.

"Ride with the Sun" becomes the official slogan of South Pasadena.

South Pasadenan Philip F. Dodson is elected state commander of the American Legion.

1928

The Record Publishing Company introduces the *Foothill Review*, a merger of its two weekly newspapers, the *Record* and the *Courier*.

El Centro School is rebuilt, and South Pasadena opens its first junior high school.

South Pasadena forms a Girl Scout Council, with Miriam Purcell as director.

Harry Ben Gronsky, fifteen-year-old South Pasadena violinist, makes his concert debut in the Hollywood Bowl.

South Pasadenan Rayma Wilson, woman's national 800-meter champion, wins a bronze medal at the Amsterdam Olympics.

The Edward H. Rust Nursery moves to Pasadena after forty-two years in South Pasadena.

1929

The Rialto Theatre shows its first talkie.

The Masons collect pledges of $100,000 for a temple.

Anna and Ormand Lewis opened an antique shop in 1928 in a building inspired by architecture Mrs. Lewis had admired in England. The Lewis-Markey Building, opposite the Baranger Studios on Mission Street, is a Cultural Heritage Landmark. *Photograph by Tom M. Apostol.*

Construction of a flood control channel in the Arroyo Seco provided work for a number of South Pasadenans during the Great Depression. The channel was designed to carry a peak flow of 13,500,000 gallons a minute. *Courtesy of South Pasadena Public Library.*

VI

THE DEPRESSION YEARS: 1930-1939

Remember we are not talking about some slum community, but about the fair home city of South Pasadena—the city that boasts about the economic independence of its people. . . . We are talking about good, substantial citizens.　　　　　　　　W. A. ANDERSON

"THE PRESENT WEEK has witnessed the greatest stock-market catastrophe of all the ages," a financial journal reported on November 2, 1929. Despite the crash, South Pasadena moved with brisk confidence into the thirties. The Masons built a $100,000 temple (its cornerstone first sprinkled with "the corn of sustenance, the wine of refreshment, and the oil of joy"), the public library rebuilt and enlarged its twenty-two-year-old structure at a cost of $55,000, and the telephone company put up a half-million-dollar exchange with the latest dial equipment. South Pasadena got its first drive-in market in 1930 and its first miniature golf course. A ticket to the Rialto Theatre included admission to the course, built by Walter Gillette on the lawn of his Fair Oaks residence. Players enjoyed a Wild West ambience as they drove golf balls through a deer's antlers, a mule's skull, and muleskinners' freight wagons.

Some people still believed the city's name hampered development, giving the impression that South Pasadena was part of Pasadena, and on the wrong side of the tracks at that. There already had been three serious attempts to rename the city, and in 1931 the *Foothill Review* sponsored yet another effort. More than a thousand people mailed ballots to the paper, a majority favoring a name change. Most people suggested the city be called Oneonta or San Pascual, but there were scattered votes for such imaginative alternatives as Floresta, San Raymo, El Raymond, Lodena, Bajadena, Pasa Losa, and San Pasahamgeles.

Businessmen wanted "a go-getter name for a bigger and better city," according to one observer. He doubted, however, that any of the names proposed would lure factories, shops, and skyscrapers to Mission Street or Fair Oaks Avenue. "Let us go boldly after what we want," he facetiously advised, "and call our prospective metropolis Zenith City, say, or New Babylon." He then continued:

> The proposal may be logical, but the trouble is that about ninety percent of our people have no yearning for the bigger and better city suggested—they would flee from it if it should come to pass. Otherwise we would be in Alhambra, perhaps, which already has a Main Street miles long and several fine factories in the direction of the bigger and better life. No, gentlemen, no. You may sell us shoes and Chevrolets and insurance, but you cannot sell us that idea.

Despite the *Foothill Review*'s enthusiastic efforts, the name-change campaign failed, and the paper turned its attention to more pressing matters. Chief among these was the local economy. Perhaps nothing better symbolized the effect of the Great Depression

20c 20c 20c 20c 20c 20c 20c 20c 20c 20c 20c 20c 20c 20c 20c 20c 20c 20c

FEBRUARY 1932

This coupon will be accepted at its face value, 20c, at any food or clothing store displaying a sign to that effect, or will be exchangeable at the Treasurer's office at the City Hall for a bank check with which to pay Rent, Light, Heat, and Water bills. It will be redeemed for 98% of face value when presented by the merchant accepting same, within three months from date printed hereon.

SOUTH PASADENA CITIZENS ORGAN-IZATION FOR UNEMPLOYMENT RELIEF

Redemption limited to a fund derived from the sale of these certificates.

Chairman

During the Depression, some South Pasadena workers were paid with employment scrip, redeemable for food and clothing. *Facsimile courtesy of TMA Graphics.*

102

on South Pasadena than the closing of the Raymond Hotel. As tourism dwindled, Walter Raymond could no longer meet the mortgage payments on the hotel. The bank foreclosed in 1931, and three years later a wrecking crew tore down the magnificent old landmark.

South Pasadena struggled to cope with rising unemployment. In the spring of 1931 the city opened a job registry and tried to give work, on a rotating basis, to the neediest applicants. The city encouraged people who did have jobs to spend money and not hoard it. Echoing President Hoover, City Manager O. S. Roen advised, "Good times are just around the corner, and if you buy and spend now we'll all soon get around the corner." Throughout 1931 South Pasadena advertisers proclaimed, "Idle dollars make idle men," and one headline bluntly ordered, "BUY—BUY—SPEND—SPEND—NOW—NOW."

By the first of January 1932 more than a hundred South Pasadenans had reached the end of their resources. In three weeks the number had doubled, and by April it had nearly quadrupled. "Remember," said W. A. Anderson, editor of the *Foothill Review*, "we are not talking about some slum community, but about the fair home city of South Pasadena—the city that boasts about the economic independence of its people. We are not talking about chronic pauperism; we are talking about men and women who have never before faced the economic situation that now confronts them—we are talking about good, substantial citizens."

The city manager hoped to squeeze $12,000 from the budget to hire part-time workers from among the jobless, and a hundred regular employees of the city pledged 5 percent of their salaries to an employment fund. At best, however, there would be enough to support only twenty-five families for a year. Early in 1932 a number of concerned citizens organized the South Pasadena Emergency Relief Committee, with McIntyre Faries as chairman. The committee hoped to create jobs in the community and also to boost home trade. Borrowing an idea already adopted in Anaheim, the committee issued employment scrip in denominations of twenty and forty cents. It urged residents to offer paint-up, fix-up jobs to the unemployed and to buy scrip with which to pay the workers. The suggested rate of pay was forty cents an hour for unskilled labor, sixty cents for skilled. Workers could spend the scrip in South Pasadena for food and clothing or exchange it at City Hall for checks with which to pay utility bills.

The *Foothill Review* encouraged the purchase of scrip "to help meet a situation that has no right to exist here in South Pasadena." Local teachers, who already had pledged $1,700 to the faltering Community Chest, now agreed to take $3,000 in scrip as well. Few others in the city were as generous. In one year scrip sales amounted to only $7,900, and early in 1933 the project was abandoned. Work became increasingly scarce during the summer of 1932, but one makeshift job was available in July and August. People trudged door to door in South Pasadena peddling window stickers that advertised the Olympic Games being held in Los Angeles. The stickers cost a dime, of which the seller kept seven cents.

South Pasadena's Layne Foundation sponsored a relief project in Los Angeles. Bertha Layne (widow of inventor, manufacturer, and philanthropist Mahlon E. Layne) opened a center with a chapel, an employment bureau, and a kitchen serving free coffee and pancakes. The pancakes were made on an automatic griddlecake machine invented by the Laynes' son Ollyn. From 1931 to 1933 the Layne Foundation served an estimated half a million meals and found work for more than three thousand people, 60 percent of them women.

The Red Cross and the Community Chest gave some help to the needy in South Pasadena, as did church groups and the American Legion. The Home Service Circle, a women's group long active in welfare work under the leadership of Hannah Pearson, provided food and clothing and helped with expenses like utility bills. The South Pasadena Cooperative Relief Association exchanged staple foods and vegetables for sixteen hours of work a week. (Some of the vegetables came from other cooperatives, and some from gardens planted in vacant lots on Mission Street.) The South Pasadena Unemployment Unit put men to work cutting firewood for sale. When a devastating earthquake hit Long Beach in March 1933, the men generously donated more than twenty-five cords of wood to help quake victims suffering from lack of fuel.

The number of jobless in South Pasadena continued to grow, and volunteer efforts to solve the problem proved woefully inadequate. South Pasadena welcomed the employment aid program begun by Los Angeles County in the summer of 1932. County funds put South Pasadenans to work, at thirty cents an hour, repairing roads in the Arroyo Seco and replacing curbs and gutters in the city. South Pasadena also hoped to receive federal funds for a post office building after President Hoover signed the Emergency Relief Act in July 1932.

Voters turned out in record numbers for the presidential election in November. Franklin Delano Roosevelt swept the country, and even in Republican South Pasadena the Democrats made great gains, but the city voted for Herbert Hoover by two to one. He received 4,283 votes to Roosevelt's 2,155 and Norman Thomas's 176. The Prohibitionists limped in with 51.

Prohibition had been the official policy of South Pasadena ever since it incorporated as a city in 1888. Over the years a number of transgressors were brought to justice—among them, the hotel keeper who served drinks without a special license (only the Raymond qualified for one), the druggist who dispensed alcoholic "tonics" without a prescription, and the owner of a fruit and soft drink stand on the Arroyo who made under-the-counter sales of his own fruit brandy (said to be of excellent quality).

Since 1920, when the Eighteenth Amendment went into effect, prohibition had been national policy. By 1933, however, public opinion was turning against the "noble experiment." Congress submitted a repeal amendment to the states, and in the period before final ratification it legalized the sale of beer with an alcoholic content of 3.2 percent. South Pasadena maintained that its own prohibition ordinance still prevailed within the city, but the Superior Court ruled otherwise. "We are of the opinion," the judges observed, "that none of the procession of ordinances passed by the city of South Pasadena is now effective to prohibit the sale of beer." Two weeks later the city council abandoned nearly half a century of tradition by passing an ordinance to license and regulate the sale of beer in the city.

National prohibition ended in December 1933 with ratification of the Twenty-First Amendment. Liquor control in California was now vested in the state, with no provision for local option. South Pasadena had voted for repeal by a slim majority, but

Graduates of a homemaking class given in 1931 by the American Red Cross pose with their teachers in the Japanese Center at Meridian Avenue and El Centro Street. *Courtesy of Pasadena Historical Society.*

All mail sent from South Pasadena on July 18, 1936, received a special cachet showing the new post office and the one-room building used at the turn of the century. *Courtesy of Barbara Ketchum Pearce.*

support for temperance remained strong and vocal. On several occasions the city council led impassioned—and successful—battles against licenses for cocktail bars. The protesters denounced liquor as a moral hazard. Although they did not directly quote Hiram Reid, they reaffirmed sentiments expressed by him in 1888:

For truth and right, for HOME we fight
And NO SALOON IN THE VALLEY.

Of course saloons did come to the valley. Bars and liquor stores have existed in South Pasadena since the thirties, but they have always been few in number.

Between 1933 and 1940, FDR's New Deal alphabet became a familiar part of South Pasadena life. Banner headlines announced local response to the NRA—the National Recovery Administration—which the *Foothill Review* described as "the greatest national adventure of all time—the resolution of 120,000,000 people to break the shackles of depression." Store windows throughout South Pasadena displayed the NRA Blue Eagle and the slogan "We do our part."

Federal relief agencies—CWA, PWA, WPA—put the jobless to work on numerous projects. The largest one affecting South Pasadena was the flood control channel built in the Arroyo Seco from Devil's Gate Dam in Pasadena to the Los Angeles River. The project cost $1,500,000 and employed several thousand men, including a number of South Pasadenans. Federal grants helped pay for the high school's science and fine arts buildings, as well as its grandstand, running track, and other athletic facilities. Nearly $600,000 in federal aid went for work on municipal projects such as improving the water system, building a swimming pool at Orange Grove Playground, enlarging the War Memorial Building, and constructing sidewalks, storm drains, and sewers. Other projects ranged from rebacking sheet music in the public library to building a terrace and walkways in South Pasadena's newest park—the estate at Edgewood Drive and Chelten Way bequeathed to the city in 1934 by Ellen Mary Eddie.

The federal government also agreed to give South Pasadena a post office building. The city donated a site at Fremont and El Centro, then threatened to take it back unless the building design met its architectural standards. Critics deplored the government's first design, calling it drab, characterless, and boxlike, with no ornament except a slab of black marble over the entrance. "We don't want any barn on El Centro," the city announced with some asperity and demanded a more attractive building. After looking at photographs of South Pasadena buildings and street scenes, the architect submitted a design that the city accepted without enthusiasm.

The new post office, at 1001 Fremont Avenue, was dedicated on July 18, 1936. All outgoing mail that day received a special cachet designed by teen-ager Barbara Ketchum, a graduate of South Pasadena High School. Her pen-and-ink drawing showed the new building and also the one-room post office that stood at Meridian Avenue and Center Street in 1894. The *Foothill Review* devoted much of its July 17 issue to the post office, tracing the history of mail service in South Pasadena back to 1882, when six volunteers took turns riding horseback to Pasadena to collect the mail.

Artist John Law Walker, a former postal clerk, was commissioned by the Treasury Relief Art Project to paint a mural in the post office lobby. His work shows a Concord mail coach—a vehicle that the new postmaster, George Hugh Banning, and his uncle, Captain William Banning, had written about in their book *Six Horses.*

107

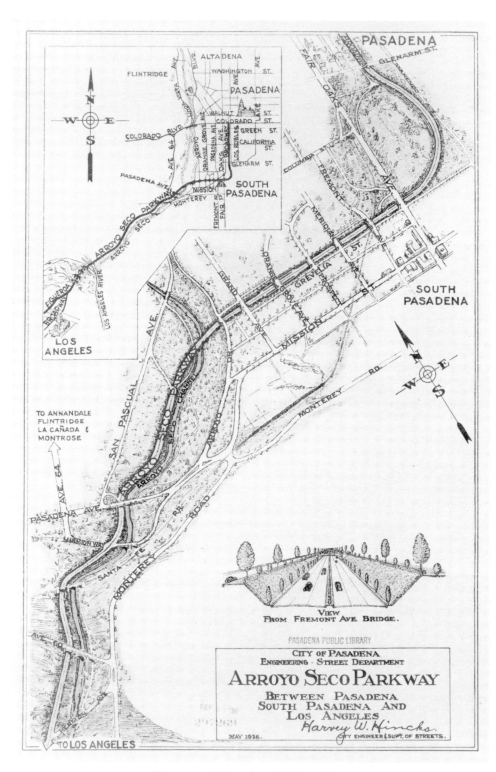

Courtesy of Pasadena Public Library.

The new post office was not the only highlight of 1936. The year opened triumphantly when South Pasadena captured its first Sweepstakes Award in Pasadena's Tournament of Roses. The prize-winning float—designed, built, and decorated by volunteers—portrayed Marie Antoinette and Louis XVI in the gardens of Versailles. City news continued good, with building permits up and business at its highest level since 1932. August marked the end of a nine-year campaign to have the Pacific Electric move its trolley poles from the center of Fair Oaks Avenue to the curb. (Trolley tracks and overhead lines disappeared from Mission Street and Pasadena Avenue in 1935, when the PE replaced the Big Red Cars on that route with modern motor coaches.) Thirty-seven vehicles had crashed into the poles on Fair Oaks since 1927, with the loss of two lives. To celebrate the end of a serious traffic hazard, the Merchants Association sponsored a Kids Koaster Kontest. Ten thousand spectators lined the street as twenty-five soapbox racers sped down Fair Oaks from Columbia Street to Monterey Road.

The Depression Years: 1930-1939

The eventual demise of the Big Red Cars was foreshadowed by plans involving city, county, state, and federal governments for what became the first freeway in the West—the Arroyo Seco Parkway from Pasadena to Los Angeles. There had been talk for years of linking the two cities with a major highway through the Arroyo or alongside it. A route was first surveyed in 1895 and a scenic boulevard was proposed, with an electric railway down the center and sidewalks, bicycle paths, and roadways on either side. This splendid plan was shelved in 1897. At the same time, Horace Dobbins acquired a six-mile right-of-way along the route and began construction of his famous elevated cycleway. The first expressway in the area, it went from downtown Pasadena to the foot of Raymond Hill but was never completed to Los Angeles, as Dobbins had intended.

The idea of an Arroyo Seco highway persisted. In 1924 Los Angeles voters approved traffic plans for major roads in the city and a dual highway through the Arroyo. The route as originally proposed followed the Arroyo from the Los Angeles River to Devil's Gate Dam in Pasadena. A number of Pasadena businessmen and civic leaders wanted an Arroyo highway, but along some other route. They hoped to spare the Arroyo within the Pasadena city limits and thus by-pass Busch Gardens, the Rose Bowl, and the golf course in Brookside Park. In 1934 Carl Hinshaw, a member of the Pasadena Realty Board (and later a congressman), sketched an alternative route that followed the Arroyo from Los Angeles to Sterling Place in South Pasadena, cut across South Pasadena parallel to Grevelia Street, and entered Pasadena at Glenarm and Broadway (now Arroyo Parkway). The Pasadena group had Hinshaw's sketch redrawn by the Los Angeles County Regional Planning Commission. In this way, one of the men later told historian H. Marshall Goodwin, the route could be presented to South Pasadena as the county planning commission's idea, rather than as Pasadena's. The strategy proved successful. In August 1934 the city councils of both Pasadena and South Pasadena passed resolutions in favor of the Grevelia route. South Pasadena appeared to welcome the idea of a great boulevard through the city and construction of a beautiful bridge over the Arroyo that "would rival the world-famous Colorado Street Bridge in its architectural features."

In 1935 Governor Frank Merriam signed legislation that included the Arroyo Seco Parkway in the state highway system but did not specify its exact route. Shortly afterwards, the *Foothill Review* complained that the Pasadena city engineer was drawing up plans for the route but refused to show them to the paper "because it is not desired to get the people stirred up until after a route through the city is determined definitely."

People were indeed stirred up when they realized the route through South Pasadena would make a cut sixteen to twenty feet deep, nearly two hundred feet wide, and extending from the western limits of the city at Sterling Place to the eastern limits at Raymond Hill. The city council (with Mayor John C. Jacobs abstaining) approved a resolution whose words would echo in later freeway battles. The proposed route, said Councilman Burton E. Heartt, "would definitely segregate a substantial part of the city of South Pasadena from the remainder thereof, destroy valuable property and property rights, create many dead-end streets, and would be of no local benefit or advantage." Councilman Sydney G. Parshall made the further observation that the route would cut South Pasadena's Arroyo Seco Park in half.

At a mass meeting held in February 1936, opponents denounced the "speedway" through South Pasadena as a menace, an eyesore, and "just another big ditch." Many people favored the route, however. Morris K. Benagh, who organized the South Pasadena Arroyo Seco Parkway Association, called the freeway "a sunken garden with a scenic driveway in its center" and predicted it would mean "the erection of GREAT and beautiful apartment houses and fine single homes, along the Arroyo and in west South Pasadena."

In March 1936 the city council voted general approval of the Arroyo Seco Parkway by a vote of three to two—with Heartt and Parshall on one side and Mayor Jacobs, E. E. Washburn, and David L. Butler on the other. Seven candidates, including Heartt, Washburn, and Butler, ran for city council in April. An acrimonious campaign focused on issues pertaining to the freeway and to more open council sessions. More than four thousand people voted—the largest number yet for a council election—with Heartt defeated for reelection and victory going to the slate backed by freeway proponents.

Meanwhile, the California Highway Commission approved the Grevelia route through South Pasadena. Efforts to reroute the freeway up the Arroyo failed, and a ground-breaking ceremony for the Arroyo Seco Parkway was held two years later, on March 22, 1938, at Arroyo Drive and Sterling Place in South Pasadena. Rose Queen Cheryl Walker of South Pasadena pulled the lever of a giant tractor, and work on the first freeway in the West was under way.

Minerva Hamilton Hoyt, who lived on the old Benjamin S. Eaton property on Buena Vista Street, campaigned hard against the Grevelia route, which took a portion of her estate. She was more successful in her long campaign to preserve the beauty of the desert. Outraged by widespread theft and destruction of desert flora, Minerva Hoyt organized the International Deserts Conservation League in 1930. In recognition of her work, the University of Mexico made her an honorary professor of botany and named a new species of cactus *Mammillaria hamiltonhoytea*. Mexico's president, Pascual Ortiz Rubio, announced he would set aside ten thousand acres near Tehuacán as a desert reserve in honor of the league and its founder, whom he called "The Apostle of the Cacti."

The year 1936 brought a happy conclusion to Minerva Hoyt's battle to have an area

Construction of the Arroyo Seco Parkway began in March 1938. This view is from Los Angeles, looking south. *Courtesy of Huntington Library.*

Employees of the Cawston Ostrich Farm pose around 1910 outside the feather factory. At that time annual gross sales averaged half a million dollars. Fashions changed, however, and by 1916 ostrich feathers were no longer in demand. *Courtesy of South Pasadena Public Library*.

east of Palm Springs declared the Joshua Tree National Monument—a desert reserve that now covers more than 870 square miles. At Salton View, the highest point in the monument, grateful citizens placed a marker honoring Minerva Hamilton Hoyt and quoting her words about the desert: "I stood and looked. Everything was peaceful, and it rested me."

South Pasadena was fifty years old in 1938. It celebrated with a Golden Fiesta, whose theme was the golden California poppy. A pageant, parade, and street dance enlivened the Fiesta. The pageant dramatized three events associated with South Pasadena history: the arrival of Portolá, the wedding of Manuel Garfias and Luisa Avila, and the city's Flag Day Celebration in 1909. A final scene, which represented a South Pasadena garden party, featured performers doing the latest dance steps, from trucking to Big Apple. On May 6, 1938, the *South Pasadena Review* published a Fiesta edition whose articles and photographs are a valuable source of information on South Pasadena in its first fifty years as an incorporated city.

Many reminders of South Pasadena's past had disappeared by 1938. The city's two greatest attractions—the Raymond Hotel and the bankrupt Cawston Ostrich Farm—were both gone; the hotel torn down in 1934 and the ostrich farm closed a year later. Freeway construction brought an end to South Pasadena's oldest business: dairy operations begun in the 1870s by David M. Raab. The buildings he erected in 1903 on Foothill Street were pulled down in 1938 when the state bought the land for a right-of-way.

Another bit of history ended when seventy-seven-year-old Sing Hom returned to his native China in 1934 after driving a vegetable wagon in South Pasadena for forty years. Nearly a hundred townspeople attended his farewell party, and when he left South Pasadena, an official motorcycle escort accompanied him partway.

Still another link with the past was Lincoln Park School. It took its name from one of the first subdivisions in South Pasadena, a wooded tract along the Arroyo. "We have the best of water, beautiful live oaks, the best of society, and all railroad convenience," boasted George W. Wilson, who subdivided Lincoln Park in 1885. One long-time resident of Lincoln Park was Franz Bischoff, "King of the Rose Painters," who built a home and studio-gallery on Pasadena Avenue in 1908. Before coming West in 1906, Bischoff was best known for his flower paintings on porcelain. The beauty of the Arroyo inspired him to a new career as landscape artist. Critics still praise his work for its rich color harmonies.

People living in Lincoln Park developed a strong sense of community and worked effectively for their interests, including a bridge over the Arroyo. As South Pasadena developed, Lincoln Park lost its identity as a distinct community. In 1939 Lincoln Park School was demolished and replaced by Lincoln School, which in turn became Arroyo Vista.

The old Opera House Building on El Centro was another landmark which disappeared in 1939. Built during the land boom of the eighties, it was the first brick structure in the downtown area. For years the Opera House had played an important role in South Pasadena community life. At the turn of the century it held the city council chamber, the police court, and the Free Public Library and Reading Room. A large upstairs room, complete with stage, was popular for meetings and amateur theatricals

South Pasadenan Walter Gillette held a patent on these back rests. Gillette also designed South Pasadena's first miniature golf course, which opened in 1930 on the lawn of his Fair Oaks residence. *Photograph by H. J. Kenny; courtesy of South Pasadena Public Library.*

but never saw an opera performance. Schoolchildren had classes in the Opera House in 1888 while the Center Street School was rebuilt. At one time Lu Verne S. Reid had a rug-weaving business on the second floor, and downstairs George Minier and Thaddeus Lowe manufactured and sold "the celebrated, odorless Lowe heaters and furnaces" patented by Lowe's father, Professor Thaddeus S. C. Lowe. When the Opera House was razed, the bricks were recycled and used, among other things, for walkways at the home of Walter Garmshausen, mayor of South Pasadena in 1948.

With a grant from the Public Works Administration, the city built an impressive 110-foot swimming pool in 1939, plus a mission-style bathhouse and recreation office. Opening-day ceremonies at Orange Grove Playground featured a lively water show, followed by dancing on the tennis courts to the music of a ten-piece band. The swimming pool was one of the last major projects in South Pasadena to be funded by New Deal relief agencies. In a way, the pleasant midsummer celebration of 1939 foreshadowed the end of the Great Depression.

The Depression Years: 1930-1939

In 1930 the South Pasadena Police Department moved into a Mission Street building formerly used by the Fix-It Shop. Faintly visible alongside the entrance is a sign reading "Mowers Sharpened." *Courtesy of Security Pacific National Bank Photograph Collection/Los Angeles Public Library.*

South Pasadena won the Sweepstakes Award in the 1936 Tournament of Roses. Margaret Louise Brown, former art teacher in South Pasadena, designed the float, and art students at the high school and junior high helped make the costumes. *Courtesy of Pasadena Tournament of Roses Association.*

CHRONOLOGY

1930

Census figures show that South Pasadena's population has almost doubled in ten years, going from 7,652 in 1920 to 13,730 in 1930.

The Masons build a $100,000 temple on Fair Oaks Avenue.

The American Legion Drum and Bugle Corps wins the state championship and performs for President Hoover on the White House lawn.

The public library rebuilds in the center of Library Park. Nellie Keith retires after thirty-five years as city librarian.

Former South Pasadena resident Florence Lowe ("Pancho") Barnes—the granddaughter of Thaddeus S. C. Lowe—sets a world's speed record for women flyers: 18.35 seconds for a one-mile course.

1931

The *Foothill Review* launches a drive to rename South Pasadena.

The Hotel Raymond, a casualty of the Depression, closes its doors.

The police department equips two patrol cars with radio receiving sets.

South Pasadenan Edwina Booth stars in *Trader Horn*, a motion picture filmed on location in Africa.

1932

South Pasadena mobilizes to combat rising unemployment.

The city completes negotiations for a unified water system.

1933

South Pasadena sends aid to victims of the Long Beach earthquake.

The Superior Court strikes down South Pasadena's prohibition laws, and the city passes the first ordinance in its history licensing the sale of beer.

Federal relief agencies put the unemployed to work on civic projects.

1934

The city removes the last hitching post in the business center.

The Raymond Hotel is torn down.

Ellen Mary Eddie wills her estate to the city for a park.

The city council endorses proposals for the Arroyo Seco Parkway.

1935

Teen-age actor Mickey Rooney, as Puck, rides on South Pasadena's float, "A Midsummer Night's Dream," in the Tournament of Roses.

The Cawston Ostrich Farm closes.

Buses replace trolleys on Mission Street.

Work begins on a flood control channel in the Arroyo Seco.

The Garden Club landscapes Eddie Park with six hundred rare plants.

1936

South Pasadena wins the Sweepstakes Award in the Tournament of Roses with a float depicting Marie Antoinette and Louis XVI in the gardens of Versailles.

A federal post office building opens at Fremont Avenue and El Centro Street.

Architect Herbert J. Powell helps design a 150,000-gallon water tank for Raymond Hill.

Debate rages over the route of the Arroyo Seco Parkway through South Pasadena.

The Pacific Electric moves its trolley poles on Fair Oaks Avenue from the center of the street to the curb.

Minerva Hamilton Hoyt is honored for her role in establishing Joshua Tree National Monument.

Clarita Heath, a recent graduate of South Pasadena High School, joins the United States women's ski team for the Winter Olympics in the Bavarian Alps.

1937

The city buys property at Mission Street and Orange Grove Avenue for a playground.

Philip F. Dodson, former mayor of South Pasadena, is named Assistant Attorney General of the United States.

1938

Construction starts on the Arroyo Seco Parkway, after ground-breaking ceremonies at Arroyo Drive and Sterling Place.

South Pasadena celebrates its fiftieth anniversary with a Golden Fiesta.

The *Foothill Review* changes its name to *South Pasadena Review* and publishes a special Fiesta edition on May 6.

A South Pasadena Rotary Club is organized with Charles E. Otto as president.

1939

The Graham & Mohr Opera House Building is razed.

The city builds an elevated water tank on Bilicke Hill, the highest point in the Monterey Hills.

A municipal swimming pool opens at Orange Grove Playground.

Lincoln School replaces the old Lincoln Park School.

The city council approves a Board of Recreation Commissioners.

This view, looking south, shows the elevated cycleway that ran from Dayton Street in Pasadena to the foot of Raymond Hill. Raymond Avenue is at the left, Fair Oaks to the right. Plans called for extending the cycleway to Los Angeles along the route now followed by the Pasadena Freeway. *Courtesy of Pasadena Historical Society.*

The high school class of 1945 dedicated the school annual, *Copa de Oro*, to the thirty-three former students who had lost their lives in World War II. *Courtesy of South Pasadena Public Library.*

120

➤➤➤VII➤➤

WORLD WAR II AND THE POSTWAR YEARS: 1940-1949

If the same selfless spirit were devoted to world betterment in
time of peace, what a good world we would have.

LIEUT. HENRY G. LEE

SOUTH PASADENA PROUDLY WELCOMED a new landmark in 1940, a living sign on the steep bank alongside the entrance to the city from the Arroyo Seco Parkway. Against a contrasting background of wild strawberry, a thousand dusty miller plants spelled out "City of South Pasadena" in ten-foot letters. Because the sign was visible from the air, it had to be removed during World War II, but it was replanted in peacetime and maintained until 1980, when cobblestones replaced the dusty miller.

The Arroyo Seco Parkway opened officially on December 30, 1940, when Governor Culbert Olson cut a ribbon of roses stretched across the traffic lanes. He observed that motorists could now drive from one end of the six-mile freeway to the other "in easy, nerve-free comfort and, above all, in safety." An unlikely ceremony preceded the official freeway dedication. After camping overnight in the Arroyo Seco, Indian chiefs in war bonnets smoked a peace pipe with the State Director of Public Works and grandly relinquished all Indian rights to the Arroyo. A press release explained that a Cahuilla chief requested the ceremony to express "appreciation of modern progress as exemplified by the Arroyo Seco Parkway."

Another headline event of 1940 was South Pasadena's first recall election, an attempt to oust John C. Jacobs, who had served fourteen years on the city council and six years as mayor. His friends denied charges that Jacobs behaved in an arbitrary manner and conducted public business in private sessions. Denouncing the recall movement as "improper, unnecessary and ill-advised," they urged voters to support "South Pasadena's most useful citizen" and "to save South Pasadena from disgrace." Voters heeded the appeal, and the recall lost by a vote of 2,569 to 1,775. Jacobs retained his seat on the council but was not named again as mayor. He was succeeded by Andrew Porter who, like Jacobs, had family ties going back to the early days of South Pasadena. Jacobs's father was the first city treasurer and also served on an early school board and city council. Porter's father was city attorney from 1895 to 1901, and his grandfather, A. O. Porter, headed the committee which subdivided the lands of the San Gabriel Orange Grove Association in 1874.

Perhaps nothing in the city's history so stunned the community as the school tragedy of May 6, 1940. That afternoon Verlin H. Spencer, principal of the junior high school, shot and killed superintendent of schools George C. Bush, high school principal John E. Alman, school business agent Will R. Speer, and junior high school

The Arroyo Seco Parkway, the first freeway in the West, opened in December 1940. South Pasadena's floral sign can be seen on a hillside near the top center of the picture. *Courtesy of Huntington Library.*

teachers Verner V. Vanderlip and Ruth Barnett Spurgeon. He also shot the superintendent's secretary, Dorotha Talbert, crippling her for life.

Associates described Spencer as a driven man, ambitious and insecure and unable to accept failure. He turned to violence a day after learning that he would not be kept on as junior high school principal. Spencer served thirty years in prison and during that time studied psychology and wrote several research papers. Released in 1970, he began a new life in Hawaii, where he worked in a state program to help paroled convicts.

A garden was planted at the high school to commemorate the thirty-two years George C. Bush served in South Pasadena as teacher, high school principal, and superintendent. Special gifts, including books for the junior high school library and establishment of a student loan fund, honored the other four who lost their lives.

International events soon overshadowed local news. By the spring of 1940, Hitler's troops had smashed across Europe, from Poland to the English Channel. Paris fell to the Germans on June 14, and France surrendered a week later. In July the *Luftwaffe* made its first raids on English ports, and the Battle of Britain was under way.

In the United States public opinion was shifting away from neutralism. President Roosevelt pledged to help Britain in every way short of war. Congress approved increased defense appropriations, including funds for a two-ocean navy, and voted overwhelmingly for the country's first peacetime conscription. On October 16, 1940, more than sixteen million Americans registered for the draft, and the first South Pasadenans left for training the following January.

Meanwhile, the United States took economic steps to curb Japanese expansion in the Far East. By the summer of 1941, relations between the two countries were at a flash point, and war seemed inevitable. Early on the morning of December 7, 1941, the Japanese bombed Pearl Harbor without warning and eight hours later attacked United States forces in the Philippines. With only one dissenting vote, Congress declared war on Japan, and a few days later it passed a resolution accepting the state of war "thrust upon the United States" by Japan's allies, Italy and Germany.

California had its first air raid warning and blackout on December 11, and South Pasadena's city council met that evening by candlelight. The city had already organized a defense council and posted armed guards at reservoirs and city wells. South Pasadena was divided into ten air raid districts, and more than two hundred people volunteered at once to help with emergency police, fire, and rescue operations.

In its first news from the Pacific front, the *Review* announced on December 12 that Lieut. Henry G. Lee of South Pasadena was reported safe in Manila. A few months later, Lee wrote his family a poignant letter from Bataan. He said in closing:

> Life and my family have been very good to me and have given me everything I have ever really wanted, and should anything happen to me here it will not be like closing a book in the middle. . . . In the last two months I have done a lifetime of living and have been a part of one of the most unselfish, cooperative efforts that has ever been made by any group of individuals. . . . If the same selfless spirit were devoted to world betterment in time of peace, what a good world we would have.

Stephen Vincent Benét quoted the entire letter in "Dear Adolf," a dramatic poem broadcast in July 1942 with Private William Beedle, Jr., of South Pasadena as narrator.

123

Beedle was better known by his professional name, William Holden.

Taken prisoner after the fall of Bataan, Henry Lee died when an American bomb struck the Japanese ship taking him from the Philippines. After the war the *Saturday Evening Post* published poems written by Lee and found hidden at the prison camp where the Japanese had held him captive. The poems also appeared in a limited edition entitled *"Nothing But Praise,"* a small book reprinted in 1985 by the Philippine Arts Council of the Pacific Asia Museum in Pasadena.

Early in 1942—citing patriotism and property values—the recently formed South Pasadenans, Inc., urged realtors not to sell or rent to Japanese. Modeled after similar groups in the San Gabriel Valley, South Pasadenans, Inc., had three stated aims: planning for civic beauty, publicizing the advantages of South Pasadena, and securing racial restrictions on the use of property. To its surprise, the group found its campaign for restrictive covenants met with "far more indifference than any member of the committee thought possible when the campaign was launched."

When war broke out with Japan, more than 126,000 people of Japanese ancestry were living in the continental United States, the large majority in California. Many people on the West Coast clamored for removal of all Japanese in the area, even though nearly two-thirds were American citizens. On February 19, 1942, President Roosevelt signed Executive Order 9066, which authorized removal of "any or all persons" from designated military areas. In March, Lieut. General John L. DeWitt announced that all persons of Japanese descent would be excluded from the western half of the three Pacific Coast states and from the southern third of Arizona. By May 8 the evacuation order was posted on streets and store windows in South Pasadena, and on May 14 the city's Japanese residents—about 165 people—left their homes for internment in a government relocation center.

The word "relocation" took on special meaning in the forties. Other terms in the wartime vocabulary—dimout, ration points, share-the-ride, victory gardens, V-mail—suggest some of the additional problems and concerns of the home front.

More than two thousand volunteers in South Pasadena helped cope with home-front problems. Thirteen hundred people enrolled in the Civilian Defense Corps as air raid wardens or other emergency helpers. Another eight hundred people, including five hundred women block workers, aided the Citizens Service Corps. Directed by Charlotte W. King, South Pasadena's first councilwoman, the service corps provided information and advice on everything from canning with pressure cookers to finding a job in defense industry. Still other volunteers organized a hospitality center at the American Legion clubhouse and led the campaign to furnish a recreation room for an army ordnance unit stationed at Camp Santa Anita, in nearby Arcadia.

Young people had their own service corps. Even small children helped by planting gardens and saving scrap. Older students made model airplanes for the government to use in training aircraft spotters. During summer vacations a number of high school boys helped with the harvest crusade, picking oranges for local growers.

A survey made in 1943 showed that 41 percent of the junior high school girls in South Pasadena had working mothers. Many of the women held jobs in war plants, doing work traditionally performed by men. The city had nineteen light-manufacturing plants engaged in war work. They included Day-Ray Products, which made elec-

AMERICAN RED CROSS
SOUTH PASADENA BRANCH
OF PASADENA CHAPTER

1132 Mission Street   SYcamore 9-2331

OUR GREATEST NEED
Women between the ages of 18 – 50 for Nurses Aide Training

GAUZE ROOM, SURGICAL DRESSINGS
MRS. HENRY R. ELLIOTT, Chairman
At the Woman's Clubhouse, 1424 Fremont Ave.

Tuesday	9:00 A. M. to 3:00 P. M.	Thursday	9:00 A. M. to 3:00 P. M.
Wednesday	7:00 P. M. to 9:00 P. M.	Friday	9:00 A. M. to 3:00 P. M.

SEWING
MRS. J. L. COATES, General Chairman

MONDAY—10:00 A. M. to 3:00 P. M.—St. James Church, Fremont Ave. and Monterey Rd.
(For Eastern Star Ladies and any others who wish to attend)
TUESDAY—10:00 A. M. to 3:00 P. M.—Holy Family Catholic Church, 1501 Fremont Ave.
(For members of Parish and any others who wish to attend)
WEDNESDAY—10:00 A. M. to 3:00 P. M.—St. James Church, Fremont Ave. and Monterey Rd.
(For Baptist and Presbyterian Ladies and any others who wish to attend)
WEDNESDAY—9:00 A. M. to 3:00 P. M.—Huntington House, 1925 Huntington Drive
(For Oneonta Congregational Church Ladies and any others who wish to attend)
THURSDAY—10:00 A. M. to 3:00 P. M.—St. James Church, Fremont Ave. and Monterey Rd.
(For St. James Woman's Auxiliary and any others who wish to attend. Mrs. Earley in charge)
FRIDAY—10:00 A. M. to 3:00 P. M.—St. James Church, Fremont Ave. and Monterey Rd.
(For Methodist Ladies and any others who wish to attend)

HOME WORK
Because there has been a great demand for Red Cross work that can be done at home by women who, for one reason or another, are unable to go to sewing centers and the gauze rooms, Mrs. J. L. Coates, Chairman of Sewing, has arranged a display in the South Pasadena office of all articles that women can make at home. Patterns and instructions for making any of the dozen or more articles are available at the American Red Cross office. Instructor present Monday through Friday, 1:30-4:00.

KNITTING
MRS. GUY MARTIN In Charge
Call SYcamore 9-4818 or 9-2331

NURSES AIDE, HOME NURSING, CANTEEN, FIRST AID, NUTRITION CLASSES AND MOTOR CORPS
For Information—Call SYcamore 9-2331—1132 Mission Street

SCHEDULE OF BLOOD BANK DATES FOR 1943
MRS. E. L. McDONALD, Chairman

July 8th - - - Thursday	August 12th - - - Thursday	September 24th - - - Friday
October 29th - - - Friday	December 3rd - - - Friday	

HOURS—2:00 P. M. to 6:00 P. M.—Held at the Woman's Clubhouse, 1424 Fremont Ave.

For Appointment Please Call at 1132 Mission Street or Phone SYcamore 9-2331

Courtesy of South Pasadena Public Library.

South Pasadena High School's tiger mascot encourages the war effort. *Courtesy of South Pasadena Unified School District.*

trical equipment for aircraft companies; Phillips Aviation, which made parts for airplanes and amphibious tanks; and National Technical Laboratories and the Helipot Corporation—both founded by Dr. Arnold O. Beckman—which made precision instruments for measurement and analysis. Even a company like Baranger Studios, whose peacetime specialty was window displays, now devoted its craftsmanship to ball bearings and precision parts.

A Chamber of Commerce survey of seventeen of the nineteen companies disclosed they had a combined monthly payroll of $272,000 in 1945 and employed nearly fifteen hundred people, of whom about half lived in South Pasadena. The Chamber made a concerted effort to keep the companies in South Pasadena after the war. Some stayed on for a time, but only Day-Ray has continued operating in the city.

One South Pasadena company that made a unique contribution to the war effort was the firm known as Perkins Oriental Books. P. D. Perkins had spent five years in Japan studying Japanese customs, theater, and music. In 1940 he and his wife Ione established a business in an old house on Mission Street and began supplying universities and scholars with rare and specialized works on the Orient. The company mailed so many shipments of books that the classification of the South Pasadena Post Office was raised one grade.

After the outbreak of war with Japan, the United States government asked the firm to publish books that the military could use in language training courses. Perkins and his wife reprinted Japanese dictionaries, produced thousands of pocket-sized textbooks on elementary Japanese, and supplied books in scores of other Asian languages and dialects, from Tibetan to Tagalog. The couple also issued Japanese language cards prepared by former South Pasadenan William Enking, an artist whose calligraphy is owned by a number of European museums. The governments of both the United States and Great Britain commended P. D. and Ione Perkins for their valuable wartime services.

Another South Pasadenan praised for his contributions during the war was actor Sterling Holloway. While serving in the army, Holloway helped write a comedy revue, *Hey, Rookie!* and toured with the show to entertain troops in Italy and North Africa. Benefit performances of *Hey, Rookie!* earned $450,000, which helped pay for army and navy recreational facilities. When Holloway was mustered out of the service, the army honored him with a regimental retreat review.

Nearly every day since May 8, 1941, the chimes of St. James' Episcopal Church had rung at noon, calling people to a moment of silent prayer. First suggested by South Pasadenan Lena Eggleston, the idea of the chimes spread to other cities and won national attention when written up in the *Christian Science Monitor* and mentioned on the radio by singer Kate Smith.

On June 6, 1944, the chimes rang as usual, and the El Centro schoolbell rang out, too. In patriotic assemblies held that morning, schoolchildren learned about the Allied invasion of Normandy and heard President Roosevelt's D-Day prayer. Sixth-graders at Marengo School wrote their own prayers, to be read in class in the days to come.

The chimes rang with special meaning on May 8, 1945, when President Harry S. Truman broadcast word of Germany's unconditional surrender to the Allies. Banner headlines proclaimed, "V-E DAY!" but editorials reminded readers that the war was just half over. Heeding the president's call to "work, work, work," South Pasadena abandoned its plans to close all stores and offices, and it held no public celebration.

A month and a half after V-E Day, fifty nations signed the United Nations Charter. Commencement exercises at South Pasadena High School reflected this concern for international understanding. Graduating senior Paul N. ("Pete") McCloskey spoke of the need to respect other people and their customs. He added, "Most of us will be just ordinary citizens, but a few perhaps will someday hold positions of high responsibility." McCloskey and his classmate John H. Rousselot were among those few, each serving a number of terms in Congress.

A government decree, effective January 2, 1945, had lifted the exclusion order against Japanese residents on the West Coast, and the first families returned to South Pasadena a few months later. Speakers at a meeting of the Kiwanis Club urged fair treatment of the Japanese and praised the valor of Nisei servicemen like Osawa Tabata, a graduate of South Pasadena High School, who won a Silver Star for gallantry in action with the famous 442nd ("Go for Broke") Regimental Combat Team. More support for Japanese residents came from the newly formed Council for Civic Unity, headed by G. Derwood Baker, first principal of South Pasadena Junior High School. Another local group, Friends of the American Way, helped the returning Japanese find jobs and housing. South Pasadenan Hugh H. Anderson was a founding member, as well as vice-president and treasurer of the group.

One incident marred the Japanese homecoming in South Pasadena. Vandals painted a derogatory slogan on the Diamond Market after its owner, William Kermode, dismissed two clerks who refused to serve Japanese customers. Kermode made a plea for unity and understanding and observed, "That is why the United Nations met in San Francisco—to promote world harmony."

In August 1945 the war in the Pacific ended. On August 6 the *Enola Gay*, a B-29 Superfortress, dropped an atomic bomb on Hiroshima, destroying more than half the city. A second atomic bomb devastated Nagasaki on August 9. Five days later Japan agreed to unconditional surrender. South Pasadena got the news at 4:04 in the afternoon, and by 4:30 most businesses in town had closed. "AGAIN A FREE WORLD!" the *Review* exclaimed, and a second headline urged, "Pray and Fight for Peace Everlasting." Eighteen hundred South Pasadenans served in World War II, and forty-nine lost their lives.

Veterans returning to South Pasadena faced a terrible housing shortage. By March 1946 more than a hundred people had requested help in finding a place to live. The city authorized a trailer camp for veterans, and for other emergency housing it purchased twenty deckhouses once used for gun crews aboard merchant ships. It converted the structures, which measured about six feet by eighteen feet, into two-room units with a double bunk, closet, wardrobe, sink, and hot plate. The city placed the deckhouses on a small lot near Las Flores School and added a central unit with showers and toilets.

A more ingenious—and elegant—answer to the housing shortage was the "balloon house" developed by Pasadena architect Wallace Neff. Using a large inflated balloon as a form and spraying it with Gunite, Neff could construct a four-room house in a day. His airform construction used a minimum of critical materials and was said to give added protection against everything from termites to atom bombs. South Pasade-

The Otake and Nambu families were among the first Japanese families to return to South Pasadena from wartime relocation camps. The photograph shows them in 1935 outside the South Pasadena home of Tom Tarao Otake and Helen Shizue Otake (the couple on the left). *Courtesy of South Pasadena Public Library.*

RAYMOND PARK

Immediately Adjoining the
Beautiful Grounds of the Hotel Raymond

———— ◆◆◆ ————

THIS Tract affords the best of everything an intelligent homeseeker requires. Judged by the most exacting standard the best critics may apply, the verdict will be that here the conditions are exactly right.

Why not take the time to at least make one trip to this ideal spot and learn that, in point of time, Raymond Park is closer than any of the *desirable* tracts being offered in the vicinity of Los Angeles or Pasadena.

The property is favored with an unfailing and abundant supply of pure water. Gas, electric light, and Telephones are also conveniences which are installed on the tract and are immediately available.

⊕ ⊕ ⊕

PLANS AND SPECIFICATIONS FURNISHED
INSURANCE EFFECTED
MONEY TO LOAN AT LOWEST RATES

⊕ ⊕ ⊕

S.W. Fergusson Co.

OWNERS OF THE ABOVE SUBDIVISION

505 Braly Building, Los Angeles, Cal.

Local Office at Park, cor. Palermo Ave. and Monterey Road.

SHORT-LINE CAR PASSES DOOR

A 1904 advertisement promotes a subdivision on Raymond Hill. Numerous apartments were built in the area at the end of World War II. *Courtesy of South Pasadena Public Library.*

130

na's first balloon house was built in 1946 on Alta Vista Avenue for Gordon H. Clough. The building was oval-shaped, with walls and roof forming a concrete dome.

South Pasadena helped make political history during the Congressional campaign of 1946. The Independent Voters of South Pasadena, a liberal group headed by Paul Bullock, sponsored two forums at which opposing candidates debated campaign issues. (Bullock later achieved a national reputation as a labor economist.) Nearly a thousand people crowded into the junior high school auditorium on September 13 to hear challenger Richard M. Nixon debate Congressman Jerry Voorhis. Nixon skillfully maneuvered Voorhis, one commentator observed, into fighting brush fires that did not exist. The debate marked a turning point in the campaign. "Once that debate was over," Nixon said, "I was on my way to eventual victory." And so he was. In November he defeated Voorhis by an overwhelming margin of fifteen thousand votes. The next time Richard Nixon spoke in South Pasadena—in 1954—he was Vice-President of the United States and had kind words for the city which helped launch his political career.

One of the problems facing South Pasadena in the postwar years was how the city should develop. Between 1945 and 1949 there was a surge in apartment house construction, with more than twice as many units built as in any previous five-year period. One development, with 144 rental units, opened on the crest of Raymond Hill in January 1947. That same month the city council tentatively approved a thirty-acre project on the site of the old Raymond Hotel golf course. The builder had plans for South Pasadena's largest development to date—1,500 units in apartments four to six stories high.

The plan stirred immediate controversy. The Taxpayers Association declared that South Pasadena was at a crossroads of civic development. It could become a city dominated by large apartment buildings or continue "as a residential city, with prestige which age improves rather than deteriorates." The head of South Pasadena's largest retail business, Colliau Chevrolet, stated the issue differently. In a letter to the *Review*, E. H. Colliau said, "We do not have . . . the choice between maintaining the status quo in regard to civic development or going forward. . . . If we don't go forward, we automatically go backward—because everything around us is going forward." He warned that without new residential and business developments, South Pasadena would become a backwater, surrounded by progressive and prosperous communities. Other business leaders joined Colliau in urging approval of the Raymond Hill development.

The city delayed final approval of the project until 1950. Meanwhile, the whole subject of growth, development, and zoning came under study by South Pasadena's first planning commission. During the previous five years the civic group South Pasadenans, Inc., had served as a planning body. It made a statistical analysis of the city, proposed a zoning ordinance and a plan for the Arroyo, and recommended purchase of tax-delinquent lands in the Monterey Hills. The group also spurred the city to adopt a master plan for unified street-tree planting.

In January 1947 South Pasadena appointed an official planning commission of seven members, headed by realtor Clarence E. Burke. After a year of study, it drew up a comprehensive zoning ordinance and map. One councilman hailed the ordinance—

131

the first zoning update in more than twenty years—as "the greatest thing that has ever happened to this city." The new ordinance increased the area zoned for industry, reduced the area zoned for multiple and duplex housing, and created a special zone on Raymond Hill for apartments and hotels up to seven stories tall, with a height limit of seventy-five feet.

To help preserve South Pasadena's traditional character as a residential community, the planning commission zoned nearly 55 percent of the acreage in the city for single family housing. This zoning included the Monterey Hills, where much of the land was undeveloped and put to such pastoral uses as grazing sheep. Pioneer sheep ranchers Llewellyn Bixby and his cousins, Benjamin and Thomas Flint, had wintered in the hills in 1854 with two thousand sheep they had driven overland from Illinois. One century later, flock masters still brought sheep to the Monterey Hills for spring pasturage and shearing.

When the Pacific Electric tracks reached South Pasadena in 1902, developer W. H. Carlson began selling lots in the Monterey Hills. Carlson advertised his Pasadena Villa Tract—"the coming residence suburb of Los Angeles"—in magazines and newspapers throughout the country. Maps of the subdivision showed quarter-acre lots laid out in a rectangular grid with no relation to topography. "Although on the map the land appears neatly blocked out in city streets," said George W. Glover in the *South Pasadenan*, "no such highways exist. If they did exist, they would in many cases be perpendicular owing to the steepness of the land."

Many people bought in the tract without ever having seen it. When they decided to build, they were unable to locate their property because the streets were nonexistent and boundaries could not be traced. Most owners stopped paying taxes on the land and gave it up as a bad investment. In 1943 South Pasadena acquired title to 727 parcels in the old Pasadena Villa Tract at the bargain rate of a dollar a parcel. It would take another twenty years to redevelop the area, but in 1964 the city auctioned off the first homesites in the 309-acre tract renamed the Altos de Monterey.

During the forties, attention focused on the Arroyo, as well as on the city's hillside areas. In 1947 South Pasadena authorized a "helicourt" in Arroyo Seco Park for the first local pickup and delivery of mail by helicopter. A thousand spectators gathered in the Arroyo on October 1 when the South Pasadena mail truck met the helicopter with 1,684 pieces of mail, all marked with the South Pasadena cachet. The city briefly considered use of the "helicourt" for passenger flights, but it abandoned the idea after massive protests from people living near the Arroyo.

South Pasadenans were showing increased concern for the appropriate use of the Arroyo. One controversy concerned a semiprofessional baseball team, the Rosabell Plumbers of Highland Park, which had been playing Sunday games in Arroyo Seco Park since 1941. In 1949 the team's owner offered to improve the baseball diamond and build a clubhouse in exchange for a long-term lease. He also wanted exclusive use of the ball park on Sundays and holidays and for the three months of spring training, when he hoped to rent the facilities to major league teams. The recreation commission favored the plan, which would bring in added revenues, but an editorial protested the idea of someone paying "for the privilege of denying the public the right to use their park." The city attorney agreed, ruling that the city could not lease a public park to a

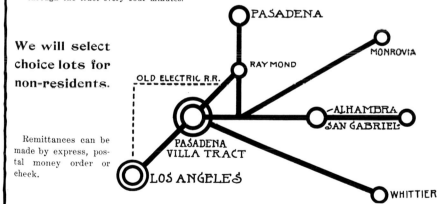

This advertisement appeared in 1902. Sixty years later a portion of the old Pasadena Villa Tract was developed as Altos de Monterey. *Courtesy of Huntington Library.*

An eighteen-hole golf course opened in Arroyo Seco Park in July 1955. The first three players began their game at daylight after camping out overnight in the Arroyo. *Courtesy of South Pasadena Public Library*.

private group for its exclusive use. In 1950 the city council adopted an ordinance providing that no change could be made in Arroyo Seco Park without a public hearing and the affirmative vote of four council members.

About fifteen acres of the ninety-six-acre park were being used for recreation, while the rest lay undeveloped. The Junior Chamber of Commerce favored using fifty-five acres for a variety of sports, ranging from handball to horseshoes, and from croquet to chess. The Garden Club wanted the area planted with native flora and kept free from commercial encroachment. Others scoffed at the idea of preserving a "birds and bees sanctuary." One entrepreneur wanted to put a polo field in the Arroyo, and another proposed a drive-in movie with space for a thousand cars. There were also suggestions for a stocked lake, a pitch-and-putt golf course, and a civic center. South Pasadena eventually agreed on an eighteen-hole golf course, and this opened in 1955 on forty-eight and a half acres in the Arroyo.

Not all the city news had to do with zoning, planning, and development. A 1947 editorial grumbled that Pasadena appeared on a recent *National Geographic* map and in the *National State Farm Atlas*, but that South Pasadena was omitted. The editor made a familiar suggestion—that South Pasadena adopt a distinctive new name. In 1948 the Junior Chamber of Commerce circulated more than 100 petitions to rename the city Las Flores, but it gathered only 400 signatures.

"Crime Comics Now Outlawed for Juveniles," read a headline in the *Review* in 1948. A new city ordinance banned the sale to youngsters under eighteen of comic books depicting violent crime. Another eye-catching headline in 1948 observed, "Dewey Favored in Big Landslide." The prediction held true in South Pasadena, which voted three to one for Thomas E. Dewey over Harry S. Truman for president.

In the spring of 1949 the Pacific Electric announced it was going to replace its trolleys with motor coaches. W. Tog Ericson, editor and publisher of the *Review*, welcomed the news. In an editorial headed "The Red Cars Must Go!" Ericson wrote, "The time has come to retire those beat-up street cars to a place where they can never again cause backaches, headaches, jangled nerves, and congested lungs." (The latter came from the "fog-like atmosphere of the smoking section.") Ericson denounced the Big Red Cars for "a minimum of comfort and a maximum of sways and bumps." Many readers took issue with the editor, and the city council adopted a resolution stating that South Pasadena opposed the abandonment of rail service. The Red Cars did continue running, but for only a few years more.

By the end of 1949, reminders of World War II were gradually disappearing from the city. The hospitality center in the American Legion clubhouse closed in December. Most of the converted deckhouses had been sold, but five veterans and their families still lived in the emergency housing on Garfield Avenue.

One piece of wartime legislation ended in 1949 when the federal housing expediter lifted rent controls in South Pasadena. His decision came too late to save the twenty-room house Edwin Cawston had built at Sycamore Avenue and Arroyo Verde Road in 1886. Industrial plants now occupied most of the famous old ostrich farm property. In buildings once used to dye ostrich plumes, the Nathan R. Smith Company turned out torpedo control equipment, magnetos, solenoids, and ignition coils. The same company owned the Cawston house and rented it to lodgers until rent control made this venture unprofitable. The company pulled down the house, and the lumber was used to build a veteran's home on another site.

South Pasadena ended the forties in a mood of confidence. Construction was at an all-time high, and the city had passed the largest budget in its history. Accenting its dedication to progress, the city voted to strip old-fashioned architectural ornament from the city hall buildings and give them a Southern California modern look. In another confident gesture, South Pasadena proclaimed itself "Hub City of Los Angeles County."

A memorial plaque at South Pasadena High School honors George C. Bush, who was superintendent of schools at the time of his death in 1940. *Photograph by Tom M. Apostol.*

THE SECRET WEAPON THAT WILL WIN THE WAR

Morale

Congress can't vote it
Dollars won't buy it
It's OUR job to build it

PUT UNITY INTO YOUR COMMUNITY

Unity starts with U. To win the war, stop private wars at home, on the job, with neighbors.
Honest apology ends friction—starts teamwork.
If we all pull together, we'll all pull through.

BE A RUMOR-STOPPER

Rumors help the enemy. Trace the facts. Face the facts.
Don't exaggerate.
Make your community—
Gossip-proof
Smear-proof
Panic-proof
Fear-proof.
Every patriot shoots a rumor dead on sight!

MEET SHORTAGE BY SHARING

Use all of everything. Don't hoard. If everybody cares enough, and everybody shares enough, everybody will have enough.
No waste in ice-box, cash-box, brain-box!

KEEP THE MORAL STANDARDS OF THE NATION HIGH

It's sabotage on the home front to wangle something for ourselves on the side.
Dishonesty and indulgence in us saps the nation's fighting strength. A decent world tomorrow depends on how each one of us lives today!

THE SECRET OF STEADINESS AND INNER STRENGTH IS ON EVERY PENNY:

"In God we trust." Telephone wires may be cut, radio stations off the air, but no bombardment can stop us from being directed by God.
To listen to God and obey wherever we are is our highest national service.

Andrew O. Porter

Mayor of South Pasadena and Chairman of War Council
HANG THIS IN YOUR HOME, OFFICE, STORE OR FACTORY

A copy of the morale card was printed for every house in South Pasadena. Similar cards were used throughout the country and were issued by the millions in Great Britain. *Courtesy of South Pasadena Public Library.*

CHRONOLOGY

1940

The census records the population of South Pasadena as 14,356.

The South Pasadena Tournament of Roses Association organizes.

Disgruntled voters petition for the city's first recall election. The recall loses at the polls.

Two junior high school teachers and three school administrators die in a mass slaying.

Young men register on October 16 for the country's first peacetime conscription. The city gears for national defense.

The Arroyo Seco Parkway opens, and South Pasadena plants a floral sign at the freeway entrance to the city.

1941

The first South Pasadena draftees leave for training. A city ordinance creates the South Pasadena Defense Council.

In May the chimes of St. James' Episcopal Church begin ringing every day at noon. Residents are urged to pause for a moment of silent prayer for peace.

On December 7 the Japanese bomb Pearl Harbor. Within a few days the United States is at war with Japan, Germany, and Italy.

On December 11 California has its first blackout.

1942

The city bars trucks weighing more than 4,000 pounds from using the Arroyo Seco Parkway through South Pasadena.

Military authorities ask South Pasadena to remove its floral sign because it is visible from the air.

Charlotte W. King becomes the first councilwoman in South Pasadena history.

Volunteers open a hospitality center at the American Legion clubhouse and help furnish a recreation room at Camp Santa Anita. Thousands of volunteers enroll in the Civilian Defense Corps and Citizens Service Corps.

On May 14 South Pasadena's Japanese residents leave for relocation centers.

1943

The city acquires title to tax-delinquent lands in the Monterey Hills.

Gardeners hold a victory garden show at Eddie Park.

The army presents the city with a scroll of appreciation for helping furnish the recreation room at Camp Santa Anita.

1944

The American Legion dedicates an honor roll with the names of South Pasadenans in the armed services.

The schools have special D-Day programs on June 6.

1945

Nineteen light-manufacturing plants in South Pasadena are engaged in war work.

The city quietly celebrates V-E Day on May 8.

The first Japanese families return to their homes in South Pasadena.

The Junior Chamber of Commerce organizes, with Robert Biles as president.

The South Pasadena Public Library celebrates its fiftieth year as a tax-supported institution.

The war ends, and President Truman proclaims V-J Day on September 2.

Construction starts on a half-million-dollar apartment development at the crest of Raymond Hill.

1946

George W. Savage buys the South Pasadena *Review* from Fred Rolens.

The city converts twenty merchant marine deckhouses into emergency housing for veterans.

A large and noisy audience hears Richard M. Nixon debate Congressman Jerry Voorhis in the junior high school auditorium.

The city begins long-range planning for development of the Monterey Hills.

The South Pasadena Municipal Employees Association organizes.

1947

South Pasadena appoints its first planning commission, with Clarence E. Burke as chairman.

The city officially objects to proposed routing of the Concord Freeway, which would have run through the city on its eastern boundary.

The city authorizes a "helicourt" in Arroyo Seco Park for helicopter mail service.

W. Tog Ericson buys the *South Pasadena Review* from George W. Savage.

The Junior Chamber of Commerce holds its first annual Fiesta de las Flores to raise funds for the city's float in the Tournament of Roses.

A Business and Professional Women's Club is formed.

Mary Murdoch and Ventnor Williams organize the first Golden Age Club on the West Coast.

1948

An attempt to change the city's name to Las Flores fails.

The South Pasadena League of Women Voters organizes, with Frances Gloyn as president.

Track star Roland Sink, a graduate of South Pasadena High School, wins a place on the United States Olympic team.

In April the *Review* changes from a weekly to a semiweekly.

The city's first zoning ordinance since 1926 takes effect in September.

Merchants inaugurate Friday night shopping.

South Pasadena votes three to one for Thomas E. Dewey for president.

The Pacific Electric agrees that within five years it will stop hauling freight over its tracks on Huntington Drive.

1949

On January 11 the city enjoys its first snowfall in seventeen years. On September 7 the temperature reaches 110.

Rent control ends in South Pasadena.

One of the last vestiges of the Cawston Ostrich Farm disappears with the razing of Edwin Cawston's house at Sycamore Avenue and Arroyo Verde Road.

The South Pasadena Hospitality Center closes.

The city holds its first square dance for teen-agers, and a reporter marvels at seeing young America in some other costume than "hitched-up corduroys, flapping shirtails, or its sweaters and saddle oxfords."

Oak trees still grow in the center of two private streets in South Pasadena. *Photograph by Tom M. Apostol.*

VIII

CONTENTION AND CONTROVERSY: 1950-1959

I think that I shall never see
A Council lovely as a tree.

NATURE LOVER

SOUTH PASADENA seems to have been unusually contentious in the fifties. Tempers flared over helicopters, trucks, and freeways; over cocktail bars and movie posters; ancient oaks and young swimmers. Even an entry in the Tournament of Roses stirred up controversy.

Tree lovers fought a spirited battle in 1950 to save three oaks growing in the middle of Edgewood Drive. Just two blocks long, the street was part of the Ellerslie Park Tract subdivided by Carolyn Dobbins in 1907. Mrs. Dobbins first saw the oak groves of South Pasadena in 1886, when she was a guest at the Raymond Hotel. Shortly afterward, she and her family moved from Philadelphia to South Pasadena and built a home at the corner of Garfield Avenue and Monterey Road on a parcel covered with magnificent oaks. Several of the huge trees still standing are now designated as Cultural Heritage Landmarks.

In 1950 the city wanted to repave Edgewood Drive and cut down the oaks in the center of the street. "A modern community has no place for obstructions like that," said the city manager, who called the trees a traffic hazard. The people on Edgewood disagreed. To them the trees were an asset to be treasured. After an impassioned debate lasting an hour and a half, the city council agreed to spare two trees but insisted on cutting down the third.

When workers came to remove the two-hundred-year-old oak, they encountered an automobile blockade, a dog described as large and hungry, and people armed with brooms and rolling pins. One resident told reporters, "There is too much useless destruction going on in the world these days. . . . . In a small way we are fighting for the same things our boys in Korea are fighting for—the maintenance of freedom and the carrying out of the wishes of the majority."

The battle stirred interest across the country. Letters and telegrams poured in, all supporting the Edgewood residents. The city capitulated, and the trees remained until the early sixties, when they died of natural causes. During the fray, an anonymous poet wrote to the *Review*:

> I think that I shall never see
> A Council lovely as a tree.
> . . . . .
> The tree brings beauty to the town.
> The Council orders it chopped down.
>
> We must have progress, the tree must go!
> It interferes with traffic flow.

143

"A menace is this tree!" they cry.
"If people hit it they would die!"
. . . .

The Council hears the long debate
From lovers of the tree so great.

The people plead and beg and pray.
The Council says the tree can't stay.

Laws are made by men like these
But only God can make the trees.

Newsweek publicized another city squabble in 1952. In a report captioned "Elephants Afloat," the magazine described South Pasadena's controversial entry in the Tournament of Roses. Based on a cartoon drawn by Bruce Russell of the *Los Angeles Times*, the float showed a triumphant elephant, in rose-colored glasses, who was about to enter the White House, while a dejected donkey left by the back door. Most South Pasadenans chortled over "The Rosy Dream," but Democrats were not amused and charged the city with injecting politics in the Rose Parade. The float went on as scheduled—paid for in advance by a flood of contributions—and took first place in its municipal class. "The truth must be told, however," admitted the *Review*. "There were no other entries in that class."

On the city's next Rose Parade float, "Pulling Together," the donkey and the elephant rode a bicycle built for two. The sensitive question of which animal took the front seat was to be determined by the outcome of the 1952 presidential election. General Dwight Eisenhower trounced Adlai Stevenson in November (by a margin of almost four to one in South Pasadena); so on New Year's Day the elephant steered the bicycle, and the donkey helped him pedal.

Posters in the lobby of the Ritz Theater stirred a censorship battle in South Pasadena in 1950. Outraged by advertisements for a coming attraction, *French White Cargo*, the city manager proposed a censorship board to protect South Pasadena from films "not in keeping with the character of the community." In an editorial response, W. Tog Ericson wrote, "Censorship of movies here does not seem desirable. The free choice of a free people is still the foundation of our liberties." He added that local censorship was not only dangerous but could bring notoriety to a city. Nevertheless, the city council appointed a censorship committee, with representatives from service clubs, the Woman's Club, and the PTA. Theater managers were supposed to consult with the committee before showing films that might be controversial. No provision was made for failure to consult the committee, or for a committee deadlock on the merits of a film.

Another dispute in 1950 concerned the planning commission. The Realty Board thought it should be abolished, or else reorganized to be more representative of local business and industry. After intense discussion the city council voted to continue the planning commission, to reappoint three members whose terms had expired (an attorney, a purchasing agent, and a member of the League of Women Voters), and to choose someone from business or industry when next a vacancy occurred. The mayor lauded the commission and its purpose: designing a pattern for the future of the city.

In 1950 the planning commission turned its attention to the old Pasadena Villa

South Pasadena's entry in the 1952 Tournament of Roses provoked both laughter and debate. *Courtesy of Pasadena Tournament of Roses Association.*

Altos de Monterey was a pioneering redevelopment project. Work on clearing the brush-covered hills began in 1962. *Courtesy of South Pasadena Public Library.*

Tract, a brush-covered expanse of more than three hundred acres in the Monterey Hills, about five miles from downtown Los Angeles. The commission urged redevelopment of the Monterey Hills property—to which South Pasadena had acquired title in 1943—suggesting it could bring the city at least four hundred new homes and millions of dollars in revenue, instead of remaining "blightful, unusable, inaccessible, unmarketable, and without value."

After debating the issue for several years, the city council authorized a Community Redevelopment Agency in 1953. Its first chairman, Verne E. Robinson, served only briefly and was succeeded by Charlotte W. King, who headed the agency from September 1953 until her death in 1969. Unable to secure private capital for the project it envisioned, the CRA applied for federal funds. It did not seek an outright grant but a straight loan, to be repaid with the proceeds from property sales in the new development. In 1958 the South Pasadena Community Redevelopment Agency obtained a federal loan of $4.5 million for the country's first open-land project. Under a rarely used provision of California law, this area qualified as blighted because it had been subdivided (fifty years earlier) with no regard for the contours or other physical characteristics of the land. Not only was the Monterey Hills Redevelopment Project the country's first open-land, straight-loan project, but it was one of the first designed for single-family housing, and it covered one of the largest areas handled by the Urban Renewal Administration. The development—later named the Altos de Monterey—was formally dedicated in April 1962 and hailed as "the minor miracle of the Monterey Hills."

More than sixty years after South Pasadena passed its first antisaloon ordinance, the city continued to legislate against liquor. In 1950, after a successful fight against a beer license for the local bowling alley, the city council declared "No more bars!" and amended the zoning ordinance to prohibit any new bars or cocktail lounges without a special variance. For the time being, this limited the number of bars to three.

In 1955 Marion E. Jackson, who owned a cafe and bar at Huntington Drive and Fremont Avenue, decided to move from that location and open a $150,000 restaurant and cocktail lounge a block away at the corner of Huntington and Fair Oaks. For the next two years residents of nearby Oneonta Knoll battled to halt Jackson's project, saying it would create a disturbance to health and well-being, depress property values, and "cater to customers foreign to South Pasadena and its interests."

After a hearing which lasted until two in the morning, the city council denied Jackson a variance. He promptly filed suit, challenging the validity of the amendment against cocktail bars, and he also appealed to the California Department of Alcoholic Beverage Control. After one of the longest hearings on record, the department granted Jackson a liquor license transfer and lambasted the zoning amendment as "arbitrary, unreasonable, and invalid."

The city council responded by hastily passing an emergency ordinance "for the protection of public safety, health and welfare." The ordinance changed the zoning on twenty-one lots—including the property at Huntington and Fair Oaks—from general commercial to limited commercial, a new category that prohibited any establishment where goods were displayed, served, sold, or serviced. Oneonta Knoll residents enthusiastically endorsed the interim ordinance and petitioned to make it permanent.

Ninth-graders from San Marino once rode the PE Special to classes at South Pasadena Junior High School. This photograph was taken in the forties. *Courtesy of Huntington Library*.

The planning commission declined to study the ordinance or make recommendations concerning it. The Realty Board and the Chamber of Commerce denounced the measure, calling it discriminatory, indefensible, and of dubious legality. They also felt the measure set a dangerous precedent because it had been passed without public notice or hearing. Nevertheless, by a vote of four to one, the council made the ordinance permanent in August 1957.

A long preamble to the measure defined South Pasadena as a community where families wanted to live "relatively undisturbed by the noise, congestion, hazards, and confusion usual to commercial areas." The preamble justified the new limited commercial zone as an essential transition between purely residential and purely commercial zones. Without such a transition, the preamble said, "an unwholesome family atmosphere would be created. Vacancies would occur. Property values would decline. The community interests would be impaired."

Unable to build a new restaurant at the disputed corner, Jackson remodeled his café and bar at Huntington and Fremont. It reopened as the Crossbow Steak House in 1960 and won a Beautiful Building Award from the Chamber of Commerce. Tog Ericson wrote a congratulatory editorial and cheerfully quoted Samuel Johnson, whose opinion some readers may have found subversive: "There is nothing which has yet been contrived by man by which so much happiness is produced as by a good tavern or inn."

On occasion, schools caused as much dissension in the community as cocktail lounges. Despite studies showing that Las Flores School lay above an earthquake fault, many parents were angered by a decision to close the school. They thought the earthquake danger exaggerated and petitioned to have the building strengthened and kept open. Las Flores students made an eloquent plea for their schoolhouse and even sent the school board $19.56 to start a reconstruction fund. Petitions and pleas were unavailing, and Las Flores School was abandoned at the close of the spring term in 1950. Five years later, however, the district established the Las Flores Primary Unit to help ease overcrowding at Marengo. For the next quarter of a century, neighborhood children from kindergarten to third grade met in classrooms built on the old Las Flores playground.

The future of the high school and the junior high provoked a bitter controversy in 1951. When San Marino joined the South Pasadena High School District in 1921, the school had a four-year program. In 1928, however, ninth-grade classes were made part of the new junior high. Most San Marino parents preferred the continuity of a four-year high school, and in 1950 a joint committee of South Pasadena and San Marino citizens began a year-long study of the school situation. The committee recommended adding the ninth grade to the high school and making the seventh and eighth grades part of the elementary system.

In June 1951 San Marino and South Pasadena voted on a bond issue for a four-year high school. The bonds won in San Marino but lost in South Pasadena, where many people were reluctant to give up the junior high. The two cities held a second election in December 1951. The bonds again fell short of a two-thirds majority, and San Marino withdrew from the union district and established its own high school.

One controversy in the fifties involved a charge of racial discrimination. According

149

to a lawsuit brought against the city in 1955, a Highland Park child was denied admission to South Pasadena's municipal swimming pool and told Negroes could not swim there. The city denied the charge, saying the girl was turned away only because she did not live in South Pasadena. The courts ruled in favor of the city. To avoid legal difficulties in the future, the city issued identification cards to all children in the South Pasadena schools; and the council passed a resolution—no longer in effect—that restricted the use of the pool, the War Memorial Building, and the Eddie Park Clubhouse to residents.

The volume of truck traffic through South Pasadena in the fifties brought a storm of protest. Helicopters and buses also stirred complaints. People living near the Arroyo denounced a plan to use the city heliport, not only for the twice-daily mail flights, but for passenger service as well. "Intolerable!" residents said, and Los Angeles Airways dropped the plan. Electric trolleys made their last run through South Pasadena on September 30, 1951. "Our faithful Pacific Electric BIG RED CARS bow to the lowly and poisonous gas bus," one commuter mourned. "Instead of a comfortable seat, and protection on the old Red Cars, we now must stand on other people's feet, and risk accidents on the public streets. And TRY to read your newspaper!"

The PE removed its tracks from Fair Oaks Avenue in 1952, and the city planning commission suggested landscaping the median strip from Columbia Street to Monterey Road. Merchants opposed the idea, saying Fair Oaks was too narrow and was meant "not for glamour but for service." One shopkeeper's wife demanded, "What do these planners want? A park with geese running around in the middle of our main street?" Another skeptic wondered if the city might not do better to landscape the existing traffic lanes and pave the center of Fair Oaks to accommodate fast trucks.

In 1953 Pasadena, South Pasadena, and Los Angeles passed ordinances that closed the Arroyo Seco Parkway to heavy trucks. The state required an alternate route through South Pasadena, going from the city's western limits at Pasadena Avenue, across Mission Street to Fair Oaks, and north on Fair Oaks. South Pasadena tried to negotiate a master truck plan with neighboring cities but admitted defeat when San Marino closed Huntington Drive to trucks, and Pasadena closed San Gabriel Boulevard. Soon more than two thousand heavy trucks were traveling through South Pasadena every weekday. Residents complained bitterly about increased noise and pollution and the danger to pedestrians. The *Review* attacked what it called the Fair Oaks Turnpike and the Truck Thru-Way, and editor Tog Ericson wrote, "Map makers can't find space to put us on a map (other than our own city maps) yet we have to make room for all the trucks of the county."

Between 1953 and 1959 the city council held fifteen meetings on traffic problems, and the Chamber of Commerce conducted seven traffic surveys. The Chamber also met with representatives of the trucking industry, who agreed that drivers should try to avoid South Pasadena between four and seven in the morning and between twelve and two in the afternoon.

Meanwhile, Pasadena ruled trucks off its streets between ten in the evening and six in the morning. "Where will these trucks wait to get into Pasadena?" Ericson wondered. "Will they line our curbs . . . from Columbia Street to Huntington Drive?" He suggested overnight parking zones for trucks and asked, "Will the city create a new job

The center of Fair Oaks Avenue was repaved in December 1952 after the Pacific Electric removed the streetcar tracks. *Photograph by John C. Shaw.*

The prize-winning garden office building designed by Smith & Williams has a steel-framed metal mesh canopy which cuts off light from the south and transmits 87 percent of the light from the north. *Photograph by Marvin Rand.*

and have an employee go to the top of the hill at Columbia and Fair Oaks and wave a green starting flag at six o'clock in the morning? This will give all the trucks that spent the night in our city a roaring flying start."

In 1959 the city council debated a proposed ordinance to ban heavy trucks from Fair Oaks south of Mission for a trial period of one year, but voted down the proposal by three to two. Resigning itself to an unhappy situation, it then voted to synchronize the traffic signals on Fair Oaks to speed trucks through.

Nothing in the history of South Pasadena has produced more dissension than the subject of freeway routings through the city. More than a decade after the Arroyo Seco Parkway was built, people still resented the way it slashed through the city, taking property, and dividing South Pasadena in two. Some people were annoyed, also, when in 1954 the Parkway was renamed the Pasadena Freeway after years of lobbying by Pasadena.

The city council opposed routing the Long Beach Freeway through South Pasadena as early as 1947, when the freeway was first proposed. After construction started, a headline in the *Review* asked, "Will So. Pasadena Be Split Again by Another Freeway?" The refrain was taken up in 1957. A front-page article ended with the query, "Will the Long Beach Freeway plough a big path right through this City to reach the Freeways in Pasadena?" Official maps showed the freeway going from the Pacific Coast Highway in Long Beach to Huntington Drive in El Sereno, but with no route specified through South Pasadena. The *Review* pressed the city to come up with its own plan and suggested having one developed by the Stanford Research Institute, which recently had moved its Southern California laboratories to Mission Street.

John J. McCrory, president of the South Pasadena Realty Board, seems to have made the first definite proposal for a westerly freeway route through South Pasadena. In 1959 he suggested that the freeway go through the Monterey Hills—then sparsely settled—dip into the Arroyo Seco near Arroyo Verde Street, and follow the Arroyo to Devil's Gate Dam in Pasadena. Pasadenans, however, preferred a route running somewhat west of Fremont Avenue, then north to an intersection with Pasadena Avenue. "Just why anyone would want to recommend this proposed route is hard to understand," McCrory said, "unless it would be to clear out, with a freeway, some of the older and more obsolescent buildings in that section of Pasadena."

McCrory thought the proposed route west of Fremont Avenue would bring economic ruin to South Pasadena. "We now have the Pasadena Freeway cutting us in two, north and south," he said, "and with this division, east and west, dividing our city of only 3.44 square miles into four parcels, we might as well go out of business as an independent city." For the next quarter of a century, South Pasadena fiercely battled against any freeway going through the center of town.

Not all local news in the fifties provoked contention and controversy. Golfers welcomed an eighteen-hole golf course in Arroyo Park; Girl Scouts celebrated completion of their Little House, in Garfield Park; and hillside residents rejoiced in a new high-rise stairway, with 249 steps and 15 landings, between Monterey Road and Alta Vista Avenue. In 1950 the library gained a support group, the Friends of the South Pasadena Public Library. Its first speaker was distinguished author and UCLA head librarian Lawrence Clark Powell. The holder of South Pasadena library card No. 3089, Powell

Professor Frank C. Baxter of USC enjoyed making the scale models he demonstrated in his English classes and on his award-winning television programs. This model of an early wood-pulp machine was used for a lecture on papermaking. *Courtesy of University of Southern California Archives.*

Industrial designer Henry Dreyfuss is shown working in his South Pasadena studio. Dreyfuss influenced the basic style of numerous familiar objects, from tractors to telephones. *Courtesy of John Dreyfuss.*

154

Estelle Barden Watson and Lena Crossley Harris, who graduated from Center Street School in 1890, helped place the old school bell on a permanent mount in 1952. *Courtesy of South Pasadena Public Library.*

recalled the days when Nellie Keith allowed him to borrow as many books as a six-year-old could carry.

South Pasadenans earned a number of special honors in the fifties. On Scout Day in 1958 the city recognized Frank C. Stoney's thirty-six years of work with the Boy Scouts by naming a street in the Arroyo for him. Charlotte Hoak, a founder of the South Pasadena Garden Club and dean of San Gabriel Valley horticulturists, had a begonia named for her in 1955. A lily that she discovered in the mountains of Southern California also bears her name, and so does a five-acre section of pygmy forest—a unique stand of ancient conifers in Van Damme State Park, near her birthplace in Mendocino County.

In 1956 Professor Frank C. Baxter of the University of Southern California won the George Foster Peabody Award for his lively program "Shakespeare on TV," the first television course in Southern California given for college credit. Despite Baxter's prediction that his audience would consist of "three retired librarians and a bedridden old man," more than a thousand people registered for the course when it was first given in 1953. Of that number, 332 enrolled for credit and took the final exams. By September 1954 the program had won eleven awards. This was no surprise to Baxter's USC students, who once voted him the person "who should teach all the courses in the university."

Architects Whitney R. Smith and Wayne R. Williams have designed projects ranging from a teahouse to a complete city. Their numerous honors include an Award of Merit given in 1959 for an office building described by one juror as providing an ideal setting for creative work. The building, at 1414 Fair Oaks in South Pasadena, was designed for Community Facilities Planners—a group formed by architects Smith & Williams; landscape architects Eckbo, Dean & Williams; and city planning consultants Simon Eisner & Associates. In 1963 an international jury of architects honored the Fair Oaks building for its outstanding design, which features such elements as a sun screen roof over gardens and enclosed spaces.

Henry Dreyfuss (described by the *Los Angeles Times* as "a kind of jet-propelled Renaissance man") also earned international recognition. In 1952 Queen Juliana of the Netherlands presented him with the order of Orange-Nassau for his advice to Dutch manufacturers on industrial design. Dreyfuss received many other awards, including two gold medals from the Architectural League. In a converted barn on his four-acre estate on Columbia Street, and in his New York studio, Dreyfuss designed products ranging from fly swatters to missile sites, from tractor seats to a streamlined train. He designed for people, not just for style, and his products won praise for their comfort, safety, and efficiency, as well as for their restrained good looks. In 1972 Dreyfuss published a guide to international graphic symbols, a book he dedicated to Doris Marks Dreyfuss, his wife and business associate of more than forty years.

During the fifties South Pasadena entered three spectacular floats in Pasadena's Tournament of Roses. For the 1957 parade the high school football queen—in a rickshaw borrowed from the studios of 20th Century Fox— accompanied a floral dragon described by various commentators as "a beautiful mechanical marvel," "the outstanding float of the day," and "the most unusual float of all time." Local boosters denounced the judging procedure when the dragon won no major prize. The next year,

156

however, South Pasadena captured the Queen's Trophy for its float, "June in January," a bridal scene created with ten thousand white roses, narcissi, chrysanthemums, and sweetpeas. In 1959 South Pasadena won the Mayor's Trophy for the most original entry—a magnificently decorated floral elephant representing the Indian Festival of Dussehra.

South Pasadena commemorated two landmarks in the fifties and let two others vanish without ceremony. When the city removed the stump of the old Cathedral Oak in 1952, the Oneonta Park Chapter of the Daughters of the American Revolution placed a monument nearby—a simple cross set in a base of Arroyo boulders. The cross echoed a shape once carved in the bark of the oak tree, and it recalled the legend that Portolá had worshipped at the site in 1770.

More than three hundred people gathered at El Centro School in May 1952 when the old school bell was dedicated as a permanent monument. The quarter-ton bell, which had summoned children to classes for sixty years, was removed from the bell tower in 1949 on the advice of safety engineers. In 1952 the Junior Chamber of Commerce rescued the bell from storage and placed it on a concrete base in front of the school. Honored guests at the dedication included Estelle Barden Watson and Lena Crossley Harris, members of the first graduating class of 1890.

Despite valiant efforts by the SOS Committee (Save Our Station), in 1954 the Santa Fe tore down the picturesque old structure that Margaret Collier Graham described in 1887 as a $1,300 Gothic depot building. The station at El Centro Street and Glendon Way was familiar to moviegoers from having appeared in such Hollywood classics as *Pollyanna* and *Ruggles of Red Gap*. The Santa Fe offered the building to the city, and there was talk of moving it to Garfield Park for use as a historical museum, but fundraising efforts failed, and the station was demolished.

One year earlier, the Hermosa Vista was taken apart timber by timber. South Pasadena's first hotel and site of the first post office, the Hermosa Vista had been a private residence since 1898, and between 1908 and 1936 was owned by astronomer George Ellery Hale—a founder of the California Institute of Technology, one of the original trustees of the Henry E. Huntington Library and Art Gallery, and the first director of the Mount Wilson Observatory. Hale loved the rambling old house, its L-shaped library, and the front verandah from which he had an unobstructed view of the observatory nine miles away. The Hermosa Vista was razed in 1953 to make way for a subdivision.

As the fifties ended, South Pasadena focused on another subdivision: the pioneering redevelopment project in what some people grandly called "the hills of promise."

The Santa Fe Depot, near El Centro Street and Glendon Way, served South Pasadena for more than half a century. The city's first post office building can be seen in the background. *Courtesy of Huntington Library*.

CHRONOLOGY

1950

The census records South Pasadena's population as 16,935.

The Huntington Library exhibits work by South Pasadena resident Will Bradley, the dean of American typographers.

Girl Scouts dedicate their Little House, in Garfield Park.

The city celebrates its first annual Boy Scout Day.

The Friends of the South Pasadena Public Library holds its first meeting, with Lawrence Clark Powell as speaker.

The school board closes Las Flores School because of earthquake hazard.

Residents of Edgewood Drive win a battle to keep the city from cutting down three oak trees growing in the middle of the street.

The first South Pasadenans are called to serve with United States forces aiding the United Nations "police action" in Korea.

The planning commission recommends redeveloping the Monterey Hills.

The city institutes voluntary film censorship.

An amendment to the zoning ordinance prohibits new bars and cocktail lounges without a special variance.

A state constitutional amendment reorganizes the lower court system, and the city council requests that South Pasadena be made part of the Pasadena judicial district.

1951

Work begins on an apartment house development on twenty-nine acres on Raymond Hill.

The Big Red Cars make their last run through South Pasadena.

The Pacific Electric removes the trolley tracks from Huntington Drive.

South Pasadena and San Marino vote to maintain separate school districts.

1952

The El Centro school bell is relocated in the schoolyard.

A monument on the east bank of the Arroyo commemorates the Cathedral Oak.

The Pacific Electric removes the trolley tracks from Fair Oaks Avenue.

1953

Trucks are banned on the Arroyo Seco Parkway.

The Hermosa Vista is razed.

The city establishes the Community Redevelopment Agency with Verne E. Robinson as chairman. He is succeeded by Charlotte W. King.

The Korean War ends.

1954

The Santa Fe tears down a picturesque depot built in South Pasadena at the turn of the century.

The Arroyo Seco Parkway is renamed the Pasadena Freeway.

1955

An eighteen-hole golf course opens in Arroyo Seco Park.

The last San Marino students graduate from South Pasadena High School.

1956

The Federal government approves South Pasadena's application for redevelopment funds.

1957

The city council rezones twenty-one lots, specifically to prevent the opening of a new restaurant and cocktail lounge at Huntington Drive and Fair Oaks.

Debate intensifies over the Long Beach Freeway and how it should be routed through the city.

1958

South Pasadena wins the Queen's Trophy for its Rose Parade float, "June in January."

The Community Redevelopment Agency receives a federal loan of $4.5 million for the country's first open land project.

1959

South Pasadena wins the Mayor's Trophy with its Rose Parade float, "Festival of Dussehra."

The city council votes down a proposal to ban heavy trucks from Fair Oaks north of Mission for a trial period of one year.

South Pasadena's prize-winning entry in the 1959 Tournament of Roses represented a splendidly decorated elephant in the Indian Festival of Dussehra. *Courtesy of South Pasadena Public Library.*

A freeway through South Pasadena would connect with this portion of the Foothill Freeway in Pasadena. *Photograph by Tom M. Apostol.*

THE CHANGING FACE OF A CITY:

1960-1969

The world worries about the endangered species. So do we. But we also worry about the small endangered cities and towns being buried under tons of concrete.

SOUTH PASADENA REVIEW

IN THE NEW DECADE South Pasadena considered problems as diverse as widening Monterey Road, shortening schoolboys' hair, and lengthening schoolgirls' dresses. Debate over the Long Beach Freeway became increasingly shrill, and zoning provoked the usual controversy. There was also cause for celebration. South Pasadena held its diamond jubilee during the sixties and also launched its most ambitious civic enterprise, the Monterey Hills Redevelopment Project.

The 309-acre project lay between Monterey Road and Huntington Drive, adjoining the El Sereno district of Los Angeles. Transforming the area from wilderness to residential suburb involved a decade of planning and two years of site preparation. One of the largest jobs was contouring the hills while preserving their natural beauty. Nearly four million cubic yards of earth were moved to prepare the land for building.

Work started in 1962 after the Community Redevelopment Agency of South Pasadena formally dedicated the project—named Altos de Monterey to distinguish it from other areas in the Monterey Hills. In January 1964 five hundred people attended the first in a series of land auctions held by the CRA. As a headline in the *Los Angeles Times* phrased it, "For Sale: One Fifth of a City—South Pasadena!" By October 1964 almost half the 631 lots were sold, bringing in receipts of more than $4.5 million. Fifteen houses had been built, seventy-one more were under construction, and two families had moved in.

Because it had received a federal loan, Altos de Monterey was open to any qualified buyer, regardless of race, creed, or color. Only two decades earlier, many South Pasadenans had openly campaigned to prevent non-Caucasians from buying or renting property in the city, and at first the Altos policy caused an undercurrent of apprehension. To help meet the challenge of what it called "the possibility of changing conditions in the city," the South Pasadena Ministerial Association formed the South Pasadena Council of Human Relations. It defined human relations as "the way in which people 'get along' with people, ideally with mutual understanding and respect."

Some people from minority groups did move into Altos de Monterey. By 1969 twenty-one black children and fifty-seven Asians had enrolled in the Monterey Hills School. Small as the number was, it represented a significant change in South Pasadena's ethnic makeup.

Whatever doubts people may have had about their new neighbors proved

The Community Redevelopment Agency formally dedicated Altos de Monterey in 1962. Participating in the ceremony are Virginia Delano, executive director of the CRA; John E. ("Bud") Collier, State Assemblyman; and Charlotte King, chairman of the CRA. *Courtesy of South Pasadena Review.*

unfounded. Advertised as a prestige development (lots sold for an average price of $15,000), Altos de Monterey attracted business and professional people interested in good schools and a pleasant environment. According to a CRA survey made in 1969, more than a quarter of the residents in Altos de Monterey owned their own business or were engaged in sales and management, one-quarter were engineers, and about 10 percent were teachers or school administrators.

In 1965 the CRA repaid its federal loan in full. The necessary funds came from lot sales and a $3.4 million bond issue, which the CRA retired in 1969. The following year the agency and the city agreed to deposit net profits from Altos sales in a separate fund whose income could be used by the city for special projects such as downtown revitalization or improving parks. On the recommendation of the South Pasadena League of Women Voters, the surplus fund was named the Charlotte King Development Fund. It was a fitting memorial to the woman who guided the CRA for sixteen years and helped transform one-fifth of the city from tax-delinquent lands to a flourishing residential community.

South Pasadena celebrated its seventy-fifth anniversary on March 2, 1963, with a Diamond Jubilee organized by a Chamber of Commerce committee headed by architect R. Van Buren Livingstone. The grand marshal of the Jubilee parade, Herbert J. Vatcher, had worked in South Pasadena's first bank and as a youngster had lived at the Cawston Ostrich Farm, where his father was superintendent for many years. Young Vatcher eventually became a stockholder in the ostrich farm, and he later served as its president and general manager. Two people in the parade drove ostrich-drawn carts, but Vatcher rode in a gold Rolls-Royce borrowed from the Hollywood Wax Museum.

In honor of the Jubilee, the *Review* featured a series of articles on South Pasadena written by two longtime residents, Sally Clouse and C. Milton Hinshilwood. A local firm, Liljenwall and Shane, published a souvenir booklet, *SP 75*, which included a brief history of the city and reproduced a large number of historic photographs. Advertisements in the booklet gave a picture of local business and industry, with products ranging from Fosselman's ice cream to Microdot's electronic components for satellites and missiles.

SP 75 also carried an advertisement for the South Pasadena Americanism Center, a bookstore and lending library that opened on Mission Street in 1961. The idea of South Pasadenan Jane Crosby, the center was founded "to educate citizens of the community on the subject of Americanism and by all means of communication convey to them the concepts of freedom established by the framers of the Declaration of Independence and the United States Constitution." Even dialing the center was a lesson in American history, for the last digits in its telephone number were 1776.

A nation-wide recession in the late fifties seriously affected South Pasadena. Between January 1958 and December 1962 the number of business establishments in the city declined from 242 to 189. To revitalize the downtown area, the Chamber of Commerce discussed various plans, from painting storefronts to building a shopping mall. The city council rezoned three acres on the outskirts of South Pasadena for a supermarket, but downtown merchants rallied in protest. Urging the city to confine all business to a centralized area, they petitioned for a referendum on the zone change.

One letter to the editor denounced the move for a special election. "South Pasadena is a great 'No' man's land," the writer said. "Our first reaction is always 'No.' You can always count on a 'No' vote here. You can always get a signature on a petition to stop something. . . . Let's stop this costly nonsense. It is stunting the growth of our village."

Despite this outburst, the merchants succeeded in having a special election called. Committees with impressive titles organized for and against the zone change: South Pasadena Good Government Committee; Realtors for Sound Zoning; Committee for Preservation of the Cultural, Residential, and Economic Unity of South Pasadena. After a heated campaign, voters went to the polls in January 1963 and overwhelmingly approved the ordinance to let Ralphs Grocery build at Huntington Drive and Atlantic Boulevard, the former site of the San Marino Hall School for Girls.

At another election in 1963, South Pasadena voted to join the Metropolitan Water District. Along with other San Gabriel Valley communities, South Pasadena pumped all its water from wells. The water table had dropped alarmingly in recent years—as much as eight to ten feet annually. In 1959 Long Beach, Compton, and Downey sued the upstream communities for pumping excessive amounts of water from the common basin, with a resulting increase of salt water intrusion in the coastal areas. In response to the suit, South Pasadena and sixteen other communities formed the Upper San Gabriel Valley Municipal Water District to study ways of bringing supplemental water to the area. They considered salt water conversion, water reclamation, and contracting with the state for Feather River water, but decided the cheapest and most practical solution was annexation to the Metropolitan Water District. In the special election held in 1963, the Upper San Gabriel Valley Water District voted by a ratio of four to one to annex to the Metropolitan Water District. In South Pasadena the vote for annexation was an impressive 95 percent: 2,670 to 121.

In 1965 the city council adopted a comprehensive general plan prepared for South Pasadena by Simon Eisner & Associates. The goals proposed for the next twenty years included a new civic center, a distinctive plan for the central business area, and alignment of the freeway along the city's western border. The plan also urged the city to maintain its suburban identity and single-family environment.

Apartment houses had proliferated in South Pasadena since the end of World War II, especially on Raymond Hill; along Pasadena Avenue, Monterey Road, and Huntington Drive; and in the vicinity of Grevelia Street. Construction boomed during the forties and continued with even more vigor in the fifties. Between 1945 and 1965, builders put up 380 multiple-family projects, with a total of 3,053 units. During the record-breaking period from 1950 to 1955, there were 129 new multiple-family projects, with a total of 978 units. In sharp contrast, only 37 projects—with 664 units—went up in the decade following adoption of the general plan.

In 1965 the city council took steps to widen Monterey Road, an action precipitating four years of controversy. The city had talked of widening the road as early as 1921 but had not authorized preliminary studies until 1963. Two years later, South Pasadena and Los Angeles County signed an agreement for joint financing of the road project.

Plans called for widening a 1.1 mile stretch of Monterey Road between Fair Oaks and Pasadena avenues. Property owners were furious that the council held no public

166

One of the local companies advertising in South Pasadena's Diamond Jubilee booklet was Boller & Chivens, which built this 90-inch optical telescope for the University of Arizona's Steward Observatory. *Courtesy of South Pasadena Public Library.*

hearing on the plan to replace the existing two-lane road with a four-lane divided highway and to extend the right-of-way from 60 feet to 108 feet. "Are city problems too complex for laymen?" opponents demanded. "Is open discussion an outmoded institution?"

In the face of growing opposition, the council called a public meeting and later offered to consider a right-of-way just eighty feet wide. Meanwhile, the newly organized Citizens for South Pasadena asked, "Shall South Pasadena remain a city of homes or become the traffic interchange of the San Gabriel Valley?" The group filed an initiative petition for an ordinance prohibiting the city from widening any street beyond sixty feet, or any right-of-way beyond seventy feet, without approval of the voters. When the city attorney ruled the petition invalid, the group ran a black-bordered advertisement stating, "Representative government for South Pasadena died on October 20, 1965."

In municipal elections held in 1966, Citizens for South Pasadena endorsed the three winning candidates for city council: William Harker, John L. Sullivan (co-chairman of the citizens group), and Lila Cox, who became South Pasadena's first woman mayor. The new council voted four to one to widen Monterey to eighty feet. Sullivan held out for seventy-two feet, the figure preferred by residents on Monterey. Eventually both sides were able to claim success because of a compromise that Sullivan helped negotiate. In 1969 the Los Angeles County Road Department agreed to specify the right-of-way as eighty feet, but actually improve only seventy-two feet: a roadway sixty-four feet wide, and sidewalks four feet wide next to the curb on both sides of the road. The remaining eight feet in the right-of-way would be designated as utility areas, one alongside each stretch of sidewalk. Semantics thus ended an impasse of four years, and work finally proceeded on widening Monterey Road.

In 1967 the *Review* quoted a Santa Cruz newspaper: "School boards have a tough job these days monitoring the length of girls' dresses and boys' hair." A headline in the *Review* had already announced, " 'Hippie' Look On SPHS Campus Out This Fall." The dress code for boys outlawed beards, mustaches, and long hair (as well as shoes without socks). The rules for girls were more detailed: no long nails or excessive makeup, no shorts, slacks, muu-muus, or low-cut dresses, and no skirts shorter than an inch above the kneecap. Over the months a beleaguered school board gradually modified its rules, even abandoning a definite length for skirts, provided they covered underclothes and stocking tops. By 1970 boys were allowed to have long sideburns, small mustaches, and collar-length hair. In 1971, after a student at South Pasadena High School won a court case to wear his hair as long as he wanted, the school board stopped enforcing its restrictions on hair length.

During the summer of 1968—concerned about racial tension in the country—a few South Pasadena young people started the Hometown Project. The two leading spirits, Don Farrow and Charles Black, graduated from South Pasadena High School in 1965, the year the Watts riots brought death and destruction to Los Angeles. Now the young people proposed reaching out to groups in Watts and Pasadena that were working for social and economic stability in the black community. The Hometown Project held a seminar attended by eight hundred people, encouraged South Pasadenans to open savings accounts in the Watts area, and helped with the tutorial program at Pasadena's

Westside Study Center. In 1969 Don Farrow and Charles Black received the Raymond Pitts *Star-News* Human Relations Award for the outstanding accomplishments of South Pasadena's Hometown Project.

Other South Pasadenans received recognition in the sixties, especially for literature and the arts. Jerry Cohen and a colleague on the *Los Angeles Times*, W. S. Murphy, wrote *Burn, Baby, Burn*, a compelling account of the Watts riots. Henri Coulette's first book, *The War of the Secret Agents*, was the Lamont Poetry Selection for 1965. Charles Webb's first novel, *The Graduate*, won praise as "a stunning little tour de force" and became a hugely successful motion picture. Artist Susan Peterson, whose ceramic pieces are in major museum collections, was made a Knight of the Lion of Finland for furthering Finnish and American design in her television program "Wheels, Kilns, and Clay."

An Outstanding Professor Award went to both Walter Askin and Paul Zall, faculty members at California State University, Los Angeles. Both men won further recognition as well. A prize-winning painter and printmaker, Askin has exhibited widely, both in this country and abroad. Zall has published a number of scholarly works with such lively titles as *A Hundred Merry Tales* and *Comical Spirit of Seventy-Six*. He has also edited the first complete and accurate edition of Benjamin Franklin's *Autobiography*.

On her eighty-first birthday, South Pasadenan Nelbert Chouinard received a scroll from the Los Angeles City Council for helping make Los Angeles an acclaimed art center. In 1921—with $200 in the bank and a widow's pension of $75 a month—Nelbert Chouinard rented a two-story house in downtown Los Angeles and opened the Chouinard School of Art. She persuaded artists with national and international reputations to teach at what has been called the first really great art school in the city. Admired as "a kind of Mother Superior of Art in Los Angeles," Nelbert Chouinard was active in the work of the school for forty years. In 1961 the Chouinard School of Art and the Los Angeles Conservatory of Music amalgamated to become the California Institute of the Arts, now located in Valencia.

In 1960 California observed the twentieth anniversary of the first freeway in the West, the Pasadena Freeway (originally called the Arroyo Seco Parkway). At the same time South Pasadenans worried about the approaching Long Beach Freeway, whose route had been adopted as far north as Huntington Drive in El Sereno. "Isn't one ditch through our town memorial enough to poor engineering?" Tog Ericson asked in a front-page editorial in the *Review*. He urged South Pasadena to study paths the freeway might take through the city and to work aggressively for a route that was not economically disruptive. "It's later than you think," he warned and suggested if the city would not fight for its own interests, it should change its name to Milquetoast, California.

The Property Owners Association also called for decisive action to keep South Pasadena from being "quartered and chewed to pieces" by a route dividing the city east and west, as the Pasadena Freeway had divided it north and south. Many people feared the state would approve a straight-line route, generally along Meridian Avenue. Such an alignment would not only bisect the city but would pose a threat to the public library, El Centro School, a number of historic landmarks, a residential section of twenty-three acres, and numerous business and commercial establishments. The Property Owners Association estimated the loss to South Pasadena at over $6 million in personal property and at least $125,000 to $150,000 a year in taxes.

As an alternative to the Meridian Route, the Property Owners Association proposed that the freeway go west of the Monterey Hills, curve northeast along the Arroyo Seco, and connect with the Foothill Freeway near Devil's Gate Dam in Pasadena. In 1962 the city formally asked the State Division of Highways to consider the route, and over the next quarter of a century South Pasadena battled to have some variation of this plan adopted.

Although most South Pasadenans favored a westerly route, some people worried about its impact on the Monterey Hills and the Arroyo Seco. The *Review* had no sympathy for anyone wanting "to save a bit of dried grass and dead brush in the Arroyo," and for several months it ran photographs contrasting the worst scenes in the Arroyo—old barns, broken fences, and trash dumps—with the homes and commercial buildings which a freeway along the Meridian Route would destroy. Twelve-year-old Billy Clanton accused the paper of giving an unfair impression of the Arroyo and asked why it did not show views of Arroyo Seco Park, the baseball diamond, and the golf course. He pointed out that the Arroyo contained the last land in the city not yet built on and asked, "If you do take the Arroyo, where are all the kids in South Pasadena going to play ball?"

His was a minority voice, however. In August 1964 the city council declared the Meridian Route unacceptable and said if it were adopted, the city would not agree to the closing of any streets for freeway ramps. The school board and the library board also opposed the Meridian Route, and seven thousand of South Pasadena's eleven thousand registered voters signed petitions against it.

The California Highway Commission scheduled an all-day hearing in September for public testimony on three possible routes through South Pasadena: a westerly route, the Meridian Route, or a combination of the two. Nearly three thousand people from South Pasadena and neighboring communities turned out and clamored to be heard. A significant number of speakers opposed any freeway link at all. Their sentiment was best expressed by Dr. Robert Freeman, a member of the Pasadena Board of Education, who called on the state to discontinue all north-south freeway proceedings until it could justify the need for "an eight-lane, truck-bearing, smog-producing freeway from South Pasadena to Sunland."

In November 1964 the highway commission announced approval of the Meridian Route. South Pasadena expressed shock and disappointment but pledged continued opposition to the choice. The *Review*'s first editorial in 1965 urged readers to fight the freeway, and scarcely a month passed for the rest of the year without another editorial attacking the Meridian Route through South Pasadena.

In 1966 South Pasadena proposed an alternative it claimed would save eight hundred houses. This "city-saving route" would angle across the Monterey Hills and follow the city's western border to the intersection of York Boulevard and the Pasadena Freeway. From there it would run parallel with the Pasadena Freeway, or be double-decked above it, and enter Pasadena near Fair Oaks Avenue and Columbia Street. Unimpressed with the plan, the California Highway Commission reaffirmed support

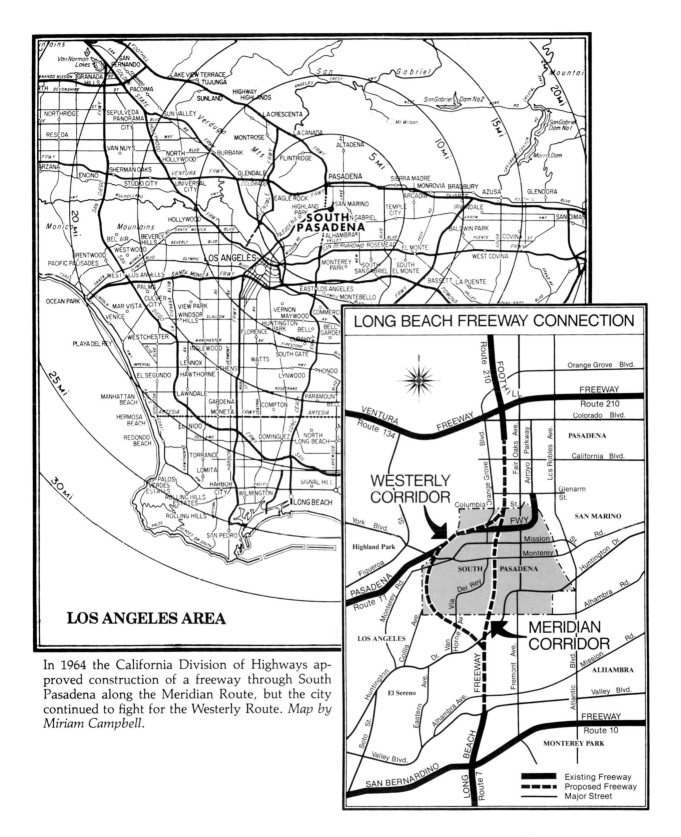

LOS ANGELES AREA

LONG BEACH FREEWAY CONNECTION

In 1964 the California Division of Highways approved construction of a freeway through South Pasadena along the Meridian Route, but the city continued to fight for the Westerly Route. *Map by Miriam Campbell.*

171

for the Meridian Route, which provided a straight-line connection between the Long Beach and Foothill freeways.

South Pasadena next turned to the California legislature for help. State Senator John L. Harmer introduced a bill designating the Westerly Route the official freeway route through South Pasadena, but the bill died in committee. The Senate Transportation Committee was no more successful in winning a new hearing for South Pasadena before the highway commission. Determined to battle on, the city appointed a freeway study committee to recommend further action. "We have just begun to fight!" said committee member AlvaLee Arnold, who later served as city councilwoman and as mayor of South Pasadena.

The freeway committee reported to the city council in 1968. Six members signed the minority report, which recommended that the city end its battle for a westerly route and settle with the highway commission on the best terms possible. It also urged the city to revise its master plan and zoning laws and to work to attract light industry, which would help equalize the tax burden. "Let's realize that the horse and buggy days are gone," the report concluded, "that South Pasadena is part of a great metropolitan area, and that we must plan for a community in that metropolitan area."

Eight members signed the majority report, which denounced the Meridian Route and stated once again that it would change the character and environment of South Pasadena and damage its economy, school system, and cultural welfare. Designer Henry Dreyfuss agreed with the majority. "A highway system should be beneficial to all," he said. "Freeways that transport us on the one hand, but are ruinous to the community on the other, cannot be considered an asset. The operation may be successful, but the patient will surely die."

The question of the freeway dominated a special election held in 1969 to fill a vacancy on the city council. Frank Randall, who won by nearly a thousand votes, favored the Westerly Route. As a first order of business, the city council chose William Harker, who was firmly committed to the Westerly Route, as the new mayor. The council then appointed a City Freeway Commission, with attorney Michael B. Montgomery as chairman, to study the freeway problem once more and recommend a compromise solution.

After consulting with the Los Angeles City Engineer and the District Engineer of the Division of Highways, the City Freeway Commission proposed a modified westerly route. From Huntington Drive it would enter the southwest corner of South Pasadena, and staying within the city limits it would continue as far as the Arroyo Seco golf course. It would then go northeast through the golf course, emerge parallel to the Pasadena Freeway, and swing north to rejoin the adopted route along Meridian Avenue to the Pasadena border. Without endorsing the plan, Pasadena, Alhambra, and Los Angeles agreed to South Pasadena's request for a detailed study of the route by the State Highway Commission. The commission unanimously agreed to make the study, and the city hoped for acceptance of a westerly route at last.

The most traumatic event of the decade—the war in Vietnam—provoked bitter debate in some communities, but seems to have stirred little controversy in South Pasadena. In 1967 the mayor proclaimed Support Our Servicemen Week, and in 1968 students at South Pasadena High School adopted a battalion of nine hundred men

172

The Buena Vista district is one of the historic areas threatened by completion of the Long Beach Freeway along the Meridian Route. Two houses designed by Charles and Henry Greene stand side by side on Buena Vista Street. The house on the left was built in 1897 for Howard Longley; the Craftsman bungalow in 1906 for Lucretia Garfield. *Courtesy of Greene and Greene Library.*

fighting in Vietnam. In 1971 the city council declared No Substitute for Victory Day, in connection with the showing of a film by that name. Just three people publicly criticized the council action, saying it was taken without a mandate and without following proper procedures—or as one critic gently phrased it, without showing due discretion. Records show that four South Pasadenans lost their lives in Vietnam, but there is no way of knowing what other scars the war may have left on the community.

From 1963 to 1980 the Friends of the South Pasadena Public Library held an annual book fair on the library lawn. Alla Hall is the customer in this 1963 photograph, and Robert Wayne, Mary Helen Wayne, and Mary Murdoch are the volunteer workers. *Courtesy of South Pasadena Public Library.*

CHRONOLOGY

1960

The Pasadena Freeway marks its twentieth anniversary.

The official census count for South Pasadena is 19,706.

1961

The South Pasadena Americanism Center opens.

1962

The city asks the State Division of Highways to consider a westerly freeway route through the city.

The Community Redevelopment Agency dedicates Altos de Monterey.

1963

South Pasadena celebrates its Diamond Jubilee on March 2.

The city votes to join the Metropolitan Water District.

The Friends of the South Pasadena Library holds its first book sale.

A tree in the Ancient Limber Pine Forest, near the summit of Mount Baden-Powell in the Angeles National Forest, is named for South Pasadenan Michael H. Waldron, active for forty years in the Boy Scout movement.

Churches stay open for prayers in memory of President John F. Kennedy, assassinated on November 22.

1964

The CRA auctions off the first lots in Altos de Monterey.

The Ministerial Association forms the South Pasadena Council of Human Relations, with Ruth Swenson as chairman.

Fight the Freeway headquarters open in Pasadena and South Pasadena.

The California Highway Commission adopts the Meridian Route through South Pasadena. The city council declares it unacceptable and says it will not agree to the closing of any streets for freeway ramps.

Eighteen-year-old Tom Hutton joins the Los Angeles Dodgers organization and becomes the first graduate of South Pasadena High School to sign a Big League baseball contract.

1965

South Pasadena Beautiful organizes and elects Fred Golding president.

The CRA repays its federal loan in full with funds from lot sales and a $3.4 million bond issue.

The city council adopts a general plan for future development of the city.

1966

South Pasadena wins the Mayor's Trophy for the most original entry in the Tournament of Roses—a float with astronauts landing on another planet.

The new South Pasadena-San Marino YMCA opens at Garfield Avenue and Oak Street, where an orchard flourished at the turn of the century.

Lila Cox becomes the first woman to serve as mayor of South Pasadena.

1967

South Pasadena wins the Sweepstakes Award for beauty at the Tournament of Roses with its float, "A Voyage to Atlantis."

South Pasadenan Julie Lyn Holmes becomes United States National Ice Skating Champion.

Monterey Hills School opens on Via del Rey.

South Pasadena High School bans the "hippie look" on campus, but after a court case suspends enforcement of the dress code rules.

The mayor proclaims Support Our Servicemen Week.

1968

The city's Freeway Study Committee votes 8 to 6 against the Meridian Route.

Los Angeles plans redevelopment in the Monterey Hills adjacent to Altos de Monterey.

Young people in South Pasadena organize the Hometown Project, which receives a human relations award.

The Associated Student Body of South Pasadena High School adopts a battalion that is fighting in Vietnam.

1969

The city and county agree to widen Monterey Road.

Union Pacific stops running trains through South Pasadena.

The State Highway Commission agrees to study a modified westerly route proposed by South Pasadena's new City Freeway Commission.

Assembly, California Legislature, 1967 Regular Session

Resolution

Relative to commendation of the City of South Pasadena

By Honorable John L. E. Collier, 54th District; Honorable Robert E. Badham, 71st District; Honorable E. Richard Barnes, 78th District; Honorable Frederick James Bear, 79th District; Honorable Carlos Bee, 13th District; Honorable W. Craig Biddle, 74th District; Honorable John V. Briggs, 35th District; Honorable Carl A. Britschgi, 26th District; Honorable Willie L. Brown, Jr., 18th District; Honorable Robert H. Burke, 70th District; Honorable John L. Burton, 20th District; Honorable Charles Edward Chapel, 44th District; Honorable Eugene A. Chappie, 6th District; Honorable Charles J. Conrad, 57th District; Honorable Kenneth Cory, 69th District; Honorable Earle P. Crandall, 25th District; Honorable Robert W. Crown, 14th District; Honorable Pauline L. Davis, 1st District; Honorable Wadie P. Deddeh, 77th District; Honorable James W. Dent, 10th District; Honorable Gordon W. Duffy, 21st District; Honorable John F. Dunlap, 9th District; Honorable Edward E. Elliott, 40th District; Honorable March K. Fong, 15th District; Honorable John Francis Foran, 23rd District; Honorable Joe A. Gonsalves, 66th District; Honorable Bill Greene, 53rd District; Honorable Leroy F. Greene, 3rd District; Honorable James A. Hayes, 39th District; Honorable Stewart Hinckley, 23rd District; Honorable Harvey Johnson, 38th District; Honorable Ray E. Johnson, 4th District; Honorable William M. Ketchum, 29th District; Honorable John T. Knox, 11th District; Honorable Frank Lanterman, 47th District; Honorable Ken MacDonald, 37th District; Honorable Patrick D. McGee, 64th District; Honorable George W. Milias, 22nd District; Honorable Ernest N. Mobley, 33rd District; Honorable Robert T. Monagan, 12th District; Honorable Carlos J. Moorhead, 43rd District; Honorable Don Mulford, 16th District; Honorable Frank Murphy, Jr., 31st District; Honorable David Negri, 41st District; Honorable Alan G. Patton, 34th District; Honorable Walter W. Powers, 8th District; Honorable Paul Priolo, 60th District; Honorable Newton R. Russell, 62nd District; Honorable Peter F. Schabarum, 49th District; Honorable Alan Sieroty, 59th District; Honorable Kent H. Stacey, 28th District; Honorable John Stull, 80th District; Honorable Vincent Thomas, 68th District; Honorable L. E. Townsend, 67th District; Honorable Jesse M. Unruh, 65th District; Honorable John Vasconcellos, 24th District; Honorable John G. Veneman, 30th District; Honorable Victor V. Veysey, 75th District; Honorable Floyd L. Wakefield, 52nd District; Honorable Charles Warren, 56th District; Honorable Pete Wilson, 76th District; Honorable Edwin L. Z'berg, 9th District; and Honorable George N. Zenovich, 32nd District.

WHEREAS, It has come to the attention of the Members of the Assembly that South Pasadena, the little city adjacent to the site of the Rose Bowl Parade, won the sweepstakes prize in the 78th Tournament of Roses with an imaginative, flower-frosted entry; and

WHEREAS, South Pasadena's winning effort was a float depicting Atlantis, the lengendary island kingdom which sank into the depths of the sea centuries ago; and

WHEREAS, South Pasadena has contributed greatly to the enjoyment of parade lovers by having participated in the Rose Bowl Parade for forty-seven years; and

WHEREAS, South Pasadena's prize entry consisted of eight lovely Grecian maidens riding the main portion, a giant clamshell and four flowery fish, two on each side moving independently along with the main float, all using a myriad of majestic flowers; now, therefore, be it

Resolved by the Assembly of the State of California, That the Members send their heartiest congratulations to the City of South Pasadena for this climactic award following many years of exemplary efforts; and be it further

Resolved, That the Chief Clerk of the Assembly shall transmit a suitably prepared copy of this resolution to the City of South Pasadena.

❡ *House Resolution No. 11 read and adopted unanimously January 16, 1967.*

❡ SIGNED:

Jesse M. Unruh
JESSE M. UNRUH
Speaker of the Assembly

❡ ATTEST:

James D. Driscoll
JAMES D. DRISCOLL
Chief Clerk of the Assembly

Courtesy of South Pasadena Review.

South Pasadena's living sign, planted in 1940, was replaced by cobblestone letters in 1980. *Photograph by Tom M. Apostol.*

ROUNDING OUT ONE HUNDRED YEARS:
1970-1988

The praises of South Pasadena have been sung by all who have visited our fair little city since the earliest settlement of the old colony known as the San Gabriel Orange Grove Association. That for advantageous location it is superior to all the surrounding country, was proven by the fact that many of the shrewdest men of that old association chose it as their future homes.

GEORGE W. GLOVER

In April 1888—just one month after South Pasadena incorporated—a news story boasted, "Every week makes an addition to the business houses of South Pasadena. The latest is a boot and shoe store, which is being opened by Messrs. Crossley & Barden, in the Wotkyns building on Mission Street." Prospective customers included some four hundred workmen employed to level hills and fill arroyos in a tract adjoining the Hotel Raymond grounds.

Eighty years later, business news was less encouraging. During the 1960s a number of large companies—including Beckman Instruments, Stanford Research Institute, and Microdot—had moved to other locations when they found it difficult to expand in South Pasadena. According to one estimate, the departure of Beckman Instruments meant an annual tax loss to the city of $100,000. South Pasadena was at an industrial crossroads, said the president of Microdot in 1966. He complained that all land zoned for industry was occupied, and that an area zoned for manufacturing research and development (by Mission Street and Meridian Avenue) might be taken for the Long Beach Freeway; so firms were reluctant to locate there.

In addition to the loss of industry, retail business also had been declining. An economic study made in 1972 revealed that only 13 percent of South Pasadena's revenue came from the sales tax, while in neighboring communities the figure was around 25 percent. South Pasadenans were spending as much as $19 million a year outside the city because local merchants did not meet their needs. Over the next decade the city considered, and abandoned, various ideas to revitalize the downtown center and attract new business and new customers.

The most ambitious proposal, suggested by the Community Redevelopment Agency in 1973, would have placed more than a quarter of the city's land under its jurisdiction. Presenting its plan as an amendment to the highly successful project launched in the Monterey Hills in 1958, the CRA hoped to finance downtown revitalization with as much as $400,000 a year in tax increments from Altos de Monterey development properties. Council candidate David Card and the ad hoc South Pasadena Citizens Defense Group filed a legal challenge to the plan. They won a court

179

The four-block revitalization project considered in 1974, but never built, had the orange tree as its theme. *Courtesy of South Pasadena Public Library.*

ruling that tax revenues from a completed residential project could not finance commercial redevelopment.

As a result of the lawsuit, the CRA reduced the scope of its plan for downtown revitalization to the four blocks between Mission, Oxley, Fair Oaks, and Fremont. Whitney Smith, architectural consultant to the CRA, recommended developing the area as a superblock, with consistent architectural design and with Mound and El Centro closed to traffic. Smith proposed an orangery as a central focus for the block, with walkways radiating from the grove under latticed canopies. The plan was approved in 1975 as Downtown Revitalization Project No 1. Fifty people gathered at El Centro and Mound in November 1977 for the Orangery Shopping Center ground breaking. The *South Pasadena Review* observed that a sign on the premises read like a Rialto Theatre announcement, with "Coming Attraction" at the top and "A CRA Production" at the bottom.

The coming attraction never materialized. Downtown merchants became increasingly skeptical about the new project: their right to participate, the rents they would have to pay, and the benefits they would receive if forced to relocate. Due in part to pressure from the merchants, the city council disbanded the CRA board in 1978 and assumed its authority. Still displeased with redevelopment plans, some merchants threatened to sue to have the plans modified to their liking. The threat halted the sale of bonds for the project and effectively ended the city's efforts to develop a superblock with a unifying theme.

In 1984 merchants did agree with the CRA on one effort to help local business. This was the construction of an improved parking area for stores along the west side of Fair Oaks Avenue, from Mission Street to Oxley. The city financed the project with a combination of federal funds and CRA money available for public facilities. As their contribution, the merchants agreed to improve store entrances facing on the new parking lot, which is known as the Mission Oaks Center.

In a move aimed at encouraging private developers, the city council— sitting as the CRA—in 1981 relinquished architectural control and the power of eminent domain within the downtown area. Much of the construction that took place in the seventies and eighties was along Fair Oaks Avenue. The first to build and anchor new shopping centers were a Vons Market, a Safeway Store, an Ole's Home Center, and a Thrifty Drug & Discount Store. Another symbol of renewed business activity was the shopping center that opened in 1985 at Fair Oaks Avenue and Grevelia Street, where for seven years there had been an empty market building and a vacant parking lot. The new cluster of stores featured a Bristol Farms market, which brought South Pasadenans a variety of specialty foods, from bagels to sashimi.

Just west of the central downtown area is the business district that grew up around Mission Street and Meridian Avenue at the turn of the century. Credit for one of the first improvement efforts on Mission Street goes to Harry Goldfarb, the philosopher shoemaker. In 1935 Goldfarb planted flowers between his shop and the Santa Fe railroad tracks, added a bench, and dedicated his small garden plot to the public as West Mission Street Park. Goldfarb also enlivened his windows with samples of his own verse. One bit of doggerel ended with the lines:

> I am content and happy without booze,
> And all I want is to Repair Your Shoes.

181

The Mission West area has enjoyed a modest renaissance since the early seventies, with the old brick buildings put to use as offices, studios, and workshops, and as salesrooms for antiques and contemporary crafts. Charles Crozier, owner of the building originally known as the Mission Hotel, led the drive to preserve and promote South Pasadena's Historic Business District, which is now listed in the National Register of Historic Places.

Historic preservation was bolstered by formation of a city commission to identify and designate the city's historic landmarks. Inaugurated in 1971 with architect Raymond Girvigian as chairman, the Cultural Heritage Commission was the result of a year's planning and research by a South Pasadena Beautiful subcommittee headed by architect Jean Driskel. In 1974 the Cultural Heritage Commission published a brochure describing twenty-five South Pasadena landmarks—a number since expanded to thirty-two, plus the Historic Business District.

Moviegoers and architecture buffs rallied in 1977 to save the half-century-old Rialto Theatre, which the CRA wanted to bulldoze for a drugstore parking lot. More than three thousand people signed petitions to save the theater, described by *Los Angeles Times* critic Charles Champlin as a cultural resource that South Pasadena and its neighbors could ill afford to lose. Responding to public sentiment, the city voted against demolishing the building. The Rialto's landmark status was recognized in 1978 when it was listed in the National Register of Historic Places.

One old structure did come down in the seventies—the glazed-brick Ong Building at the southwest corner of Mission and Fair Oaks. Built at a cost of $30,000, the building was hailed in 1911 as the pride of South Pasadena, its finest and largest business structure. Tenants in 1911 included the South Pasadena Savings Bank, Chaffee's Basket Grocery, and Washburn Brothers (purveyors of real estate, automobiles, and clean, filtered gasoline), who in one month sold four new Buicks, two second-hand Buicks, and two pieces of property.

The Ong Building gave way to Security Pacific National Bank in 1974. One of the displaced tenants was Fosselman's ice cream and coffee shop, a city institution since 1937, when a malt cost a dime and a double cone cost a nickel. On Fosselman's last hour of business in South Pasadena, the shop filled with a hundred devoted patrons, including the mayor, who presented Bill Fosselman with an official commendation.

When South Pasadena celebrated its ninety-fifth birthday in 1983, the oldest family-owned business was seventy years old. Founded in 1913 as Smith & Coots, and continued as South Pasadena Plumbing, it was owned by members of the Coots family until 1983, when the business closed. Citizens Dry Cleaning now holds the record as South Pasadena's oldest family-owned business. Originally Citizens Dye Works, it was started by Max and Zona Schmiedeberg in 1917 and is run today by their son Donald.

A number of other businesses have been in South Pasadena for fifty years or more. The *South Pasadena Review* is a direct descendant of the *South Pasadenan*, founded by George W. Glover in 1893. The Braewood Convalescent Center evolved from a sanitarium started in 1906 by Dr. Thomas W. Bishop, who introduced such features as a roof garden with tents for patients who needed open air. Oneonta Transfer & Storage opened for business in 1913 and in 1925 acquired the pioneering South Pasadena Transfer Company, which operated one of the first motor vans in the city. Black and

The Mission Hotel opened in 1923 in what is now designated as South Pasadena's Historic Business District. The ground floor of the building was planned for shops, and the upper floor for lodgings. The old hotel building is now a Cultural Heritage Landmark. *Photograph by H. J. Kenny; courtesy of Huntington Library.*

Young patrons line up outside the Rialto Theatre for a Saturday matinee in 1931. The Rialto is a Cultural Heritage Landmark and on the National Register of Historic Places. *Photograph by H. J. Kenny; courtesy of Huntington Library.*

This dray was converted to a motor van by mounting the barn-red wagon body on the chassis of a Mack truck. *Courtesy of Edwin H. Carpenter.*

White Cleaners, begun in 1923, has changed ownership several times since then, but the original building is still in use. The plumbing firm started by Percy Markowitz in 1926 has been continued as Morrow & Holman.

Two banks have a long association with the community. The Home Commercial & Savings Bank of South Pasadena, founded in 1923, ultimately became the South Pasadena Branch of the Bank of America. Security Pacific National is linked, through merger, with South Pasadena's first bank, founded in 1904. Security has another special tie with the city, for in 1922—under the name of Security Trust & Savings—the bank published a souvenir history of South Pasadena.

There has been a drugstore in the Ozmun Building, at Mission Street and Fair Oaks Avenue, since 1915: first the South Pasadena Pharmacy, and then the Raymond Pharmacy, which became the Fair Oaks Pharmacy in the fifties. A restaurant has operated at one address on Fair Oaks since 1929. The first owner (C. T. McCulley) called his establishment Hamburger Mac's, and the second owner (Gus Tripodes) renamed it Gus's Barbecue.

The Rialto Theatre will be sixty-three years old at the time of South Pasadena's centennial. Another old-timer—Balk's Hardware—will be fifty-two, tracing its history back to a pet and garden shop run by Les Balk in 1936. With such pleasant traditions as providing freshly popped popcorn to Saturday customers, Balk's Hardware conveys a small-town feeling that the city cherishes.

South Pasadena has always prided itself on being a residential community. "The City of Happy Homes," read a booster ad in 1906. "All the advantages of City Life, plus a Purer Atmosphere, Better Water, and a quiet home among the Native song birds." The long-range general plan adopted in 1965 urged South Pasadena to retain its suburban identity, and the Mayor's Committee on Revitalization recommended in 1971 that the city prohibit high-rise buildings and commercial density.

High-rise did not become an issue until 1982, when South Pasadena businessman Ted Colliau proposed building two office towers on Fair Oaks Avenue just south of the Pasadena Freeway. One structure was to be a ten-story building 129 feet tall, and the other a twelve-story building 216 feet tall. To build higher than 45 feet he needed a conditional use permit, and this the city readily granted, believing the towers would give a much-needed boost to the economy. The city council also granted Colliau a 21 percent reduction in the number of parking spaces he had to provide.

For nine months people hotly debated the merits of high-rise construction. Those in favor of the towers argued they would create jobs, attract other investors, improve a depressed business area, and bring the city as much as $500,000 a year in added tax revenues. Opponents focused on one argument: that the towers would destroy South Pasadena's residential character and small-town atmosphere.

Opposition to the towers was led by the Save South Pasadena Committee, organized by real estate agent Norman Getchell and attorney Helen Simmons, who was a former councilwoman. Circulating an initiative petition, the committee gathered enough signatures for a referendum on high-rise construction. The grass-roots campaign resulted in an upset victory in July 1983. By a margin of 269 votes, the electorate approved a measure banning construction higher than 45 feet and placing a 5 percent limit on parking variances. "When nearly 40 percent of the voters turn out on a hot

July day," Colliau said after the election, "you know it has to be an emotional issue." With passage of the new ordinance, Colliau modified his building plans and in 1986 began construction of a four-story office building on Fair Oaks.

The city council decision to build a new civic center provoked another bruising battle and another referendum. A civic center had been under consideration since 1972, when Arthur L. Pereira, consulting architect to the CRA, advised selling the property at Mission and Mound—occupied by the city hall, police department, and fire department—and building a new complex "to provide more open space and to give an attractive identity to the focal point of South Pasadena's public facilities."

Interest in a civic center rekindled in 1977 when the old brick city hall, which had been built in 1914, was declared structurally unsafe. The city offices moved next door into the CRA Annex on Mission Street, but the fire station remained in the old building. Advocates of a new center claimed that rebuilding would be cheaper than modernizing the existing facilities, and that a new center would enhance South Pasadena's image. In 1981 the city bought a million-dollar site at Meridian and El Centro, near the library and the school administration building. On the same property, in 1877, George Lightfoot had built his South Pasadena Hotel, whose location he advertised as the garden spot of Southern California. A more recent owner of the same property was Boller & Chivens, which in 1957 built the country's first satellite-tracking cameras.

City acquisition of the property stirred little debate at the time, except from Robert Wagner, a member of the planning commission, who threatened a lawsuit against the city. He called $1.1 million a gross overpayment and complained that the transaction had never come before the planning commission or been presented for a public hearing. The matter languished until 1983, when the city razed the buildings at El Centro and Meridian, hired an architect for a new civic center, and approved his preliminary design. In response, Wagner cosponsored a drive to put the question of the civic center to a public vote.

Opponents of relocating the city hall gathered more than twice the signatures needed for a referendum. "For the first time in 20 years," said the Los Angeles Times, "the proposed extension of the Long Beach Freeway through the middle of town has taken a back seat to other election concerns in South Pasadena." Meanwhile, there was a heated battle for the two council seats to be filled in April 1984. Mayor AlvaLee Arnold, a strong supporter of the new civic center, ran for reelection. Seven other candidates were also running. Among them was Robert Wagner, in his fourth try for the council. He and political newcomer Lee Prentiss won election, and Mayor Arnold was unseated. The long and bitter dispute over a new civic center ended in November 1984, when 63 percent of the voters turned down the proposal to rebuild at Meridian and El Centro. In 1986 the city council approved senior citizens housing for the corner, where a large hotel (with birdcage elevator) had stood a century earlier.

During the council election of 1984 a new citizens' group emerged: the Committee for Responsive Government, which was founded by Thomas Biesek. Members of the group were variously described as civic watchdogs and as "anti-everything dissidents." The committee helped elect Wagner to office, it fought for a public vote on the civic center, and it claimed credit for the resignation of city manager Charles Martin, who had served for twenty years as South Pasadena's city attorney and for eight years

A proposal to build these office towers on Fair Oaks Avenue led in 1983 to an ordinance banning construction higher than forty-five feet. *Courtesy of Ted Colliau.*

Janet and Scott Ziegler helped youngsters make up as clowns during the Fourth of July celebration at Garfield Park in 1982. *Courtesy of Ted R. Shaw.*

as the city manager and as director and attorney for the redevelopment agency.

At the same time that he held these posts in South Pasadena, Martin was on the payroll of a number of other San Gabriel Valley communities. Early in 1983 he held sixteen positions in six different cities. His supporters praised Martin as "the foremost city attorney in California" and as a capable administrator who had put South Pasadena on a sound financial footing. Opponents charged, however, that Martin devoted too little time to the problems of South Pasadena and received "full-time wages for part-time work." In 1983 Martin divested himself of all but one of his posts outside South Pasadena. With the council's knowledge and consent, he also performed legal work for two other cities. The Committee for Responsive Government claimed this was a breach of contract. Stung by what he felt was unfair criticism, Martin resigned from all his South Pasadena posts in October 1984. He was succeeded by John Bernardi, the assistant city manager, who had experience as city engineer, head of the public works department, director of the building and planning department, and executive director of the CRA.

Rancorous debate has often divided the community, but some events have brought residents together in joyful celebration. During the country's bicentennial, three thousand people took part in Fourth of July festivities in Arroyo Seco Park. In a salute to local history, an award was made to former mayor Walter Garmshausen, whose father came to South Pasadena in 1894 and soon owned one of the first bakeries in town. Walter Garmshausen had lived in South Pasadena since 1903, but the Board of Realtors later found someone who beat this record by two years. Myrtle Coots arrived in South Pasadena in 1901, and eighty-five years later she still occupied the house her father bought when Milan Avenue (then called Elm Avenue) was surrounded by orange groves and vineyards. Settling down in one place for a long period of time—although untypical of Southern California as a whole—is not uncommon in South Pasadena, where a surprising number of people live in houses passed down from one generation of the family to another.

Three happy events highlighted the summer of 1982: a Fourth of July Extravaganza, a high school grand reunion, and dedication of the newly rebuilt library. Mayor Ted Shaw, Joan Shaw, and City Councilman David Margrave proposed the Extravaganza. It may well have been the best Fourth of July celebration since 1912, when four thousand people swarmed to Garfield Park for a free barbecue, and entertainment ranging from Shakespearean drama to the Pantages vaudeville act of Leon Morris and his wrestling ponies. In 1982 a good part of the town marched in the Fourth of July parade, picnicked at Garfield Park, and watched fireworks at the high school athletic field. The crowd also enjoyed the music of a jazz band (led by School Superintendent Tom Brierley); watched a demonstration by a new member of the police department (Belker of the K-9 Corps); and cheered members of the city council and the school board, who engaged in a vigorous new sport (trying to propel a suspended barrel by water shot from firehoses).

Twenty-five hundred people attended the dedication of the library on July 31, 1982. Opening-day events included a story hour, a magic show, a film created by Oneonta fourth-graders, and a Dixieland band with the Chamber of Commerce executive manager, Grice Axtman, on clarinet, and former mayor Burton Jones on trumpet. The

A reporter interviews Congressmen John H. Rousselot and Paul N. McCloskey, class of '45, during the high school reunion in 1982. *Photograph by Daniel F. Castle*.

master of ceremonies was Henry J. ("Duke") Wheeler, immediate past president of the library board, who had helped guide the building program to its successful conclusion.

The high school reunion, held in May 1982, had a parade said to stretch seventy-five years. Riding at the head were homecoming queen Edna Munger Goldman, class of 1907, and homecoming king John Coots, class of 1909. Behind them, in antique cars or on foot, came six thousand people accompanied by the Tiger Marching Band. Among the paraders was a California Supreme Court justice, Frank C. Newman, class of 1934. Two of the best-known marchers—both from the class of 1945—were Paul N. McCloskey and John H. Rousselot, the only congressmen in the nation's history to have graduated together from high school and served together in Washington. Rousselot presented the school with a flag flown over the Capitol, and student Randy Marrs—whose father, grandmother, and great-grandfather had also attended South Pasadena High School—led the flag salute.

During the festivities, lighthearted tribute was paid to Mary and Robert Mills, who came the farthest distance to the reunion (from Djakarta); to Mary and Tom Bryce, who came the shortest distance (from across the street); and to Athelia and William Tanner, "who gave the most to the high school" (their thirteen children). The idea for the grand reunion originated with Mary Ida Phair as an expression of gratitude to the school from which she, her husband, and their two sons had graduated, and in which she served for twenty years as librarian. The media center she helped create at the high school was named in her honor when she retired in 1983.

Another community event in 1982 was the opening of a Senior Citizens' Center, adjacent to the library. By 1986 more than a thousand people had joined the city-run center, which offered classes, recreational activities, a hot lunch program, and other special services.

In the early history of South Pasadena, any thought of a saloon in town provoked outrage and righteous indignation. Similar passion has greeted every attempt to build a six-lane freeway through the center of South Pasadena to connect the Foothill (210) Freeway in Pasadena with the Long Beach (710) Freeway, which ends just south of Valley Boulevard in Alhambra. For almost a quarter of a century South Pasadena has battled the state-adopted Meridian route, which would bisect the city, and has urged instead a route along its western border. As AlvaLee Arnold stated the choice in 1977: "We can survive the loss of an arm and a leg, which would be the case if the Westerly Route is adopted; but we cannot survive losing our heart—the center of our city—as would happen with the Meridian plan."

The *South Pasadena Review* has consistently opposed the Meridian Route, often in colorful prose. It has compared the effects of a freeway built through the center of town to the devastation wrought by a juggernaut, a cyclone, or a tornado uprooting everything in a two-block-wide swath for the length of the city. When twelve freeway bridges collapsed during the San Fernando earthquake of 1971—the worst earthquake in California since 1933— the paper wrote, "Just think, if our city council had signed for the Meridian Avenue route . . . those concrete dominoes would be lying across our city." When the Supreme Court halted construction of a dam on the Little Tennessee River, to save an endangered species of fish, the *Review* suggested that South Pasadena was endangered by a freeway that would split it in half and destroy its essential char-

DON'T LET THEM
BREAK THE HEART
OF OUR CITY

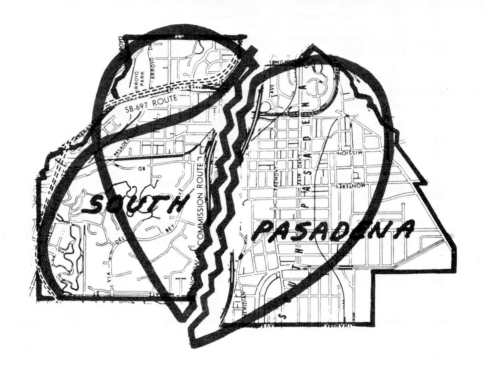

We Can Save It With A By-Pass

The Facts Are On Our Side

Time Is On Our Side

The Final Decision Is Ours

A pamphlet issued by the Committee for the Westerly Route opposes building a free-way through the center of South Pasadena. *Courtesy of South Pasadena Public Library.*

192

acter. An editorial asked, "Do you suppose the residents of the city of South Pasadena would get the same consideration that a tiny fish, the Snail Darter, received from the Supreme Court?"

In the 1973 Tournament of Roses, South Pasadena entered a float called "The Perils of Pauline." It was a wryly appropriate subject for a city that already had struggled for thirteen years against the Meridian Route, considered by many residents a dangerous assault on the virtues and values of South Pasadena. In the continuing freeway drama, South Pasadena achieved small victories, only to see them snatched away. In 1972 a citizens' committee succeeded in placing on the ballot an initiative measure designed to settle the freeway controversy for good. Nearly 90 percent of the electorate went to the polls. By a vote of 7,240 to 4,334, residents approved an ordinance forbidding the city to close any of fifteen east-west streets along the proposed Meridian Route for a period of ten years. It was an effective countermeasure at a time when state policy opposed building a freeway through a city without a signed agreement.

A decade later state policy changed. Meanwhile, attorneys from the Center for Law in the Public Interest filed a lawsuit on behalf of South Pasadena, the Sierra Club, Stamp Out Smog, and the Pasadena Freeway Committee. The lawsuit sought a halt in further construction of the Long Beach Freeway until it met requirements of the National Environmental Policy Act of 1969 and the California Environmental Quality Act of 1970. The state agreed in 1973 to prepare a new environmental impact report on the Meridian Route and specified alternatives. It also agreed that until final approval of the environmental impact statement, it would halt construction on the Long Beach Freeway except for work already under contract.

Additional work did take place, however, after the 210 Freeway opened through Pasadena in 1975. The courts granted permission to Caltrans (successor to the California Division of Highways) to build interim ramps to relieve traffic congestion near the Pasadena interchange of the 134 and 210 freeways. By widening two streets in Pasadena, near its border with South Pasadena, and making the streets one-way, Caltrans created a "wishbone" link with the interchange. Although it eased traffic in Pasadena, the wishbone funneled as many as twenty-five thousand additional cars a day through South Pasadena.

For eighteen years South Pasadena had stalled construction of a freeway through the middle of the city by refusing to sign an agreement with Caltrans. To end the stalemate, the California legislature in 1982 passed the Martinez Bill, which authorized the state to build through a city without a signed agreement. As originally proposed, the bill virtually ensured final adoption of the Meridian Route. South Pasadena successfully lobbied for an amended version that required consideration of alternative routes, a new environmental impact report, and additional public hearings.

A Caltrans hearing in 1983 made clear the importance of the completed freeway for the port of Long Beach, which already was handling nearly all the truck cargo from Southern California and the southwestern states. One spokesman predicted that Long Beach would handle more cargo than any other port on the Pacific Coast—in excess of fifty million metric tons a year— when the freeway was completed and joined to nine other freeways between Long Beach and Pasadena.

South Pasadena gained an impressive ally in 1983: the federal Advisory Council on

Historic Preservation. Although acknowledging that regional economic needs justified completion of the freeway, the council recommended against both the Meridian Route and the Westerly Route proposed by Caltrans. Either plan, according to the council, would have a devastating effect on historic properties and cultural resources. Council members accused Caltrans of giving insufficient study to prudent and feasible alternatives, in particular a westerly alignment that included double-decking of the Pasadena Freeway. Double-decking would not only spare historic properties, said the council, but would displace 900 fewer people than the Meridian Route, take about 500 fewer homes and 20 fewer businesses, and cost $60 million less to build.

The idea of double-decking was not a new one. South Pasadena first suggested the alternative in 1966, and the idea was elaborated by Jess Reynolds in 1973. A retired design engineer, formerly with the California Division of Highways, Reynolds served ten years as South Pasadena's unpaid freeway consultant. Under his plan, a small segment of the freeway would have been built in the Arroyo Seco. To prevent this encroachment, the California legislature passed the Arroyo Seco Parklands Preservation Law in 1975. When the Advisory Council on Historic Preservation revived the idea of double-decking, Reynolds said it could be accomplished by taking only two-thirds of a mile of the Arroyo—an area already being used for the Pasadena Freeway, the flood control channel, and various city structures such as a recycling center. Posing the issue as a slight effect on the Arroyo as against a major displacement of people, Reynolds suggested that voters might agree to a modification of the Parklands Preservation Law.

In 1984 Caltrans reaffirmed the Meridian Route as its choice for closing the freeway gap. The Advisory Council on Historic Preservation again rejected the Meridian Route, calling it highly destructive and the least desirable plan for completing the freeway. "If it came down to the Meridian or nothing, nothing is desirable," said the council's director of the office of cultural resource preservation. "The current traffic problem is not so serious that it warrants tearing the heart out of South Pasadena."

Because the Federal Highway Administration will pay 86 percent of the $400 million cost of the freeway project, Caltrans cannot proceed without federal approval. Yielding to necessity, in 1986 it proposed a Meridian Variation that would loop slightly to the west and spare the Historic Business District and most of the landmark homes north and south of Mission Street. The new route, however, would severely damage the Buena Vista Street neighborhood and destroy hundreds of homes in Altos de Monterey. A decision on the Meridian Variation is expected in 1987. Meanwhile, in November 1986, South Pasadena citizens overwhelmingly approved a ballot measure that asked, "Shall the City of South Pasadena continue to oppose the Meridian Route of the Long Beach Freeway?" Heartened by an impressive vote of 6,184 to 2,537, the city prepared to fight on for a route more acceptable to the majority of residents. Whatever route ultimately may be selected, construction is unlikely to start before the mid-1990s.

With the freeway issue unresolved, South Pasadena began focusing on other concerns. In 1985 the city completed the largest road project in its history—the reconstruction of Fair Oaks Avenue between Columbia Street and Monterey Road. The heavily traveled one-mile stretch of road was paved with concrete, brick crosswalks

The only example of architect Rudolph Schindler's work in South Pasadena is the house he designed in 1928 for David N. Grokowsky. The California Department of Transportation owns the Grokowsky house, which is a Cultural Heritage Landmark. *Photograph by Henk Friezer.*

At the turn of the century Aaron F. McReynolds had a grocery store in what is now the Meridian Iron Works. McReynolds also served as ticket agent and telegrapher. *Courtesy of Huntington Library.*

The Meridian Iron Works building, a Cultural Heritage Landmark, was restored in 1986 under the direction of architect Robert E. Tryon. *Photograph by Ralph Tillema; courtesy of South Pasadena Cultural Heritage Commission.*

were installed, sidewalks were improved, and flowering trees were planted at the curbside. The project took seven months and cost $1.3 million.

In 1986 the city completed a half-million-dollar refurbishing of Arroyo Seco Park. More than forty volunteers worked with the Parks and Recreation Commission to draw up the plans, which included better parking and lighting, three improved baseball diamonds, and two championship soccer fields. The park will be further improved in 1987 with a new picnic area, another soccer field, and two more baseball diamonds.

Most ambitious of the new municipal projects is a $2.8 million civic center that will house the city offices and the police and fire departments. It is scheduled for completion in 1987. The new complex is at Mission Street and Mound Avenue, site of the city hall designed by Norman Foote Marsh in 1914. Paying tribute to a historic building, architects Peter deBretteville and Stefanos Polyzoides saved bricks from the old civic center for use in the new one.

South Pasadena's first historical museum opened in 1986 in the hundred-year-old Meridian Iron Works, a building owned by the city and leased to the South Pasadena Preservation Foundation. In the 1880s, when the building was new, orange groves and vineyards still covered much of South Pasadena. The little town had one school, two churches, a few businesses, and about five hundred people. A century later, South Pasadena had seven public schools, a dozen churches, and a population of more than twenty-three thousand. It also had about fifteen light manufacturing plants and several hundred business establishments. Although squeezed between the metropolis of Pasadena and the megalopolis of Los Angeles, South Pasadena still retained much of its pleasant small-town atmosphere.

In its spirit and concerns, the South Pasadena of today is not too unlike the newly incorporated city described by George W. Glover in 1893. "Our Schools are of the very best," he wrote. "Society is excellent, and we have numerous churches. . . . All in all there is no better place to live if you desire to do business or work on a salary in Los Angeles. The location is equally good for those who desire to engage in the growing of fruits, raising chickens, or any of the lighter industries."

For more than a hundred years South Pasadenans have taken pride in their community and worked for its enhancement. They formed a school district in 1878, opened a free reading room in 1889, and planted a thousand street trees in 1894. The dedication and spirit of independence shown by the pioneer residents is still manifest in citizens today. These qualities should help South Pasadena maintain its special character, preserve its heritage, and adapt to meet the challenges of its second hundred years.

197

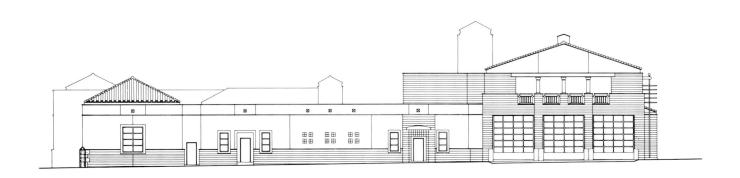

A new civic center opened in South Pasadena in 1987 at the corner of Mission Street and Mound Avenue. It houses city offices and the police and fire departments. *Architects' drawing courtesy of deBretteville and Polyzoides.*

CHRONOLOGY

1970

The population of South Pasadena increases by more than 3,000 in ten years, going from 19,706 in 1960 to 22,979 in 1970.

South Pasadena Beautiful organizes a Cultural Heritage Committee, chaired by Jean Driskel.

The California Highway Commission agrees to study the feasibility of a westerly route for the Long Beach Freeway.

The CRA board voluntarily terminates, and the city council assumes its duties.

1971

A severe earthquake strikes the San Fernando Valley. Seventy-five chimneys topple in South Pasadena.

The mayor appoints a committee on downtown revitalization.

Monterey Road is widened to four lanes.

The city forms a Cultural Heritage Commission and appoints Raymond Girvigian as chairman.

1972

The city council appoints a new CRA board for downtown revitalization but retains authority to dissolve the board and to supervise its functions.

The Jean Driskel Cultural Heritage Foundation is established to raise funds for preservation and restoration of South Pasadena landmarks.

A youth center opens at El Centro and Mound in the old Baptist church building purchased by the city.

Arthur L. Pereira, consulting architect to the CRA, presents a preliminary plan to revitalize sixty-nine acres in South Pasadena.

By a vote of 7,470 to 4,234 South Pasadena voters approve an initiative measure forbidding the city to close east-west streets along the proposed Meridian route.

1973

South Pasadena has its first snowfall since 1949.

The city joins in a lawsuit to stop further construction of the Long Beach Freeway until the state files an adequate environmental impact report.

The city council approves a revitalization plan that would place 25 percent of the city under jurisdiction of the CRA.

1974

The Cultural Heritage Commission publishes a brochure on city landmarks.

The old Baptist church is razed.

The city approves plans proposed by CRA architect Whitney Smith for a downtown superblock.

The Ong Building at Fair Oaks and Mission is demolished to make way for a bank.

The courts rule against South Pasadena's plan to use tax increments from Altos de Monterey to finance downtown revitalization.

1975

Friends of the South Pasadena Public Library celebrates its twenty-fifth anniversary.

The California Legislature passes the Arroyo Seco Parklands Preservation Act, which forbids highway construction in the Arroyo.

The last United States combat troops leave Vietnam. Four South Pasadenans lost their lives in the conflict.

1976

A trophy for humor goes to the city's Rose Parade float, "Saturday Night in South Pasadena," which shows the town constable rolling up the sidewalk.

Caltrans builds a wishbone connection that links the 210 interchange in Pasadena to the South Pasadena border at Columbia Street.

The county agrees the CRA may impound tax increments from Altos de Monterey to finance a public facilities construction program.

The city council votes to close Via del Rey to through traffic. Los Angeles retaliates with barricades on Alpha Street.

Three thousand people enjoy a bicentennial celebration in Arroyo Seco Park on the Fourth of July.

1977

Caltrans proposes a cut-and-cover freeway through South Pasadena.

1978

After receiving a petition with over three thousand signatures, the city council votes to save the Rialto Theatre from destruction.

A threatened lawsuit halts the sale of bonds to revitalize the business center.

Passage of Proposition 13, a California tax-limitation measure, results in severe budget cuts for the South Pasadena schools, library, and city hall services.

The *South Pasadena Review* goes from a semiweekly to a weekly paper.

Preservationists honor restoration consultant Rodger Whipple for rebuilding a turn-of-the-century bungalow to reflect Craftsman-era charm. Now the Raymond Restaurant, the building once was a caretaker's cottage on the Hotel Raymond grounds.

1979

South Pasadena's float, "The Great Ostrich Race," wins the Founder's Day Trophy in the Tournament of Roses.

Tamara Asseyev, graduate of South Pasadena High School and the first woman in the Motion Picture Producers Guild to work on feature films, coproduces *Norma Rae*, which wins two Academy Awards.

Oaklawn Bridge is closed to traffic.

El Centro and Lincoln schools merge as Arroyo Vista School.

1980

The population of South Pasadena is 22,681—slightly lower than the census figure for 1970.

The old El Centro School becomes the School Administration Center.

Honoring her efforts on behalf of the cultural heritage of South Pasadena, the city council names Margaret Fay official city historian.

The South Pasadena Educational Foundation is inaugurated to help finance projects designed to stimulate learning and creativity in the South Pasadena public schools.

Under the auspices of South Pasadena Beautiful, the city sign on the banks of the Arroyo is restored.

1981

The city council purchases a site for a new civic center.

The CRA gives up its rights to condemnation, eminent domain, and architectural control in the downtown business center.

The city commends Raymond Girvigian for his efforts to put South Pasadena at the forefront in the field of historic preservation.

1982

The California Legislature passes a bill allowing completion of a freeway through a city or a county without its signed agreement.

Six thousand people take part in the High School All-Years Reunion held in May.

Andy Zall, South Pasadena High School graduate, receives his third Emmy award, which honors his special achievement in videotape editing.

Sally and Clifton Clouse are honored by the Los Angeles County Board of Supervisors, the city of Los Angeles, and the city of South Pasadena as outstanding older Americans and as seniors of the year.

The newly rebuilt library opens on July 31. On November 5 the Senior Citizens Center opens in Library Park.

The city celebrates one hundred years of postal service in South Pasadena.

The community-owned First Arroyo Bank opens.

1983

Oneonta School closes.

South Pasadena votes a height limit of forty-five feet on buildings in the city.

LePore Lane is dedicated in memory of Vincent LePore, long active in civic affairs.

1984

The city holds Jess Reynolds Day to honor its unpaid freeway consultant for ten years of service.

The Jean Driskel Cultural Heritage Foundation is renamed the South Pasadena Preservation Foundation.

South Pasadenan Kelly Kittridge is chosen as a member of the United States Olympic team for women's bicycle road racing.

The fifty-seven-year-old school administration building on Diamond Street is demolished despite attempts by preservationists to save it.

Administration of the police and fire departments is consolidated under a Director of Public Safety.

1985

In the largest road project ever undertaken by South Pasadena, Fair Oaks Avenue is repaved and landscaped between Monterey Road and Columbia Street.

1986

The city completes a half-million-dollar renovation of Arroyo Seco Park.

The city council approves a hiring policy giving preference to nonsmokers.

The city's first historic museum opens in the Meridian Iron Works Building.

South Pasadena architect Lee Hershberger wins a national award for a home designed in the Craftsman tradition and emphasizing the visual and textural beauty of wood.

Trader Joe's, whose main office is in South Pasadena, celebrates the twenty-eighth anniversary of its *Fearless Flyer*, an unsolemn newsletter whose cartoons and puns help advertise the market's specialties.

Grant Thompson, a native of South Pasadena, becomes the first man to serve as executive director of the national League of Women Voters.

1987

A new civic center opens on the old city hall site at Mission Street and Mound Avenue.

Part II

The elementary school built on Columbia Hill in 1883 was later used as a Presbyterian college, an academy, and a private residence. *Courtesy of South Pasadena Public Library.*

XI

SOUTH PASADENA PUBLIC SCHOOLS

*The colony settlers of Pasadena were of that class of people
who regard public schools not as a mere appendage, but as one
of the prime necessities of a civilized community.*

HIRAM A. REID

WITHIN A FEW MONTHS OF CHOOSING THEIR HOMESITES, members of the San Gabriel Orange Grove Association had formed a school district, hired a teacher, and arranged for a temporary classroom. Pupils began school in September 1874, meeting for lessons in the home of their teacher, Jennie Clapp. In January 1875 classes moved to the new schoolhouse, a rough board structure that had cost about three hundred dollars to build. It enjoyed a pleasant site, close to a great oak tree that grew in the middle of Orange Grove Avenue near California Street.

In 1876 B. D. Wilson donated a school site at the Colony's emerging business center—Fair Oaks Avenue and Colorado Street—and the little schoolhouse was moved to the new location. Reluctant to send their children so far, the colonists south of California Street petitioned for their own school district. As established by the County Board of Supervisors in 1878, the new district lay west of present-day Fremont Avenue and south of California Street and extended to the Los Angeles city limits.

The supervisors had named the original school district San Pasqual—for the rancho settled by the Indiana Colony—and they named the southern district Pasadena. O. R. Dougherty observed with some annoyance, "More properly theirs should have been named Pasadena and ours San Pascual. Both we & they were displeased with the naming." Dougherty and his neighbors below California Street had a strong sense of local pride and already thought of themselves as South Pasadenans, although cityhood lay ten years in the future.

The first school in the new district opened on March 5, 1878, in the Columbia Street home of architect and builder Clinton B. Ripley. Public subscription raised $248.20 for the first year's expenses, which included a salary of $50 a month for the teacher, Bessie Harris. Classes continued in Ripley's house for another year, but in 1880 the district built a schoolhouse on four and a half acres bordered on the north by Columbia Street and on the east by what is now Orange Grove Avenue. A school tax raised $250 for the site and $250 for the building. Voluntary contributions paid for trees to beautify the grounds.

In 1883 twenty-two voters unanimously approved a $4,000 bond issue for a larger schoolhouse. Clinton B. Ripley, who had built the first school, also built the second, which could accomodate more than fifty students. It was located on a six-acre parcel and boasted decorative stick work, a chimney, and a bell tower.

Deciding in 1884 to relocate classes in the center of town, the board of education

The Columbia Hill Tennis Club entered a decorated six-in-hand in the 1893 Tournament of Roses. *Courtesy of Pasadena Historical Society*.

Lily Martin, in the back row at the left, was principal of the Center Street School built in 1888. *Courtesy of Security Pacific National Bank Photograph Collection/Los Angeles Public Library*.

posted auction notices (one on the school, the others on two live oaks in the neighborhood) and sold Schoolhouse Hill and the schoolhouse for $2,000 in gold. The successful bidder, P. M. Green, bought the property on behalf of Sierra Madre College, a school just established by the Los Angeles Presbytery. The college opened on September 17, 1884, with twenty-five students and a faculty of six. According to Hiram Reid, instruction was of a high order; "but the fact was, this college was mislocated, was premature, was not on a plan in touch with the times, and had no money behind it—hence.it was born with failure in its bones."

Attorney C. D. Daggett bought the property and renamed it Columbia Hill. He enlarged and altered the schoolhouse for a residence, and he built a tennis court for his children and their friends. The first South Pasadena organizations to have entries in the Tournament of Roses were the Raymond Hotel and the Columbia Hill Tennis Club—both taking part in the parade in 1893, and the club winning second prize for the best decorated six-in-hand.

Daggett's wife, Mary Stewart Daggett, wrote several novels with a California setting, and in *The Yellow Angel* she tried to combat anti-Chinese prejudice. The Daggetts' son John conducted a radio program for children, and their daughter Maud was a well-known sculptor. One of her carvings is above the fireplace in the children's room of the Pasadena Public Library.

*South Pasadena
Public Schools*

EL CENTRO SCHOOL

South Pasadena's first downtown school opened on October 1, 1885, on a one-acre lot at Center Street and Oak Hill Avenue (names more familiar today as El Centro and Fairview). The little building was used not only for classes, but for town meetings, church services, and social gatherings. In 1886, almost a decade after O. R. Dougherty and others had grumbled at the name bestowed on their school district, it was renamed the South Pasadena School District. At the same time its northern border was established at Columbia Street. Soon after South Pasadena incorporated in 1888, the voters passed bond issues to enlarge the Center Street schoolgrounds and put up a more substantial building. Until the new school was finished, children attended classes in Graham and Mohr's brick Opera House Building, two blocks farther west on Center Street. The Santa Fe tracks ran by the building, and the school board prudently established rules that forbade students to jump on and off the railroad cars.

The new schoolhouse was ready for fall classes in 1888. The first principal was Lily Martin, a rancher's daughter from Visalia. On opening day, according to one old-timer, Miss Martin hung a riding quirt behind her desk and warned, "God help the boy who makes me take it down." The quirt remained in place until Miss Martin's death several years later.

In 1902—the year South Pasadena boasted, "Watch us grow!"—townspeople met to discuss a proposed $15,000 bond issue for enlarging the Center Street School and campus. "The trustees were commended for the modesty of their request," the paper reported, "and instead of voting to raise $15,000 by bonding, it was unanimously decided to make the amount $20,000 so that the trustees need not feel hampered for the want of funds, and so that the best of everything may be had in the purchase of the necessary materials and supplies."

Norman Foote Marsh designed the new building, which opened in 1903. A cautionary news report advised, "The public are requested to drive slowly by our schoolhouse so they will not run over the marble players, who prefer the hard streets to the deep dust of the schoolyard."

By 1916 there was talk of moving the school, which faced on Mission Street and the Pacific Electric trolley tracks. Noise from the electric cars interfered with studies, and every time the Santa Fe went through, recitations had to stop.

During a school bond campaign in 1917, administrators called El Centro a firetrap and said, "The building is old, out-of-date, three times made over, and is actually patch upon patch." Nevertheless, the bonds were defeated. In 1920 money was voted for repairs, and in 1928 the old wooden structure was finally torn down and replaced by an arcaded brick building designed by Marsh, Smith & Powell. One link with the past remained: the original school bell, cast in 1889, was rehung in the new tower. A highlight of the dedication ceremony was a march, "The Bell of El Centro," composed by music teacher Norine Clarkson Merritt.

After the devastating Long Beach earthquake of 1933, the California legislature passed the Field Act, which set building standards to make schools more earthquake-resistant. Bond issues to rehabilitate elementary schools in South Pasadena failed in 1935 and again in 1937, but in 1946 a bond issue won overwhelming approval by a vote of 1,555 to 484. El Centro was strengthened in 1949, its tower removed, and the school bell stored away. In 1952 the Jaycees rescued the bell from storage and mounted it on a low platform in front of the school. At graduation time a new tradition started. Sixth-graders marched from the auditorium to the front lawn, and each student struck one triumphant blow on the old bronze bell.

In 1979 El Centro School marked the end of one era and the beginning of another. Enrollment was declining, and the board decided to close the school—whose history spanned ninety-four years—and send its two hundred students to Lincoln School, near the Arroyo. In one of the last ceremonies at El Centro, the student body and staff observed Arbor Day by planting a bottle brush tree on the campus. Beneath it they buried a time capsule, with the names of staff and students and with news of such current events as a recent eclipse of the sun.

In the fall, El Centro merged with Lincoln School, and the combined student body voted to rename the school Arroyo Vista. The old El Centro building was converted to use as the administration center, official headquarters for the unified school district. The quarter-ton bronze bell is still mounted in front of the building.

Arroyo Vista School

During the land boom of the eighties, property sold briskly, not only in the center of town, but on the outskirts as well. Schoolmaster George Wilson gave up teaching at the Center Street School to sell acreage in Lincoln Park, a tract near the Arroyo Seco. "The Pasadena Brass Band will furnish the music," read one of his auction notices. "A fine lunch will be served under the grand old oaks, free of charge."

In 1887 Lincoln Park School opened in a rented storefront by the Arroyo. The following year students had a real schoolhouse: the old Center Street school building which had been moved to a site on the Arroyo near the Cawston Ostrich Farm. (Caw-

The brick schoolhouse built on El Centro Street in 1928 now serves as the school administration center. *Courtesy of South Pasadena Unified School District.*

Lincoln School was renamed Arroyo Vista when the student bodies of Lincoln and El Centro merged in 1979. *Photograph by Tom M. Apostol.*

Until 1947 Marengo students attended classes in this mission-style schoolhouse. *Courtesy of South Pasadena Public Library.*

Emily Pryor, seated at the left, posed with her students at Marengo School around 1925. Miss French is at the piano. *Courtesy of Priscilla Roth Feigen.*

ston Street, on the eastern boundary of the present school, is a reminder of its early neighbor.) School bonds passed in 1908 paid for a modern building at Lincoln Park, and its old schoolhouse was moved to Orange Grove Avenue for youngsters living at the Boys' and Girls' Aid Society. Abandoned as a school in 1918, the building was converted to a residence. The old hopscotch squares can still be seen in the paving outside 1016 Orange Grove Avenue.

In 1909 Lincoln Park parents organized the first kindergarten class in South Pasadena. With the permission of the school board, the Lincoln Park Improvement Association selected a teacher and raised funds to pay her. Lincoln Park also had the first Parent-Teacher Association in the city. Eighteen parents formed the group in 1911 and chose Mary Gardner as president. The PTA led a campaign to beautify the schoolgrounds, and in 1915 Lincoln Park School boasted that it had the only fish pond and Japanese garden in the city.

From 1913 to 1915 Lincoln Park had a principal later acclaimed as "Portia of the West" and as "first legal lady of the land." Mabel Walker Willebrandt studied law in evening classes while working days at Lincoln Park School. In 1915, just four years after women won the right to vote in California, she was admitted to the state bar and appointed assistant public defender in Los Angeles. Six years later, President Harding appointed her Assistant Attorney General of the United States, heading the division which enforced tax laws and prohibition laws.

In 1939 the name Lincoln Park disappeared from South Pasadena. The old tract had long ago lost its separate identity, and its name survived only on the school. When the building was torn down in 1939, the new Lincoln School took its place. That name disappeared, too, when El Centro merged with Lincoln in 1979, and the school adopted the new name of Arroyo Vista.

Marengo School

By 1909 the area east of Fair Oaks Avenue was rapidly changing from groves and pastures to town lots, and new homes were going up almost daily. Residents were eager to have a school, but less eager to have one in their immediate neighborhood. Some property owners refused to sell land to the school board, and the people of Oneonta Park threatened a lawsuit if the board attempted to build there. Henry E. Huntington finally agreed to sell a lot at Marengo Avenue and Bank Street, but only on the condition that the school board not attempt to build in Oneonta Park.

The eight-room school opened in September 1910. It was surrounded by orange groves and had a streambed—the San Pasqual Arroyo—on its eastern border. Crossing the gully was a great adventure. Youngsters would slide down one bank and clamber up the other. Stratford Avenue eventually covered part of the arroyo, and from Oak Street to Huntington Drive an open concrete flume was built in the streambed. To the children this was the "sankey," a word corrupted from the Spanish *zanja*, or irrigation ditch. It was an ideal setting in which to play Paris Sewers.

In 1919 eighth-graders Ward Ritchie and Pat Kelley founded the *Marengo Literary Leader*, which sold for five cents a copy. A fellow eighth-grader, Lawrence Clark Powell, published his first writings in the paper. His contributions ranged from

211

MARENGO LITERARY LEADER

Volume I | South Pasadena, Calif., October 28, 1919 | Number 4

THE HALF MOON

Harold Kelley

(Continued from Last Week)

Dick Allen after his successful discovery thought everything would be all right again, but after all, he decided the little silver key could not do so much.

Dick made up his mind to try first and find out who the murderer was.

His friend, Bob Campbell, came over to see him the next night, and after an hour's talk, they strolled over to Bob's house, where they parted.

Dick was just starting up the walk to his house, when someone grabbed him from behind and a smelly fish sack was thrown over his head.

Dick fought like mad, but it was of no avail, as he could not see what to hit.

He was thrown to the ground and someone snatched the sack off his head and he found himself looking up at two big men.

"It's no use to try and back out now, kid; we know you have Ruth Madarin's papers," said one, fiercely.

Luckily for Dick, he had left the key at home, and after a thorough search through his clothes, the men gave up, and with a quick turn batted him over the head with a club.

He did not regain consciousness again for many hours, but finally stumbled into his house.

The next afternoon Dick thought he would go down to Ruth Madarin's old home and see if there still might be some papers there.

When he was within a few doors of the house he saw a man come out of it, and on a little closer view saw it was none other than Ezra Jenkins.

He waited till Jenkins was out of sight and then went up to the same house.

The lady who came to the door said: "Why, that man said he was a detective and a partner of yours."

(To Be Continued)

Hollywood, Cal., Oct. 22, 1919.

My Dear Friend:

I am sure you are entirely forgiven. I understand exactly how you did it on the impulse of the moment.

Your letter was greatly appreciated by me, because I know it is often difficult to acknowledge your wrong and make an apology.

Please do not think any more about it, for I shall not, except to remember you as the little boy who wrote me a very charming letter.

Sincerely,

(Signed) MARY PICKFORD.

Frances Vail is too interesting for Richard. He can't keep from turning around. Miss Sheppard threatened to change his seat, but he did not seem to like the idea. Better be careful, Fannie, if you want him to sit there.

A TONGUE TWISTER

I knew a gnu that another gnu knew, but the gnu knew a new gnu who knew another new gnu that neither I nor the other gnu knew.

LOCAL NEWS

The students of the Marengo School wish to extend the sincerest smypathies to Lawrence Mulling and Wilfred Horn in their recent bereavement.

Mr. Whsat and Mr. Knepper, Assistant County Superintendents, visited South Pasadena schools for three days. We certainly were very proud to have these gentlemen with us.

Miss Reece was ill on Tuesday, the 21st, and was obliged to stay at home. Miss Ballard taught her class all day.

We wonder if Dick Bellamue will come running back to California after reaching Chicago?

Did you know that Lieutenant Maynard took a little over a day in his actual flying time in crossing the confinent?

THE DESERT SUNSET

As the sun sank mid billows of golden clouds it cast its last rays of light on the distant purple peaks. A lone night bird, the harbinger of the night, hooted in the distance. Gray cliffs, and gigantic piles of boulders stood out indistinct in the hazy twilight. The mournful wailing of a wolf in the foothills was the only sound that broke the silence. The sun finally disappeared entirely from view. The wailing of the wolf ceased and silence reigned supreme.

LAWRENCE POWELL.

Jacobs Electric Company
CONTRACTORS & DEALERS
1126 MISSION STREET.
THOR WASHERS
HOOVER CLEANERS

YOUR MOTHER
BUYS HER POTS
AND PANS HERE
Live Hardware Co.

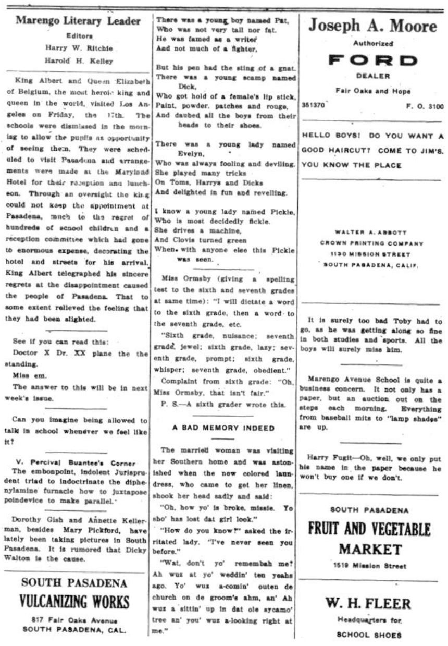

Marengo Literary Leader

Editors
Harry W. Ritchie
Harold H. Kelley

King Albert and Queen Elizabeth of Belgium, the most heroic king and queen in the world, visited Los Angeles on Friday, the 17th. The schools were dismissed in the morning to allow the pupils an opportunity of seeing them. They were scheduled to visit Pasadena and arrangements were made at the Maryland Hotel for their reception and luncheon. Through an oversight the king could not keep the appointment at Pasadena, much to the regret of hundreds of school children and a reception committee which had gone to enormous expense, decorating the hotel and streets for his arrival. King Albert telegraphed his sincere regrets at the disappointment caused the people of Pasadena. That to some extent relieved the feeling that they had been slighted.

See if you can read this:

Doctor X Dr. XX plane the the standing.

Miss em.

The answer to this will be in next week's issue.

Can you imagine being allowed to talk in school whenever we feel like it?

V. Percival Buantee's Corner

The embonpoint, indolent Jurisprudent tried to indoctrinate the diphenylamine furnacle how to juxtapose poindevice to make parallel.

Dorothy Gish and Annette Kellerman, besides Mary Pickford, have lately been taking pictures in South Pasadena. It is rumored that Dicky Walton is the cause.

There was a young boy named Pat,
Who was not very tall nor fat.
He was famed as a writer
And not much of a fighter,

But his pen had the sting of a gnat.
There was a young scamp named Dick,
Who got hold of a female's lip stick,
Paint, powder, patches and rouge,
And daubed all the boys from their heads to their shoes.

There was a young lady named Evelyn,
Who was always fooling and devilling.
She played many tricks
On Toms, Harrys and Dicks
And delighted in fun and revelling.

I know a young lady named Pickle,
Who is most decidedly fickle.
She drives a machine,
And Clovis turned green
When with anyone else this Pickle was seen.

Miss Ormsby (giving a spelling test to the sixth and seventh grades at same time): "I will dictate a word to the sixth grade, then a word to the seventh grade, etc.

"Sixth grade, nuisance; seventh grade, jewel; sixth grade, lazy; seventh grade, prompt; sixth grade, whisper; seventh grade, obedient."

Complaint from sixth grade: "Oh, Miss Ormsby, that isn't fair."

P. S.—A sixth grader wrote this.

A BAD MEMORY INDEED

The married woman was visiting her Southern home and was astonished when the new colored laundress, who came to get her linen, shook her head sadly and said:

"Oh, how yo' is broke, missie. Yo sho' has lost dat girl look."

"How do you know?" asked the irritated lady. "I've never seen you before."

"Wat, don't yo' remembah me? Ah wuz at yo' weddin' ten yeahs ago. Yo' wuz a-comin' outen de church on de groom's ahm, an' Ah wuz a sittin' up in dat ole sycamo' tree an' you' wuz a-looking right at me."

HELLO BOYS! DO YOU WANT A GOOD HAIRCUT? COME TO JIM'S. YOU KNOW THE PLACE

It is surely too bad Toby had to go, as he was getting along so fine in both studies and sports. All the boys will surely miss him.

Marengo Avenue School is quite a business concern. It not only has a paper, but an auction out on the steps each morning. Everything from baseball mits to "lamp shades" are up.

Harry Fugit—Oh, well, we only put his name in the paper because he won't buy one if we don't.

SOUTH PASADENA
VULCANIZING WORKS
817 Fair Oaks Avenue
SOUTH PASADENA, CAL.

Joseph A. Moore
Authorized
FORD
DEALER
Fair Oaks and Hope
351370 F. O. 3100

WALTER A. ABBOTT
CROWN PRINTING COMPANY
1130 MISSION STREET
SOUTH PASADENA, CALIF.

SOUTH PASADENA
FRUIT AND VEGETABLE
MARKET
1519 Mission Street

W. H. FLEER
Headquarters for
SCHOOL SHOES

The *Marengo Literary Leader* helped launch the careers of several distinguished bibliophiles. *Courtesy of Ward Ritchie, once known as Harry Ward Ritchie.*

MARENGO LITERARY LEADER

Volume I | South Pasadena, Calif., December 2, 1919 | Number 7

THE PURPLE DRAGON

By Lawrence Powell

Taun Fung was pleased. The steamer, Princess Siang Nu, arrievd in the evening with a secret shipment of opium for him. It was to be thrown overboard in cans. Sing Lee, his assistant, would gather them up and bring them to wharf 10. There another servant would receive them and then into his (Taun's)' hands they would come. Opium smuggling was quite profitable for Taun Fung. There were ready customers for the dope, all over Frisco Chinatown.

On board the Princess Siang Nu deep silence prevailed. Several shadowy forms stole cautiously across the deck. They lowered what seemed to be large cans of tea over the side into the waiting hands of Sing Lee. Back they stole to their staterooms while the steamer plowed on its way. Sing Lee piloted his little launch into the harbor to wharf 10. Two autos were waiting there to convey the opium to Taun Fung.

As the autos started away a man sprang from behind a pile of boxes and leaped on the back of one of the autos. Through the mystic streets of Chinatown they wound. As they neared the den of Taun's, the man jumped off and scurried for shelter. He ran along in the deep shadows of the buildings until he came to an alley. Down this he went for a short distance then he dodged into a door and climbed two flights of rickety stairs. On the second floor he mounted a small ladder and found himself on the roof. He then walked two hundred paces south and eight paces east. According to calculations he was directly over Taun Fung's secret dope storeroom. Prying a board loose he heard the sound of voices, confering in Chinese. He could see into the room through a small crack in the plaster. He recognized Taun's voice but the rest were strange.

The room was fixed in a most resplendent Oriental style. The odor of incense was heavy in the air. Many Chinamen lay in the bunks with pipes of poppy weed in their mouths. Great piles of opium cans were piled in all corners. Suddenly the lid to one of the cans wos raised, out jumped a man with a brace of automatics levelled at the startled Chinamen. At the same instant the man on the roof dropped through the plaster with another pair of revolvers in his hands.

"Who are you that intrudes in the domain of the Purple Dragon?" said Taun Fung.

"The Messrs. Patrick and Donald Sherman of the Department of Justice," they both replied in one breath.

"Who betrayed us"?, shrieked Tuan.

"You betrayed your self," replied Don Sherman.

"I will feed your corpses to the buzzards," howled Tuan Fung.

"Wait until you get them Chinkie old sport," laughed Pat.

Suddenly Don and Pat felt themselves siezed from behind.

"Bind them," commanded Tuan.

"What shall we do with these American swine?" asked Sing Lee.

"They shall be sacrificed to the purple drogon", replied Tuan Fung.

The room was suddenly plunged into darkness. Pat and Don felt their bonds cut and they were told to run. They ran down a long corridor lighted at intervals by small lamps on the walls. The lights blinked three times and Don and Pat felt themselves falling downward. They lit in a small boat with a crash. Stars flashed before their eyes and they lapsed into unconsciousness.

When they came to they found themselves in stateroom bunks. The room was dimly lighted by small purple light. The walls were emblazoned with large dragons. A miniture dragon was belching forth clouds of sweet smelling incense. The sea was rocking the boat slightly. The door opened and in came Tuan Fung, Sing Lee and several other Chinamen. Taun Fung did not notice that Don and Pat were awake. "The Sacred and Mystic Order of the Purple Dragon has met here to decide the fate of our two enemies." He brought forth a small bottle of gluey liquid, which was opium. He then inserted a needle into the bottle and brought forth a small drop on the end. Then holding it over a candle flame he turned it slowly around until it was very hot. He brought out his dope pipe and put the opium in the bowl. The other's pipes were soon ready. Then lying down on a couch he said, "Ho!, Nang Yang bring forth the ancient volume of laws of the Sacred and Mystic Order of the Purple Dragon." When this was done he said, "Our most noble ancestors here say that all persons caught having evil intents toward the Purple Dragon in their heathenish brow shall depart by the Purple Scimter. Nang Yang go fetch the Scimter." Nang Yang returned bearing a magnificent scimter with an ivory handle inlaid with emeralds, saphires, diamonds, rubies and many other precious gems. The blade was a wonderful purple steel crescent. "Sing Lee, bring out the prisoners," Tuan ordered. Don and Pat were brought out of the bunks and were placed on a table. "I shall confer the honor upon myself to dispatch them." He picked up the Purple Scimter and bowed to the dragons on the wall. At that moment Don poked Pat and they both jumped up and made for the door The Chinamen were caught unaware. Before they could stop them our heroes were on deck running, running for the stern of the craft. They saw that they were on a fair sized yacht. A dark form sprang in front of Pat. Pat felled him like a log. "This way Pat," cried Don. Don was clambering down a rope into a small launch that was being towed behind the yacht. Pat followed him and they cut the rope and started the motor. Several bullets whistled by but no harm was done.

(Continued on page three)

prose sketches of the desert to a thrilling serial influenced by the Fu Manchu stories of Sax Rohmer.

Ward Ritchie established a fine press in 1932, setting up his first shop in a garage behind his family's home on Milan Avenue. The American Institute of Graphic Arts has honored the typographic excellence of many books designed and printed by Ward Ritchie. Over the years Ritchie published a number of Lawrence Clark Powell's books on literature, including *The Alchemy of Books*, dedicated to the memory of Nellie Keith, South Pasadena's first city librarian.

Ritchie and Powell have both paid tribute to Mattaline Crabtree, who taught at Marengo for thirty-three years. Powell once described her as "a soft-spoken steel-gripped Kentucky mountain woman" and as one of the great teachers in his life. In a letter written soon after the death of Miss Crabtree, Powell said, "I never forgot the lessons she taught us in the third grade: that all men are brothers, that work and play can be richly blended, and that the more one gets from life the more he owes it in return. She had the true teacher's supreme gift of making study a joyful activity."

When Marengo's mission-style building went up in 1910, it boasted cooled air, filtered water, and a hygienic drinking fountain. Fireproof, but not earthquake-resistant, the building was abandoned as unsafe in 1947 and demolished a year later. Classes continued in a temporary building until 1955, when Marengo erected six new classrooms and a kindergarten building.

In 1961 Marengo became the first school in the state to make use of a portable classroom that could be folded, trucked to the site, and erected in twenty-four hours. The folded roof rose slowly into place when a large balloon was placed beneath it and inflated—a process likened by the *Los Angeles Times* to a poppy unfolding in the springtime. Installed as a temporary measure, the portable buildings at Marengo were finally abandoned in 1985 and replaced by a new wing with five classrooms and a learning lab.

ONEONTA SCHOOL

In 1909 the school board announced rather tartly that influential residents in Oneonta Park had fought location of a school there. By 1921, however, people realized the need for a school south of Huntington Drive. Henry E. Huntington agreed to sell a building site on Fremont Avenue and even offered to charge nothing extra if the lot proved larger than his estimate of four acres. Measurement showed the property to be four and a half acres, and the board purchased it for the bargain price of $25,000. The electorate voted bonds for the school and also for a pedestrian tunnel under Huntington Drive and the four PE trolley tracks. At the ground breaking for the tunnel, kindergartners from Oneonta School each dug a tiny shovelful of dirt.

Many Oneonta parents volunteered as classroom aides and took part in the school's Early Childhood Education Program. In 1974 the State Department of Education praised the program, the first of its kind in South Pasadena, as exemplary and of uncommon quality.

Oneonta students had their own clubhouse—a small bungalow rescued by the PTA from the path of the Arroyo Seco Parkway. The building was moved to the campus and made into an art center and a meeting place for school and community activities.

213

Another addition to the campus was an outdoor lunch area—a building project worked on by teachers, principal, and at least a hundred parents. Instead of having a cornerstone ceremony, the school celebrated a roof-raising. A copy of the school constitution, signed by every student, was inserted in a pipe supporting the new roof over the lunch area.

A book on film making for young people features Oneonta School and a fourth-grade class taught by Nora Serra. *Lights! Camera! Scream! How to Make Your Own Monster Movies* shows Oneonta students at work on their own film projects. Although a useful text for young moviemakers, the book flunks geography, for it locates Oneonta School in Pasadena.

In 1982 Oneonta had a sixtieth birthday party attended by alumni from every class to have graduated from the school. One of the honored guests was Idelle Bock Rice, who had taught at Oneonta for half of its existence. The school's last two principals almost match her record. Maude Harris was principal for twenty-seven years. Jim Greulich was principal of Oneonta for twenty-six years, and then became principal of Monterey Hills.

By 1983 enrollment was decreasing in all four elementary schools in South Pasadena. Faced by a 7.1 percent decline in two years and by serious financial problems, the board of education voted to close one school. It decided on Oneonta, in part because there were two other elementary schools nearby and most students would still be able to walk to class. Some parents were unhappy at the closure of any school. As one father wrote in protest, "Education should be the healthiest and most vigorous 'industry' in South Pasadena . . . with constant progress toward more teachers, more innovations, and more and better classes and programs."

Oneonta School closed in June 1983. In an affectionate farewell, more than three thousand people gathered at the campus for pizza and what was billed as the world's largest banana split.

Las Flores School

Las Flores School had a dramatic baptism in September 1924. The nearby reservoir on Raymond Hill gave way just two weeks before the new school was to open, and five million gallons of water came rushing down the hill. According to a story in the *South Pasadena Courier*, "The playgrounds and terraces and the flat land to the north of the school looked Sunday like the wild untamed Arroyo itself: an assortment of sand and gravel." Mud lay two feet deep in classrooms and hallways, but school opened as scheduled.

The Arroyo Seco Parkway posed the next threat to Las Flores School. The Division of Highways wanted to build a freeway ramp at Garfield Avenue, close to the school and to the Adobe Flores. People living in the area protested that increased traffic would endanger schoolchildren, make the adobe uninhabitable, and ruin Garfield as a residential street. After much discussion, the city council went on record in 1948 against "ANY plan which proposes that South Pasadena's fine residential streets be used for heavy and continuous volume of traffic destined for parts outside the city."

Geology proved a more difficult problem for the school. Increasingly concerned about buildings that were not earthquake-resistant, the school board voted in 1950 to

214

Oneonta School opened in 1921. It closed in 1983 because of decreasing enrollment in South Pasadena's elementary schools. *Courtesy of South Pasadena Unified School District.*

Las Flores School, built in 1924, was closed in 1950 when engineers called it structurally unsafe. *Courtesy of South Pasadena Unified School District.*

Monterey Hills School opened in 1967 in the newly developed Altos de Monterey. *Photograph by Bob Worswick; courtesy of South Pasadena Review.*

The clock tower of the junior high school is a South Pasadena landmark. The photograph shows the school before its reconstruction in 1965. *Courtesy of South Pasadena Unified School District.*

close Las Flores, which lay above the Raymond Fault. Angry parents called the earthquake hazard to Las Flores "grossly over-emphasized"—no more serious for the school than for South Pasadena as a whole. More than five hundred people petitioned to keep Las Flores open, and students appealed to the school board to consider the "beautifulness of the building" and its pleasant hillside location. The children even sent the board $19.56 to help pay for strengthening the building. Despite protests and appeals, the board voted to close Las Flores School at the end of the spring term in 1950.

The name of Las Flores did not completely vanish from the school system, however, until 1981. To help ease overcrowding at Marengo, the school district opened the Las Flores Primary Unit in 1955. Neighborhood children attended kindergarten and grades one to three on the Las Flores site, in new classrooms built on the old school playground. For the upper grades, pupils transferred to Marengo School, whose principal also served as principal of the Primary Unit. The old Las Flores schoolhouse served as an education center from 1955 to 1977, when instructional services were moved to the administration building on Diamond Avenue. In 1981 the school district sold the Las Flores property, and condominiums replaced the classrooms.

MONTEREY HILLS SCHOOL

In 1967, several months after the hundredth family moved into Altos de Monterey, Monterey Hills School opened on Via del Rey. The building was planned with unusual consideration for the needs of staff and students. Its design incorporated suggestions made by teachers throughout the district.

Robert Edgar, the new principal, took over a splendid building, but an empty one. He had to order every item needed to transform a bare-walls structure into a schoolhouse. In the three weeks before classes began, Edgar, secretary Jane Clough and custodian Einer Christensen had to unpack tables, chairs, desks, flags, files, bookshelves, globes, and other furniture and supplies and put them all in place.

In 1968 Marie and Adele Axtman gave the new school a treasured heirloom: the handbell that had summoned pupils to the Columbia Hill schoolhouse in 1883. For many years sixth-graders leaving Monterey Hills for junior high were allowed to ring the bell as part of their graduation ceremony. Another tradition at Monterey Hills— the Give a Book on Your Birthday Club—helped build an excellent school library. Special bookplates and certificates designed by principal Robert Edgar honored the child in whose name a book was given.

Because a federal loan financed the development of Altos de Monterey, housing was open to all qualified buyers, without regard to race, creed, or color. Monterey Hills School reflects the multi-ethnic character of the Altos and its harmonious history. The school also serves as the hub of the community. It brings together parents, students, and other residents, not only to work for better education, but to share in the events that various ethnic groups proudly sponsor.

SOUTH PASADENA JUNIOR HIGH SCHOOL

The *Foothill Review* for October 19, 1928, featured an eight-page supplement about the new junior high school. A photograph of the Mediterranean-style building had an

South Pasadena's first high school buildings were neoclassic in style and fronted on a sweeping expanse of lawn. *Courtesy of South Pasadena Unified School District.*

inspiring caption: "Along the cloistered arcade of the junior high school, youth treads its happy way toward the fullness of life." The new school, designed by Marsh, Smith & Powell, was located on Fair Oaks Avenue, between Oak and Rollin streets. South Pasadena believed the school's location on a busy thoroughfare would advertise the educational values of the city and the progressiveness of the community.

From the outset the junior high school emphasized artistic values. The first principal, G. Derwood Baker, once said: "In thinking of the future, most of us envisage a state that is more beautiful, and a citizenry that is more appreciative of the fine and artistic things of life than the present generation of adults. To obtain this end, our junior high is attempting to cultivate the tastes and enlarge the creative capacities of the children that come under its care."

To help beautify the school, students made batik wall hangings, wove tapestries, and painted murals. Professional artists also contributed work. Millard Sheets, who was head of the art department at Scripps College, painted three frescoes on the exterior wall of the auditorium. The students suggested contemporary life in California as a theme, and they raised the money for materials. When the frescoes were dedicated in 1934, *Los Angeles Times* critic Arthur Millier praised them as art treasures. Someday, he said, when the world pays tribute to Millard Sheets, South Pasadena can say that it was here he began.

Some forty years after he painted them, Sheets said he considered the frescoes the most beautiful in Southern California. Unfortunately, they have not survived. One panel was ruined in an attempt to preserve it, and the others were plastered over when a new building went up nearby.

According to a report made in 1934, the junior high school buildings did not meet safety standards established after the Long Beach earthquake. It was difficult to pass bond issues during the Depression, however, and difficult to carry out a building program during the war years. Not until 1965 did rehabilitation of the campus finally begin. Substandard structures were replaced, but the famous old tower remained, after being repaired and strengthened. The tower not only symbolized the campus but inspired the name of the junior high school annual, *La Torre*.

Fifty years after the first graduation ceremonies in June 1929, the junior high school held an anniversary party. In honor of the occasion, alumnus William A. Myers—a railway buff, coauthor of *Trolleys to the Surf*, and coproducer of the film, *To Mount Lowe with Love*—put on a conductor's uniform and drove to the campus in a converted Pacific Electric Big Red Car. Similar cars, but without rubber tires and gas engine, had brought San Marino ninth-graders to classes at the junior high before 1951.

In 1919, when the concept was still fairly new, Superintendent George Bush had proposed an intermediate school for students in the seventh and eighth grades. Voters thought the plan too experimental and turned it down. Sixty-five years later, in the fall of 1984, the ninth grade was added to the high school, and the junior high became a middle school for grades six to eight. By student request, the school has not changed its name but is still known as South Pasadena Junior High.

South Pasadena
Public Schools

South Pasadena High School

South Pasadena High School began in 1904 with a ninth-grade class taught by the new superintendent of schools, Noble Harter. Five students met with him in a corner of the Center Street School's eighth-grade classroom to study English, Latin, algebra, and English history. The fledgling high school added two more grades in 1905 and formally organized with Noble Harter as supervising principal. Classes moved to the elementary school basement, where a faculty of five taught science, mathematics, history, languages, drawing, and music.

By the end of 1905, enrollment was up to thirty-five, and fifteen students were ready to enter ninth grade at midterm. Another twenty students were attending out-of-town high schools, where they paid tuition fees of $36 to $75 a year. Because classes in Pasadena and Los Angeles were badly overcrowded, the county superintendent of schools urged South Pasadena to build its own high school. In 1906, after twice failing to get a two-thirds majority, a $65,000 high school bond issue passed by an overwhelming vote of 201 to 41.

The school board purchased a six-acre site bounded by Fremont, Rollin, Diamond, and Bank. Building was delayed, however, by the great earthquake and fire that struck San Francisco in April 1906. This "Northern Disaster"— as the *South Pasadenan* termed it—shook down the price of Pacific Coast bonds and sent the price of building materials rocketing. Voters had to approve another $10,000 for the high school before construction could begin.

Meanwhile, classes moved into the new Taylor Building on Mission Street, upstairs from the Model Grocery. According to a student history of the high school, "Each room was heated by a small oil stove, and these stoves were very susceptible to being upset. Consequently, it was no uncommon thing to hear a crashing of glass and see a stove flying through the window, for usually when they were overturned flames and smoke filled the room, and the building had to be saved at any cost."

In April 1907 the high school boys helped load a hayrack that carried school equipment from the Taylor Building to the new campus. The three-story building, designed by Marsh & Russell, opened on April 8, 1907. Noble Harter, founder of the high school, had died just two months earlier, and George C. Bush became supervising principal. Five girls and a boy were in the first graduating class of June 1907. Their senior themes ranged from "Vergil's Debt to Homer" to "Some Evident Phases of the Japanese Question," and from "Arthur, the Ideal" to "The Use of the Barometer, Hygrometer, Aneumeter, and Thermometer in Forecasting Weather."

Twenty-seven boys signed a petition to the principal in 1909. "We, the undersigned boys attending South Pasadena High School," it read, "do hereby petition you to allow us to attend school without coats, wearing shirtwaists and belts, allowing no suspenders. Coats are uncomfortable and they interfere with our study. We base our claim of this privilege on the fact that Pasadena, Los Angeles, and Throop High Schools and Occidental College allow boys to study without coats." Judging by pictures in the yearbook, the petition was not granted.

Students published their first yearbook in 1909. A graceful drawing of the California poppy—with its golden cup, or *copa de oro*—decorates the cover. *Copa de Oro* has come out every year except 1918, when the class voted to use the money instead

The high school baseball team posed for this picture in 1909. Professor S. F. Van Patten (standing in the last row) taught history and physical culture. *Photograph by H. J. Kenny; courtesy of Huntington Library.*

Jean Gooch, standing in the center, taught languages at the new South Pasadena High School, managed the girls basketball team, and played shortstop on the faculty base-ball team. *Photograph by H. J. Kenny; courtesy of Huntington Library.*

for Armenian relief efforts. The advanced journalism class of 1915 put out the first issue of the student paper, *The Tiger*, which began as a four-page weekly, with news gathered by the journalism club.

High school athletes inspired a lead story on October 22, 1912. "South Pasadena High School Plays First Football Game," the headline read. A sympathetic article reported that although defeated by Pasadena High School 50 to 0, the home team played a classy game, made a good defense, and was not demoralized. Headlines two weeks later announced the team's first scoring game—a 13 to 13 tie with Venice Union—and in 1914 headlines proclaimed a football championship for South Pasadena. One of the high school's best-known football stars was Larry ("Moon") Mullins, varsity captain in 1926, who later coached the Notre Dame football team.

In 1912 the high school added domestic science and manual training buildings to the campus. There were no more additions until an auditorium and a gymnasium were built in 1921. The first director of manual training, Percival J. Cooney, was also a prolific author. While a teacher at the high school, he wrote *The Dons of the Old Pueblo*, inspired in part by the history of Rancho San Pasqual.

South Pasadena's first adult school, which opened on the high school campus in 1916, was organized to teach English to foreign-born residents. The school had the active interest and support of the DAR, the PTA, and the Woman's Improvement Association. Thirty people enrolled in the first class: Japanese, Russians, Mexicans, French, and Swiss. Their teacher was George W. Wilson, schoolmaster and principal of the Center Street School in 1885.

In 1917, with the United States and Germany at war, at least half the high school boys signed up for military drill and wore their khaki uniforms to school. Students refused to study German, a popular subject in former years. In another patriotic gesture, students voted against spending money on a graduation banquet, and the girls agreed to wear simple dresses for commencement. After the war, the girls voted to wear a school uniform. Military influence was evident in their costume: a blue serge skirt and a white middy blouse with stars and stripes on the collar. (Skirts were eleven inches from the floor in 1919 and rose to fourteen inches in 1921.)

For thirty-six years the head of the high school music department was Albert J. Adams, who joined the staff in 1920. Adams was well known in the community as an accomplished musician, an entertaining lecturer, and the author of program notes for Pasadena's Coleman Concerts. He won the title of South Pasadena's Victor Borge for programs in which he combined jokes, stories, and piano humor.

San Marino became part of the South Pasadena High School District in 1921. The California Legislature passed a law that year requiring any city without its own high school to annex to a neighboring school district. San Marino voted to join the South Pasadena district, and it remained part of it for thirty years. In 1928 ninth-grade classes were transferred from the high school and made part of the new South Pasadena Junior High School. The change from a four-year to a three-year high school became a source of friction with San Marino and led ultimately to formation of two separate high school districts.

One of the worst tragedies ever to strike South Pasadena occurred on May 6, 1940, when the junior high school principal shot and killed five of his colleagues. Among

An artist's sketch shows the plans made in 1954 for an enlarged and rebuilt high school campus. *Courtesy of South Pasadena Public Library.*

them was the superintendent of schools, George C. Bush, who had begun his long career in education as a teacher at the high school. In his memory a garden designed by architect Herbert J. Powell was planted on the campus.

On December 7, 1941, the Japanese attacked Pearl Harbor. Within a year three hundred South Pasadena-San Marino High School graduates were serving in the armed services, and six had lost their lives. Changes in the high school curriculum reflected the exigencies of war. The school board authorized national defense classes in machine shop and navigation, and it approved aeronautics courses for seniors planning to enter the air force. To help with preflight training, students in woodshop built a glider—aptly called the Dodo by the *Los Angeles Times*. Hopeful pilots learned the action of rudders, elevators, and ailerons when they sat in the flightless vehicle and were towed by car across the girls' athletic field.

Another vehicle made high school news in 1948. Rowdyism on the Pacific Electric School Special led to deputized civilians riding between San Marino and South Pasadena. The deputies reported the names of miscreants to the student council for punishment. "Under the old plan," said the *San Marino Tribune*, "any student reported as conducting himself in an ungentlemanly manner was denied the privilege of riding on the train for 30 days, but this punishment did not seem to have the proper effect."

By 1951 a high school designed for five hundred students had an enrollment of a thousand. The eleven-acre campus was woefully inadequate, and at least four of the old buildings were deemed unsafe. In June 1951 San Marino and South Pasadena voted on a bond measure to enlarge the campus and replace or rehabilitate the buildings. If the bond measure passed, the high school would become a four-year school, and the junior high school would be sold to the elementary district. San Marino voted overwhelmingly for the measure: 2,691 in favor and 346 opposed. Reluctant to give up its junior high school, South Pasadena voted against the measure, and it fell 201 votes short of the necessary two-thirds majority.

At the next election, held in December 1951, voters considered two issues: a bond measure for a four-year high school and a proposition for two separate school districts if the bonds should fail. In the largest turnout in its history for a local question, San Marino voted two to one in favor of building its own high school. South Pasadena voted for a union high school, but not by the necessary two-thirds majority. The union district was dissolved in July 1952, and the last San Marino students graduated from South Pasadena High School in 1955. As the South Pasadena PTA said in a farewell poem:

> It was final and fair, there was no fuss.
> We got the schoolhouse, you got the bus.

In 1954 South Pasadena voters passed a bond issue to improve school buildings throughout the city. For the high school this meant the construction of new classrooms, gymnasiums, library, and cafeteria. It also meant demolishing the columned academic building that dated back to 1907.

A four-year high school—voted down in 1951 and again in 1964—was finally approved in 1983. Because of declining enrollment in the elementary grades, the school board decided to move the ninth grade to the high school and to create a middle school for grades six through eight. The expanded senior high opened in September

1984 with a thousand more students than in 1904, when the total enrollment was five.

Six students graduated from South Pasadena High School in 1907, and four went on to college. Two entered teachers college, one entered Stanford, and one entered the Pacific College of Osteopathy. Today about 46 percent of the graduating seniors go on to study in a four-year college, and another 46 percent go to a junior college.

In 1909 boys at the high school petitioned the principal for a change in the dress code. Modern students are sometimes willing to test the rules in court. In 1970 a student at South Pasadena High School sued to wear his hair any length he wanted, and he won his case. Debate over a dress code rekindled in 1983 when the high school suspended a boy who refused to remove a small gold stud from his ear. The student was finally allowed back on campus—with his earring—when the American Civil Liberties Union threatened a court suit, and the school board decided it could not afford a legal battle.

In 1984, after a lapse of some fifteen years, Latin returned to the high school curriculum. It had been part of the original course of study, and the Latin Club was justly popular. For years toga-clad members enjoyed an elaborate Roman banquet at the close of school. Other South Pasadenans have celebrated golden anniversaries and diamond jubilees, but only the Latin Club has celebrated a bimillenium—a festival held in 1930 in honor of Vergil's birth.

A number of languages are heard on all the school campuses these days. In 1985 a total of 500 students—148 at the high school—were studying English as a second language. Most of these students had Mandarin as their native tongue. Others spoke Spanish, Cantonese, Japanese, Vietnamese, Korean, Tagalog, Arabic, Portuguese, French, or Persian.

One of the great events in the eighty-year history of South Pasadena High School was the grand reunion held in 1982. It brought together four thousand graduates, representing every class from 1907 on. They came from across the country and around the world—a remarkable demonstration of a sense of community. The day ended with dancing on the tennis courts and began with a high-spirited parade from Garfield Park to the high school's Roosevelt Field. "It was a parade that nobody watched," said school librarian Mary Ida Phair, "because everyone was in it."

Elizabeth Hoag founded a Latin club at South Pasadena High School in 1920, one year before this photograph was taken. *Courtesy of South Pasadena Unified School District.*

Children from Center Street School practice a hoop drill in 1890. *Courtesy of South Pasadena Public Library.*

Sixth-graders pose on the El Centro playground in 1935, with principal Loma Cavanaugh (in the center) and teacher Clara Ficke (on the right). The buildings in the background are on Mission Street. *Courtesy of South Pasadena Cultural Heritage Commission.*

CHRONOLOGY

1874

The Los Angeles County Board of Supervisors creates the San Pasqual School District for the San Gabriel Orange Grove Association. Classes begin in September in the home of teacher Jennie Clapp.

1875

The colonists build a schoolhouse near Orange Grove Avenue and California Street.

1876

The schoolhouse is moved to Fair Oaks Avenue and Colorado Street, on a site donated by B. D. Wilson.

1878

Settlers living below California Street form their own school district— named the Pasadena District by the County Board of Supervisors. Bessie Harris teaches the first classes, which meet in the Columbia Street home of Clinton B. Ripley.

1880

The new district builds a schoolhouse on four and a half acres at Columbia Street and Orange Grove Avenue. The school board purchases a ten-volume encyclopedia for fifty dollars.

1883

The district passes its first bond issue and builds a larger schoolhouse on the Center Street site.

1884

The school board decides to build in downtown South Pasadena, and it sells the old schoolhouse to Sierra Madre College.

1885

South Pasadena's first downtown school opens on Center Street.

1886

Pasadena incorporates as a city. The school district south of Columbia Street is renamed the South Pasadena School District.

Arethusa Burrows becomes the first woman to serve on the South Pasadena school board.

1887

Lincoln Park School opens in a rented storefront on the Arroyo.

1888

South Pasadena incorporates.

A new schoolhouse is built on Center Street, and the old schoolhouse is moved to Lincoln Park.

1890

A quarter-ton bronze bell is hung in the tower of the Center Street school.

1903

Norman Foote Marsh designs a new Center Street schoolhouse.

1904

South Pasadena High School begins with five ninth-grade students, who meet for classes in the Center Street School. Noble Harter is the first principal.

1907

The high school moves to a six-acre campus bounded by Fremont, Rollin, Diamond, and Bank. George C. Bush is appointed supervising principal.

1908

The first downtown schoolhouse—which stood originally on Center Street—is moved from Lincoln Park to Orange Grove Avenue for students living at the Boys' and Girls' Aid Society.

1909

Ada Longley forms the Child Study Association, precursor of the Parent-Teacher Association.

High school students publish the first issue of the yearbook, *Copa de Oro*. The boys petition to attend classes without having to wear jackets.

1910

Marengo School opens.

1911

Kindergarten is added to the South Pasadena school system.

The South Pasadena Federation of Parent-Teacher Associations is formed.

1912

George C. Bush is named the first superintendent of schools.

1915

The high school advanced journalism class puts out the first issue of the student paper, *The Tiger*.

1916

South Pasadena's first adult school opens, with English language and citizenship classes for the foreign-born.

1919

Eighth-graders Ward Ritchie and Pat Kelley found Marengo School's first publication, the *Marengo Literary Leader*.

The girls in high school vote to wear middy blouses and blue skirts as a uniform.

The downtown schoolhouse originally fronted on Center Street. When rebuilt in 1902, it faced Mission Street and the new Pacific Electric trolley tracks. *Courtesy of South Pasadena Public Library.*

Lincoln Park School was built in 1908 and torn down in 1939. *Courtesy of South Pasadena Public Library*

"The Farm" is one of three frescoes that Millard Sheets painted on the exterior wall of the junior high school auditorium in 1934. The other two panels were "The Harbor" and "The City." Unfortunately, none has been preserved. *Courtesy of Millard Sheets*.

232

1921

Oneonta School opens on Fremont Avenue, south of Huntington Drive.

San Marino joins the South Pasadena High School District.

1924

Las Flores School opens near the historic Adobe Flores.

1928

The junior high school opens on Fair Oaks Avenue, between Oak and Rollin streets.

The old El Centro buildings are torn down and replaced by an arcaded brick structure.

1933

A devastating earthquake hits Long Beach. As a result of widespread damage to school buildings, the state enacts the Field Act setting safety standards for new construction.

1939

The old Lincoln Park School is demolished and replaced by Lincoln School.

1940

Five staff members lose their lives in a mass slaying.

1941

An evening high school is organized for civil defense classes.

1944

Sixty-eight high school boys enroll as members of the California Cadet Corps.

1945

Roy E. Simpson, Superintendent of Schools in South Pasadena, is appointed State Superintendent of Public Instruction.

1949

The tower at El Centro is taken down and the school bell is stored away.

1950

Las Flores School is closed because of earthquake hazard.

1952

Members of the Junior Chamber of Commerce install the El Centro bell on a platform in front of the school.

South Pasadena and San Marino form separate school districts.

South Pasadena Public Schools Associates is formed to encourage interest in the public schools and promote high standards in public school education.

1955

Las Flores Primary Unit opens in conjunction with Marengo School.

The last San Marino students graduate from South Pasadena High School.

1967

Monterey Hills School opens in the newly developed Altos de Monterey.

1979

El Centro merges with Lincoln, and the school takes the name Arroyo Vista.

A swimming pool is completed at the high school.

1980

The buildings on the old El Centro campus are converted to use as the School Administration Center.

The South Pasadena Educational Foundation organizes to raise money for the schools.

1981

Las Flores Primary Unit closes.

1982

Four thousand graduates take part in the High School All-Years Reunion.

1983

Oneonta School is closed.

1984

The high school becomes a four-year school, and the junior high becomes a middle school.

1985

Monterey Hills School receives a distinguished service award from the Chinese-American Parents and Teachers Association of Southern California.

The State Superintendent of Public Instruction awards a certificate to Marengo Elementary School for its outstanding science program.

A team from South Pasadena Junior High School ranks first in California and second in the nation in a test of general knowledge.

1986

An All-Schools Celebration marks the district's hundredth year as the South Pasadena School District.

Preservationists failed in their efforts to keep the old school administration building from being demolished in 1984. *Courtesy of South Pasadena Unified School District.*

The Rev. John A. Wood paid for Diaspora Villa, his home on the Arroyo Seco, with profits from his book on salvation. *Courtesy of Huntington Library.*

XII

CHURCHES OF SOUTH PASADENA

Five religious denominations are at present represented in South Pasadena and all are highly influential in guarding the moral tone of the city.

SOUTH PASADENA RECORD, 1909

UNITED METHODIST CHURCH OF SOUTH PASADENA

In 1887 the Methodists built the first church in South Pasadena. Previously, the nearby Presbyterian church at California Street and Orange Grove Avenue had served worshippers of various denominations. When that church moved in 1885, Margaret P. Dougherty—one of South Pasadena's earliest settlers—organized a Union Sunday School, the forerunner of the Methodist Church in South Pasadena.

Sunday School members met for lectures, talks, and an occasional sermon in the old Columbia Hill schoolhouse. They had no regular pastor until 1886, when the Methodist Conference assigned the Reverend C. W. Tarr to Garvanza (now part of Highland Park) and to South Pasadena, neither of which had a house of worship. The Reverend Mr. Tarr preached Sunday mornings in one town, Sunday afternoons in the other, and within a month had organized the South Pasadena Methodist Episcopal Church. Shortly afterwards, the churchwomen formed a Ladies Aid Society. On its board—with true ecumenical spirit—were a Presbyterian, a Baptist, a Methodist, and a Universalist. The Society's first achievement was to raise fifty dollars toward the pastor's salary.

The schoolhouse soon proved too small for the growing membership, and the church bought a building site on Center Street just west of Fremont Avenue. Joseph B. Soper, a skilled carpenter—and a Methodist—built "a neat Gothic church" from plans supplied by the Church Extension Society. The Methodists dedicated the building in October 1887, and the new pastor, the Reverend A. W. Bunker, wrote a special hymn for the occasion.

By 1904 the congregation had again outgrown its quarters, and the church bought the adjoining corner lot at Center Street and Fairview. After hearing an eloquent address by Bishop C. C. McCabe, townspeople pledged $7,000 for a new Methodist church. Norman Foote Marsh designed the building, and Joseph B. Soper supervised construction. By the time the building was dedicated in November 1905, the congregation had multiplied a hundredfold, from the original 4 members to 414.

At the request of the other churches, the Methodists rehung their old church bell, which was the only one in South Pasadena. When it rang out, it summoned Methodists to their church and worshippers of other denominations to theirs. For many years the Methodists also had the only pipe organ in town. It was the gift of Andrew Carnegie and is still in use.

Calvary Presbyterian Church. *Courtesy of South Pasadena Public Library.*

A stained-glass window in the church was dedicated to the Reverend John A. Wood, a longtime member of the congregation and the author of *Perfect Love,* a best-selling book on salvation. On a visit to California in 1886, Dr. Wood attended a land auction in South Pasadena. In his autobiography he wrote:

> At the auction a table was spread and covered with eatables for a free lunch. As the men gathered around the well-spread table and were about to eat, I cried out: "Hold on, gentlemen, let us ask a blessing here. God is good, this is a grand country, and we ought to be thankful." The auctioneer said: "All right—hats off." The hats went off and I invoked the blessing of Almighty God, a new thing at an auction or land sale in California.

Dr. Wood himself bid on a lot, thinking he might retire to California. "No one would bid against me, after the table scene," he recalled, "and it was struck off to me." Before the year was out, Wood settled in South Pasadena, on the Arroyo, and built a home he called Diaspora Villa.

After sixty years at Fairview and El Centro, the Methodists moved to the old Bilicke estate, on seven wooded acres in the Monterey Hills. Until a new church was built, the Bilicke mansion served as a place of worship. In March 1967, led by the choir in song, the congregation marched from the old house to the new sanctuary for a ceremony marking completion of the church building. The Bilicke mansion—an imposing example of Mission Revival architecture—continues in use today for the Sunday School, the church offices, and the Woodsy Owl Day Care Center, which was organized in 1980 to meet the needs of working parents in the community. South Pasadena's first church bell is mounted by the walkway to the Bilicke mansion.

CALVARY PRESBYTERIAN CHURCH

Calvary Presbyterian Church can trace its history back to outdoor Sunday School classes held a century ago by a young woman who had hoped to be a missionary. The church formally organized in 1887 with nine members and one elder. The Reverend A. Moss Merwin, acting as supply pastor, held services in the Sierra Madre College building on Schoolhouse Hill.

During the winter of 1888 the Presbyterians built "a neat little church edifice" on Columbia Street, and they dedicated the building in April 1889. Over the next ten years the church had no regular pastor, and in 1897 most of the members transferred to Pasadena Presbyterian Church, although the Sunday School continued to meet in South Pasadena. In May 1902 the Reverend A. J. Compton canvassed the city to announce the resumption of church services on Columbia Street. One month later, Calvary Presbyterian Church of South Pasadena reorganized with nine charter members. The congregation elected G. A. Gilks and George W. Lawyer as ruling elders.

In 1904 the church moved downtown and for ten dollars a month rented the Nazarene chapel on Center Street, next to the city's first bank building. The following year the Presbyterians bought their own property, and in 1907 they prepared to build. It was an opportune moment because the Presbyterians in Pasadena were moving to a new location and giving up their old church building. The Sunday School wing was dismantled, hauled to South Pasadena in a horse-drawn wagon, and reconstructed at Center Street and Fremont Avenue. In its new incarnation, the building's Victorian facade gave way to the more fashionable style of California Mission Revival. Among the "furniture and fittings" that accompanied the building in its move from Pasadena were pews with ornamental carvings, and opalescent stained-glass windows with Art Nouveau designs. Calvary Presbyterian Church was formally opened in November 1907, and the Reverend Charles M. Fisher was installed as pastor.

After eighteen years on El Centro, the Presbyterians moved a block away to Fremont Avenue between Oxley and El Centro. There, in June 1925, they dedicated a Gothic-style church of brick and stone. It has a three-story education wing, named Livingstone Hall to honor the minister who served from 1916 to 1926. In 1959 the church opened a youth center and a weekday nursery school, and in 1973 it added a program of day care.

Calvary Church has sponsored a number of refugee families and helped them settle in South Pasadena. Another special activity, carried on from 1970 to 1982, involved young people of the church in a vacation work program at a small orphanage in Baja California.

Women have always played an active role in Calvary Church. Of the nine charter members, five were women. In 1959 Calvary elected a woman elder, Evelyn Shattuck, and in 1978 it installed the Reverend Joan Beebe as one of the church pastors.

Paul D. McKelvey, an elder of Calvary Church and a distinguished layman, gained national recognition in 1959. He was elected Moderator of the United Presbyterian Church in the United States of America—the highest honor the Presbyterian Church can bestow.

First Baptist Church

A Baptist church organized in South Pasadena in 1888, the same year the city incorporated. In May a visiting pastor, the Reverend John Heritage, began preaching to a Baptist congregation that met in Graham and Mohr's new Opera House Building. The church formally organized in July with thirteen charter members, and the following July the Reverend T. L. Crandall became the first regular pastor. Eager to have their own church building, members of the congregation bought property on Mission Street, between Fairview and Fremont. There in 1891 they built a little white church, at a cost of $725, and named it Memorial Baptist Church in memory of Charles Tapking, an early parishioner. A wood stove heated the church, and kerosene lamps provided light. It was the duty of teen-age girls in the congregation to keep the wicks trimmed and the lamp chimneys sparkling.

Between 1900 and 1902 the church had no regular pastor, and an ecumenical spirit again prevailed in South Pasadena. The Baptists joined the Methodists for worship, and the Episcopalians, who had no building of their own, held services in the Baptist church.

In 1902, when the Baptists again secured a pastor, the church membership numbered seventeen. By 1906 it had grown to nearly a hundred, and the Baptists bought property on Diamond south of El Centro. Here they moved their little white church and built an addition—Baraca Hall—which they helped pay for with magic lantern programs. In 1909 the city bought the Baptist property to add to Library Park. The old church was demolished, and the hall moved to another location. In 1910 the Baptists dedicated a new church at Mound and El Centro. The architect, Norman Foote

Memorial Baptist Church. *Courtesy of Huntington Library.*

South Pasadena Church of the Nazarene. *Photograph by Tom M. Apostol.*

Marsh, also designed the new Carnegie Library, a few blocks to the west.

The church—renamed First Baptist Church in 1952—continued at Mound and El Centro until 1972, when the city bought the property for its downtown revitalization program. After eighty-four years in South Pasadena, First Baptist Church dissolved, and its members joined congregations in Alhambra or Pasadena. For a time the old church building served as a youth center, but in 1974 it was torn down as a fire hazard, and First Arroyo Bank was built on the site.

South Pasadena Church of the Nazarene

In October 1895 Dr. Phineas F. Bresee, former pastor of the First Methodist Episcopal Church in Pasadena, held an evangelic meeting in Los Angeles and formed the Church of the Nazarene "with the dedicated purpose of preaching holiness, and carrying the gospel to the poor." The Reverend E. A. Girvin, a longtime friend of Dr. Bresee, noted in his diary for October 19, 1896, that the two men had gone to South Pasadena that day and visited "the residence of Brother and Sister Helm, two of the grandest old saints it has ever been my good fortune to meet. There were about thirty present, and we had a glorious prayer meeting." The following year, a Nazarene Church was organized in South Pasadena with the Reverend Mr. Clark as pastor. The congregation built a chapel on Center Street, between Diamond and Meridian avenues, and continued to meet there until 1906, when apparently the church disbanded.

A Nazarene congregation again formed in South Pasadena in 1925. Three years later it formally organized with fourteen charter members and with the Reverend James F. Black as pastor. During the thirties, the church met in a hall on Mission Street, and then in the little frame building now known as the Meridian Iron Works. In 1940 the congregation moved to El Centro Street and Palm Avenue, where members and friends had built a church in "a pleasing, simple form of ecclesiastical architecture." Carlton D. Bellamy became pastor in 1976, succeeding his father, who had served in the pastorate for sixteen years.

St. James' Episcopal Church

Although 1901 marks the real beginning of St. James' Episcopal Church, Episcopalians gathered for worship in South Pasadena more than a decade earlier. The rector of All Saints Church in Pasadena held occasional services in South Pasadena in 1887, and lay readers from All Saints held services for several years—first in the old school on Columbia Hill and later in a storefront chapel on Mission Street just west of Meridian Avenue.

In June 1901 Agnes Dunn and Lena Perkins started a Sunday School that met Sunday afternoons in the Baptist church on Mission Street. The little group reorganized on November 30, 1902, and took the name St. Andrew's Mission in honor of the day. Its first resident priest was the Reverend Milton S. Runkle, who came in 1904.

Until they had their own building, the Episcopalians met in the Baptist church or in a room of the old Opera House Building on Center Street. In 1905 Caroline W. Dobbins gave the mission a lot on the southwest corner of Fremont Avenue and Monterey Road. Here the Episcopalians erected a little wooden building that they used as a church from 1905 to 1907 and then converted to a parish house.

The present church, designed by the Boston firm of Cram, Goodhue, and Ferguson, was built in 1907 under the direction of architects Myron Hunt and Elmer Grey, who lived in Pasadena. The Reverend Charles H. Hibbard described the style of the church as Gothic adapted for Southern California. "It is thus one detects a touch of the 'Italian' or 'Mission' here and there," he told his parishioners. "If there were such a thing in architectural nomenclature as 'sub-tropical Gothic,' we suppose this could be so designated." Of the local granite used in the church, he said, "It makes a good, honest wall, massive and dignified."

Just before the Episcopalians dedicated their new church in 1907, they voted to rename it St. James' Mission, thus avoiding confusion with the Catholic parish of St. Andrew's in Pasadena. In 1909 St. James became a parish church and elected the Reverend Frederick T. Henstridge as its first rector.

A gift from Caroline W. Dobbins enabled St. James to build a bell tower in 1924. At the same time Thaddeus Lowe and his daughter, Florence Lowe Barnes, gave the parish the chimes that have become a familiar part of South Pasadena life. The chimes now ring to announce each hour during the daytime. In past years they have also rung to remind voters to go to the polls. During World War II they rang out every noon, calling the townspeople to a moment of silent prayer for international peace and justice.

The original building plans for St. James included a south aisle. This was added to the church in 1958, during the rectorship of the Reverend Gilbert P. Prince. The stained-glass windows along the south aisle are the work of artisans at the Judson Studios. Also enhancing the beauty of the church are kneelers designed by Josephine Jardine, graduate of the Royal School of Embroidery in London, who was famous for her ecclesiastical needlework.

The Reverend H. F. Knowles, who succeeded Dr. Prince, introduced an ecumenical service held every year on Good Friday. In 1970 he established the All-Parish Breakfast, which is served on Sunday mornings throughout most of the year. Father Knowles also added special commemorative services to the church program. In 1978 he won a Freedom Foundations Award for his annual George Washington Anniversary Service, which members of many patriotic groups attend.

A number of pioneering women have been members of the St. James' parish. In 1934 Rebekah Hibbard became one of the first four women elected to the National Council of the Episcopal Church. The Reverend Merrill Bittner (named one of the outstanding young women in the United States in 1974), the Reverend Barbara Mudge, and the Reverend Emily Stevens Hall were among the first women in the United States to be ordained as Episcopal priests.

South Pasadena Christian Church (Disciples of Christ)

The Christian Church, founded on the Allegheny frontier in the early nineteenth century, reached California in the gold rush years, and in 1884 a Christian Church organized in Pasadena. In January 1906 the Reverend Sumner T. Martin, minister of the Pasadena Christian Church, and J. Walter Wilson, a gospel singer, held a series of evangelistic meetings in the Opera House Building on Center Street. Sixteen people who attended the meetings formed the South Pasadena Christian Church. The congre-

St. James' Episcopal Church. *Courtesy of South Pasadena Public Library.*

Members of the South Pasadena Christian Church posed around 1910 outside the bungalow that served the congregation until 1962. *Photograph by H. J. Kenny; courtesy of Huntington Library.*

Holy Family Catholic Church. *Courtesy of South Pasadena Public Library.*

gation formally organized in March, and the Reverend H. T. Buff became its first pastor.

Initially the group met Sunday afternoons on Center Street in a little building used Sunday mornings by the Presbyterians. When Alexander R. Graham, a member of the Christian Church, finished his Alexander Building at Mission Street and Meridian Avenue, he let the congregation use two rooms on the second floor, above the post office. He also gave the church a building site at the corner of Fairview and Oxley, but the church sold the land to the city for Library Park and bought property at Fremont and Lyndon. There it built a little brown bungalow that served the congregation from 1909 to 1962, when a new sanctuary was built on the property. The bungalow continued in use as a Sunday School until 1969 and was then torn down to make room for the Edna Gish Educational Building. The name of the building commemorates a retired missionary who served the South Pasadena Christian Church as minister of education and visitation.

When the old bungalow was taken down, its wooden cross was preserved, and it now graces the wall alongside the entrance to the church.

Holy Family Catholic Church

In 1910 the Reverend Richard J. Cotter established a Catholic parish in South Pasadena. The Los Angeles Diocese had purchased a lot at El Centro and Fremont—where the post office now stands—and a remodeled bungalow on the property became the first home of Holy Family Church. In 1923 Holy Family bought a lot at Fremont and Rollin and moved the old church building onto the site. Four years later, construction of a new church was under way; and at a special service held in January 1928 the Right Reverend Joseph J. Cantwell, Bishop of Los Angeles and San Diego, blessed the altar, cross, and cornerstone. On Easter Sunday the bishop returned to Holy Family to preach the dedicatory sermon and to bless the new building, which he described as a monument worthy of the beauty of its environment.

Designed by Los Angeles architect Emmett G. Martin, the church is Spanish Baroque in style and has a bell tower ninety-two feet tall. A bronze plaque in the church vestibule pays tribute to the Reverend James B. Morris, under whose direction the church was built and a parochial school established.

In 1985 Holy Family Church observed the seventy-fifth anniversary of its founding. To celebrate its jubilee year—and to reflect new life, growth, and a reaching out of the parish community—Holy Family adopted a program to plant seventy-five trees in Arroyo Seco Park and seventy-five rose bushes in Garfield Park.

Oneonta Congregational Church

In 1910 a field secretary of the Congregational Sunday School and Publishing Society visited South Pasadena and observed, "I found a band of earnest women at work—outlook is for rapid growth." One of those earnest women was Elizabeth Bradshaw, who had called together a group of neighbors to organize a Congregational church in the vicinity of Huntington Drive and Fletcher Avenue. In March 1910 the women in the group formed the Ladies Aid Society of the Church of the Neighborhood, and shortly afterward they invited Dr. I. Curtis Meserve to come as pastor.

247

The congregation changed its name to Oneonta Neighborhood Church Congregational, then to Oneonta Neighborhood Congregational Church, and finally to Oneonta Congregational Church. All three names alluded to the Oneonta Park tract subdivided by Henry Huntington in 1904 and named for his birthplace in New York.

For twelve years the congregation met in a little church bungalow on Electric Avenue in Alhambra, just two blocks from South Pasadena's eastern boundary. In 1911 the church bought two lots on Fletcher Avenue, south of Huntington Drive, and Norman Foote Marsh drew plans for a new building. (Henry E. Huntington donated two hundred dollars to the building fund.) On Easter Sunday of 1922 the Sunday School children placed themselves where the building would go, and they set the corner stakes. In December the church was finished. A member of the Sunday School, carrying an American flag, led the other children around the block from the bungalow church to the new building on Fletcher Avenue. Elizabeth Bradshaw, the initiating founder, laid the cornerstone, which contained the first board minutes of the Ladies Aid Society.

The Oneonta Club is an outgrowth of a fund-raising drive for the new church building. Seeking contributions in the community, A. B. Culver found many of the men he called on worked outside South Pasadena and knew little about their neighbors or the city. He suggested forming a men's club to promote fellowship and encourage an interest in civic affairs. In March 1923 the Oneonta Club held its first meeting. Sixty-seven men signed the charter roll and elected Jonathan S. Dodge as president. Although many of the members belonged to the Oneonta Church, the club was not otherwise linked to it.

By 1946 the Fletcher Avenue site was no longer adequate for the church, and it explored the possibility of buying the four-acre Boothe estate, just half a mile away. The area was zoned for residential use, but after several spirited hearings, the city council granted the church a variance. Architect Herbert J. Powell, a member of the congregation, designed the new sanctuary, which he described as "modern but not modernistic." The church was dedicated on October 12, 1950, the fortieth anniversary of the founding of Oneonta Congregational Church. In 1951 the North American Conference on Church Architecture honored Powell and his outstanding design for the chancel of Oneonta Church. The organization praised the reredos, which tells the story of religious heritage in sixty-four quatrefoil windows, as "a unique contribution to church architecture."

First Church of Christ, Scientist

At year's end in 1911 a group of seventeen Christian Scientists met in the office of practitioner Millie Jean Carlson to organize a Christian Science church in South Pasadena. Progress was swift. Chartered on February 2, 1912, First Church of Christ, Scientist, South Pasadena, held services two weeks later, on February 18.

For two and a half years the congregation met on the second floor of the Jacobs Building, on Mission Street, where the church also had a Sunday School and a Reading Room. In 1914 the church found more comfortable quarters in the new Woman's Club at Fremont Avenue and Rollin Street. The Reading Room also moved from Jacobs Hall—first to Fair Oaks Avenue, and then back to Mission Street.

Oneonta Congregational Church. *Courtesy of South Pasadena Public Library.*

First Church of Christ, Scientist. *Courtesy of South Pasadena Public Library.*

Grace Brethren Church. *Photograph by Tom M. Apostol.*

In 1917 the Christian Scientists bought property at Fremont Avenue and Oak Street, one block south of the Woman's Club, and in 1922 they engaged the architectural firm of Postle and Postle to design a brick sanctuary in the Gothic style of an English parish church. It was a striking departure from the neoclassic architecture of The Mother Church in Boston, but a news story suggested that the style harmonized with the rugged hills of the surrounding landscape. The story also took note of the wrought iron fixtures in the church, the windows of straw-colored cathedral glass, and the upholstered folding chairs that were used "instead of pews, so often crowded beyond a point of comfort." When the church formally opened on October 28, 1923, it welcomed some fifteen hundred visitors.

An organ loft was completed in 1926, and an Aeolian pipe organ was installed. Pews with theater seats eventually replaced the folding opera chairs, and brighter colors and fabrics were used for the church interior. In 1961 First Church of Christ, Scientist, added a building for the Sunday School and church offices. In 1984 the Reading Room moved to 1132 Mission Street, just a few steps from its original location in 1912.

GRACE BRETHREN CHURCH

The Brethren Church was brought to the United States from Germany in 1719, and the first California congregation organized in 1858 in the vicinity of Monterey. Most Grace Brethren churches in Southern California have historic ties with a Brethren church founded in Long Beach in 1910.

Grace Brethren Church of South Pasadena evolved from a Bible class held in Pasadena in 1943. With the help of the District Mission Board, members of the group were able to form a new Brethren church. Twenty-two people met for the first regular services, which were held in January 1944 in a storefront on Mission Street in San Marino. The church formally organized in February, and it called the Reverend Charles W. Mayes to serve as pastor. Dwight Nichols, one of the twenty-two charter members, still belonged to the congregation more than forty years later.

In 1944 the Brethren bought a corner lot at Fremont Avenue and El Centro Street. On the property was a church building that dated back to 1887. Originally a wing of the Pasadena Presbyterian Church, the structure was moved to South Pasadena in 1907. Owned by Calvary Presbyterian Church until 1926, it later belonged to the Full Gospel Foundation, and then to a branch of Bethany Church of Alhambra. After the Brethren purchased the building, they dedicated it as the Fremont Avenue Brethren Church—a name changed in 1980 to Grace Brethren Church of South Pasadena. The oldest church building in the city, and the only one in Mission Revival style, Grace Brethren Church is a Cultural Heritage Landmark.

SOUTH PASADENA CHURCH OF JESUS CHRIST OF LATTER-DAY SAINTS

The Church of Jesus Christ of Latter-day Saints (Mormon) held its first services in South Pasadena in February 1950. Members gathered in the Fletcher Avenue church building they recently had bought from Oneonta Church. The two congregations shared facilities until October 1950, when Oneonta moved to its new sanctuary on the

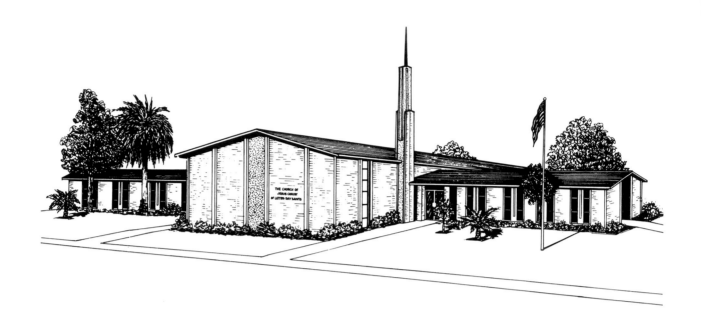

South Pasadena Church of Jesus Christ of Latter-day Saints. *Drawing by James Massey.*

Boothe estate. After taking full possession of their property, the Mormons renovated and remodeled the church building, and dedicated it in 1953.

The Church of Jesus Christ of Latter-day Saints has a lay ministry. Bishops are called to serve for various periods of time and come from all walks of life. The first bishop of El Sereno Ward, from which the South Pasadena Ward evolved, was Howard W. Hunter, a Los Angeles attorney. He now is a member of the Quorum of Twelve Apostles, among the presiding authorities of the Church of Jesus Christ of Latter-day Saints in Salt Lake City.

In 1969 Elder Hunter took part in the ground-breaking ceremonies for a new chapel for the South Pasadena Church of Jesus Christ of Latter-day Saints. One of the innovative features of the building, at 1919 Huntington Drive, is an interpretive sound system for translating sermons into foreign languages. The building also contains a cultural hall and classrooms.

Members of the church have long been active in the civic life of South Pasadena. An early contribution to the community was the organization of flag-raising ceremonies, which were held for many years before South Pasadena inaugurated an official Fourth of July celebration.

Pacific United Methodist Church

In the spring of 1978 an interdenominational group met in South Pasadena with Dr. Ha Tai Kim and formed the Korean Church of the Pacific. The congregation increased rapidly, and within a few months it organized a church school, adult Bible class, and community education programs. The church has sponsored a theological seminar for the Korean community and also has published two collections of essays written by the first pastor, Dr. Ha Tai Kim. A special concern of the church is the creation of spiritual, social, and cultural values that combine Korean tradition and American ideals in the best possible way. In 1983 the congregation adopted the new name of Pacific United Methodist Church. The following January it celebrated a charter service and installed the Reverend Moon Hee Nam as minister. The congregation meets for worship in the sanctuary of the United Methodist Church of South Pasadena.

South Pasadena Chinese Baptist Church

In July 1984 the Rev. Andrew Tsai held a Sunday worship service attended by ten adults and six children, the nucleus of the South Pasadena Chinese Baptist Church. On October 21, 1984, the Charter Service was held, with 166 people in the congregation. Pei-Shiun Chen, Charlton Lu, and Elaine Wong served on the first deacon board. The church belongs to the Conservative Baptist Association, and it holds its services in Grace Brethren Church.

South Pasadena's first church bell, cast in 1888, is mounted near the entrance to the United Methodist Church. *Photograph by Tom M. Apostol.*

CHRONOLOGY

1885

Margaret P. Dougherty organizes a Union Sunday School, forerunner of the Methodist Church in South Pasadena.

1886

The South Pasadena Methodist Episcopal Church organizes. On the board of the Ladies Aid Society are a Presbyterian, a Baptist, a Methodist, and a Universalist.

1887

The Methodists build on Center Street, just west of Fremont Avenue.

Presbyterians form an outdoor Sunday School class, forerunner of Calvary Presbyterian Church.

Episcopalians gather for worship in the college building on Columbia Hill.

1888

Baptists organize and meet for services in the new Opera House Building.

Calvary Presbyterian Church incorporates and builds a chapel at Columbia Street and Beacon Avenue.

1891

Memorial Baptist Church opens on Mission Street, between Fairview and Fremont avenues.

1897

A Nazarene church forms in South Pasadena.

1900

Swami Vivekananda, the first Indian spiritual leader to come to America, visits South Pasadena.

1902

The Episcopalians organize St. Andrew's Mission.

Calvary Presbyterian Church reorganizes.

1904

The Southern California and Arizona Holiness Association buys property in the Arroyo Seco for summer camp meetings.

1905

The Methodists move into their new church building at Center Street and Fairview Avenue.

The Bilicke mansion, on the grounds of the United Methodist Church of South Pasadena, is now used for the church offices, Sunday School, and day care center. A. C. Bilicke was part-owner of the Hotel Alexandria, at one time the most luxurious hotel in Los Angeles. *Photograph by Tom M. Apostol.*

1906

The Baptists move their church building to Diamond Avenue and Center Street.

The Episcopalians build at Fremont Avenue and Monterey Road.

The South Pasadena Christian Church organizes.

1907

The Episcopalians dedicate their new church, located at Fremont Avenue and Monterey Road. The church changes its name from St. Andrew's to St. James'.

Calvary Presbyterian Church moves into a building transported from Pasadena and reconstructed at Center Street and Fremont Avenue.

1909

South Pasadena Christian Church builds at Fremont Avenue and Lyndon Street.

1910

Memorial Baptist Church moves to a new church building at Diamond Avenue and El Centro Street.

Holy Family Catholic Church is established at El Centro Street and Fremont Avenue.

Elizabeth Bradshaw calls together a group of neighbors, who organize Oneonta Congregational Church.

1912

First Church of Christ, Scientist, organizes.

1922

Oneonta Congregational Church builds on Fletcher Avenue.

1923

The Christian Science Church builds at Oak Street and Fremont Avenue.

Holy Family Catholic Church moves to Fremont Avenue and Rollin Street.

1925

Calvary Presbyterian Church builds at Fremont Avenue and Oxley Street.

The Champions of Fundamentalism move into the church building formerly owned by the Presbyterians.

1926

The Full Gospel Foundation buys the church building at El Centro Street and Fremont Avenue formerly owned by the Presbyterians.

1928

Holy Family Catholic Church dedicates its new sanctuary at Rollin Street and Fremont Avenue.

South Pasadena Church of the Nazarenes organizes.

1935

Holy Family Catholic Church opens a parochial school.

1940

The Church of the Nazarene builds at El Centro Street and Palm Avenue.

1945

Fremont Avenue Brethren Church buys the old Presbyterian church building transported from Pasadena to South Pasadena in 1907.

1950

Oneonta Congregational Church builds at Oak Street and Garfield Avenue, on the old Boothe estate.

The Church of Jesus Christ of Latter-day Saints buys the old Oneonta church property.

1952

Memorial Baptist Church is renamed First Baptist Church.

The city churches form a United Prayer Fellowship, which inaugurates election-day prayer watches.

1962

South Pasadena Christian Church builds a new sanctuary at Fremont Avenue and Lyndon Street.

1967

The United Methodist Church completes its new sanctuary on Monterey Road, on the old Bilicke estate.

1970

The Church of Jesus Christ of Latter-day Saints dedicates its new church building at Huntington Drive and Milan Avenue.

1972

For its program of downtown revitalization, the city buys the Baptist Church property at Mound Avenue and El Centro Street. After eighty-four years in South Pasadena, First Baptist Church dissolves.

1978

The Korean Church of the Pacific organizes under the leadership of Dr. Ha Tai Kim.

1980

Fremont Avenue Brethren Church changes its name to Grace Brethren Church of South Pasadena.

1982

The Korean Church of the Pacific changes its name to Pacific United Methodist Church.

1984

South Pasadena Chinese Baptist Church organizes.

1985

Two churches celebrate their seventy-fifth anniversary: Holy Family Catholic Church and Oneonta Congregational Church.

The Vedanta Society of Southern California dedicates the Vivekananda House, 309 Monterey Road, as a shrine.

258

The Cathedral Oak Monument marks the site on the Arroyo Seco where, according to legend, Father Juan Crespí held Easter mass in 1770. *Photograph by Ralph Tillema; courtesy of South Pasadena Cultural Heritage Commission.*

T. D. Keith, husband of South Pasadena's first city librarian, photographed the laying of the library cornerstone on September 28, 1907. *Courtesy of South Pasadena Public Library.*

XIII

THE SOUTH PASADENA PUBLIC LIBRARY

The library was a challenge and a stimulation to many of us as we competed in trying to read all of the books on the shelves. We were fortunate to have peers with bookish tastes. Many of our careers were shaped by the library and our mutual interest in books.

WARD RITCHIE

"WHAT A HIGHLY EDUCATED LOT OF FARMERS YOU HAVE OUT HERE," a visitor to early Pasadena told Margaret Collier Graham. "Do they all talk so learnedly?"

Many of the first settlers in the Indiana Colony were indeed well educated, with a love of books and a delight in words. In 1876 they formed a literary society and put out a handwritten newspaper, *The Reservoir*, to which Jennie Collier and Margaret Collier Graham contributed. "That an undercurrent of genius *does* exist in this fertile ranch has been satisfactorily proved," said the first editor—or, as he called himself, the *zanjero* who tended the reservoir.

In June 1886, a few days after Pasadena incorporated as a city, its neighbors to the south launched their own Social and Literary Society. Leo Longley served as president, and O. R. Dougherty edited the club paper, the *South Pasadena Crescent*. Longley also became president of the South Pasadena Lyceum, which was founded on February 14, 1889, to open a free reading room and to circulate books and periodicals among local residents. In addition to Longley, the board included Margaret Collier Graham, vice-president; Bert Nettleton, secretary; Etta Longley, treasurer; and Jennie Collier, volunteer librarian.

Donald M. Graham gave the new library its first book, a copy of John Charles Frémont's *Memoirs of My Life*. On the flyleaf Graham wrote, "To see five thousand volumes in the South Pasadena Library on the shelves with this, its first book, is the earnest hope of the donor." Graham and his brother-in-law Richard J. Mohr provided rent-free space for the reading room in their brick building on Center Street, two blocks west of the present library. Fifty-six charter members paid one dollar each to purchase books and periodicals, and the old literary society contributed a few books and $7.70.

Margaret Collier Graham reported in June 1889 that attendance was much higher than expected—about twelve patrons in the evening, and sometimes twice that number. Most of the evening readers were young boys and men— "without exception quiet and gentlemanly." There were fewer daytime patrons. "It is hoped," said Mrs. Graham, "that the ladies of the community will discover that the Reading Room is a pleasant place in which to spend an hour."

Despite an auspicious beginning, the Lyceum soon was struggling to stay alive. Only nine people continued to pay dues after the first year, and annual contributions never exceeded twenty-five dollars. Benefit concerts and theatricals brought in a little

Margaret Collier Graham was widely acclaimed for her stories of Southern California. She helped establish a free reading room in South Pasadena in 1889, and was the first woman appointed to the city library board. *Courtesy South Pasadena Public Library.*

Jennie Collier served as volunteer librarian of the reading room and as the first president of the Woman's Improvement Association. *Courtesy of South Pasadena Public Library.*

extra money, but not enough to pay the lighting bills. By staying open afternoons only and by curtailing subscriptions, the board kept expenses down to $3.25 a month. Even so, the reading room ended 1893 with fifty cents on hand and bills of over thirty dollars.

In an impassioned plea to the community, Jennie Collier asked, "Shall the young men who have spent their evenings in the library when it was open be driven out upon the streets, and the many others who have read the 1,700 books and periodicals used during the past year be deprived of the pleasure and instruction derived therefrom?" She and her sister agreed to keep the reading room open, and Howard Longley offered to raise the necessary funds.

A number of people contributed books or money in 1894, but in 1895 the reading room was again in debt and its prospects were gloomy. At about that time, city attorney Don Carlos Porter discovered a law allowing a city to maintain a public library through taxation. Townspeople heartily endorsed the idea, and on September 10, 1895, the city council adopted Resolution 48 to establish a free public library and reading room and to create a public library fund.

The city council appointed as library trustees five men who had contributed to the old reading room: A. Moss Merwin, who became president of the board, Leo Longley, Howard Longley, Merton E. Keith, and John Wadsworth. At their first meeting the trustees voted to express regrets to Jennie Collier and Margaret Collier Graham "at the imperfection of the law in its present failure to recognize the propriety of ladies being eligible to membership on the board." In a few years the imperfection was mended, with Mrs. Graham appointed to the board in 1897, and Miss Collier in 1904.

Nellie E. Keith, the first city librarian (and mother of board member Merton Keith) was hired in October 1895 at a salary of $12.50 a month. The new library opened in the same Center Street building which had housed the Lyceum. From the old reading room it received 296 books, 40 volumes of unbound magazines, an American flag, and a portrait of Daniel Webster.

Within eight months Nellie Keith had added 424 books to the collection. Among the most popular were two by local authors: *The Land of Poco Tiempo* by Charles F. Lummis, and *Stories of the Foot-hills* by Margaret Collier Graham. By 1897 the library had over a thousand books, which Nellie Keith was cataloging by author and title. She had already prepared a booklet listing the library holdings. Published by John Sharp, South Pasadena's first newspaper editor, the booklet was financed by advertising and distributed free to patrons.

By 1902 the library owned about three thousand volumes and was in need of larger quarters. The trustees wrote philanthropist Andrew Carnegie requesting whatever sum he thought proper for a library building. They wrote once more without success, but in 1906 the Carnegie Corporation offered $10,000 for a building if the city gave the site and not less than $1,000 a year for maintenance. The city trustees promptly accepted the offer and purchased two lots at the southeast corner of Diamond Avenue and Center Street. South Pasadena architect Norman Foote Marsh designed the library, a six-room building with brick veneer and a domed skylight. Oak furnishings added $2,000 to the expected costs. Carnegie sent a check for the extra amount, and the city raised its annual contribution by $200.

The cornerstone was laid with fitting ceremony on September 28, 1907, and the library opened for business on February 17, 1908. When Carnegie visited South Pasadena in 1910, he expressed pleasure in the building and the care taken of it. Speaking at an informal reception he said, "I think some of you must have been putting a good part of your lives into the work." The library still owns the book he autographed on that occasion. In his *Problems of Today*, Carnegie wrote (with the simplified spelling he advocated), "Delited to find here in South Passedena Library one of my books." The book was in the library because Nellie Keith rushed out to buy it just before Carnegie's visit.

By 1916 the library had more than 14,000 volumes and again was running out of shelf space. The Carnegie Corporation gave $6,600 for an addition with stack rooms, a sunroom, and a basement auditorium. The addition opened on April 19, 1917, just two weeks after the United States declared war on Germany. The auditorium designed for the children's story hour now served as a meeting room for the Red Cross and the Council of Defense. Tastes in reading became more serious. Patrons checked out more non-fiction in June 1917 than ever before in the history of the library. When the community held mass meetings on home gardening, the library featured helpful books on the subject. When the Home Guard requested books on military drill, the library provided them.

In October 1918 the flu epidemic reached South Pasadena. As a precautionary measure, churches, schools, the library, and the one theater in town closed for eight weeks. They reopened early in December, one month after the Armistice was signed. That same week Jennie Collier died at Wynyate. For six years she had kept the Free Reading Room open, and for fourteen years she served as a trustee of the public library. She was also a founding member and the first president of the Woman's Improvement Association. According to an obituary for Jennie Collier, "Not a single resident of the city is not indebted to her in many little ways."

Visitors to the library enjoyed its comfortable atmosphere: the rocking chairs in the reading room and the fire in the fireplace on wintry days. One patron even composed a poem which declared, "The library seems to say howdy to me." Children received their own comfortable room in 1926. Japanese lanterns shaded the electric lights, and bright cretonne curtains hung at the windows. There were more than three thousand books on the shelves; and for the youngest readers, staff members had put together more than forty scrapbooks.

By 1930 the library had again outgrown its quarters. Library Park now covered the entire block bounded by Diamond, Fairview, Oxley, and El Centro. The trustees decided to move the building from its corner location to the center of the park and to double its floor space. Norman Foote Marsh, who had designed the first building, worked with his partners, D. D. Smith and Herbert J. Powell, on the remodeling. "Southern California architecture in the late twenties was showing a strong Spanish and Italian influence," Powell remarked fifty years later, "and it was therefore not a surprise that the library would take on a Lombard Italian flavor."

For the library's exterior, sculptor Merrell Gage made six stone panels representing literature of the past, and for the entrance to the children's room he made sculptures of a Spanish galleon and of St. George and the dragon. A frieze along the top of the

264

Nellie Keith was South Pasadena City Librarian from 1895 until the end of 1930. She was deeply admired for her sympathy and understanding. *Courtesy of South Pasadena Public Library.*

Nellie Keith is standing behind the circulation desk. An atrium in the rebuilt library has replaced the old rotunda shown here. *Courtesy of South Pasadena Public Library.*

building displays the names of writers who have contributed to California literature.

Upon completion of the remodeling, Nellie Keith retired as city librarian. Her service spanned thirty-five years, dating back to October 1895, when the library opened in one room of the Graham and Mohr Building. Georgia A. Diehl, who succeeded Nellie Keith, guided the library through the years of the Great Depression and of World War II. People were especially grateful during the Depression for the free resources of the library. Art lovers came for exhibits and talks in the new Art Room. Children came for story hours and other special programs. Many people who were unemployed came in almost daily to read magazines and newspapers and consult books which might help them find a job. The librarian noticed an increase in serious reading, with many requests for books on politics and economics.

Georgia Diehl suggested two reasons for a slight drop in circulation in 1935. Many patrons wanted only popular fiction, but the library could not afford to buy every best seller. Other patrons, she said, had been "temporary readers because of unemployment and enforced leisure." Some of these people were now back at work, and others were "read up and fed up." The latter, she said with sad eloquence, "are tired of reading to forget, to prepare for the job that could not be found, or to seek inspiration that would not come." By 1936 both circulation and registration had increased, and by 1940 almost every reader in town had a library card.

During World War II the library hung blackout curtains at the windows, turned the Art Room over to the ration board, and proceeded with its regular activities. In response to readers' interests and needs, the library bought many books on the war and related topics, from aeronautics to victory gardens. It also purchased books for armchair travelers, kept at home by the shortage of gasoline and rubber, and it bought light fiction "to relieve nerves that are taut because of uneasy days of world turmoil." To help patrons conserve gasoline, the library carried books for young people to the summer Victory Camps organized by the recreation commission, and it established book deposits in the schools.

Georgia Diehl retired as librarian in 1946. Not only had she greatly expanded the library's holdings, but she had helped arrange for reciprocal borrowing privileges with the Los Angeles and Alhambra libraries. One of her first acts as city librarian was to hire a trained cataloger. She also adopted a new registration system, "strictly alphabetical and impersonal." Previously the library had registered cardholders in two books, assigning even numbers to the ladies and odd numbers to the gentlemen.

During her sixteen years with the library, Georgia Diehl built up the children's collection and introduced library appreciation hours for students in grades three to six. She also created a separate room for young adults and had high school students decorate it with murals of local landmarks such as the Raymond Hotel, the Raymond waiting station, and the Santa Fe depot. In October 1946 the library dedicated the new reading room as the Georgia A. Diehl Room for Young People and presented Miss Diehl with an etching by South Pasadena artist Mildred Bryant Brooks. Bookplates made from the etching were placed in volumes in the young people's room.

Miss Diehl's successor, Mary Murdoch, had joined the staff in 1931 as the library's first professional cataloger. She reclassified more than twenty-four thousand books in the original collection, replaced the handwritten cards, and added thousands of sub-

The
South Pasadena
Public Library

ject headings to the catalog. As head librarian, Mary Murdoch added several outreach programs, such as mailing books to shut-ins and lending books, a hundred at a time, to a local sanitarium. For bilingual residents—who included war brides and visiting refugees—she borrowed three hundred foreign language books from the Los Angeles Public Library. Books in Spanish and German proved most popular, followed by books in Russian. She also set aside a room with technical books and magazines of interest to people working in the growing number of engineering and electronic companies in South Pasadena. For the convenience of parents, the library organized a section with books and magazines on child care. "In South Pasadena, which is chiefly a residential community," Mary Murdoch said, "books on family relations deserve to be emphasized." The library even provided a stroller to hold a child while its parent browsed.

In 1947 the library sponsored the charter meeting of the first Golden Age Club on the West Coast. The Book Review Club, the Rocket Club, a Great Books Seminar, and the League of Women Voters also met regularly at the library. In addition there were special events such as the Home Town Party given by the library in 1948 to honor local author and journalist Ed Ainsworth on the publication of his most recent book, *California Jubilee*. In later years Ainsworth won the title "Boswell of the Boondocks" for a feature column in the *Los Angeles Times* on the hill towns and desert byways of Southern California.

Over the years, patrons occasionally have demanded that the library censor books in the collection. Mary Murdoch once explained, "Book selection in South Pasadena is a cooperative effort in which seven professional librarians participate. The final decision is, of course, the city librarian's who administers under policy set down by the library board. South Pasadena is fortunate to have a board of trustees made up of library users and discriminating readers who believe adults should have free access to all points of view in books."

Recognizing the importance of a library support group, Mary Murdoch encouraged formation of the Friends of the South Pasadena Public Library. The group formally organized in March 1950 and elected Georgia Diehl as president. The Friends' first guest speaker was Lawrence Clark Powell, Chief Librarian of UCLA and Director of the William Andrews Clark Memorial Library. Reminiscing about his boyhood in South Pasadena, Powell paid tribute to the library and praised the sympathy and understanding of City Librarian Nellie Keith. "Mrs. Keith did not take rules too seriously," he recalled, "and I believe that is one reason I am a librarian today." He told the audience he used to bicycle to the library—an uphill ride from his home on Marengo Avenue—so he wanted to take out more than three or four books at a time. "Mrs. Keith in her benevolence said I could take out as many books as I could carry. She did not count on the resourcefulness of youth. My bike was equipped with a little wire basket, my brother had an old army knapsack, I borrowed Mother's string shopping bag, and I got one of those old starch boxes for the back of the bike. One night I took home close to fifty books. I recall Mrs. Keith asking me if I thought I could handle all those books, and I said of course, if she would help me on. Darned if she didn't, too!"

Over the years the Friends have enriched the library with an impressive number of books, prints, and records; they have donated equipment ranging from bicycle racks

"The reading room at this library is said to be one of the coolest spots in the city," Nellie Keith reported in 1919, "and it is a popular place for persons who have a little time they can devote to reading the current magazines." *Courtesy of South Pasadena Public Library*.

The reading room added to the library in 1930 now serves as a community room. The library still uses the oak tables and chairs seen in the photograph. *Courtesy of South Pasadena Public Library.*

to a machine that reads and prints microfilm and microfiche; and they have sponsored lectures, films, concerts and other special programs for the community, including a Japanese Day, a Chinese Culture Day, and a Festival of India. One of the earliest gifts from the Friends is still the most admired: the paintings in the children's department done by Leo Politi, whose picture book *Song of the Swallows* won a Caldecott Award in 1949.

From 1963 to 1980 the Friends raised money at a book fair held each May on the library lawn. A festive community event, the sale inspired such headlines as "Bibliophiles Brimming With Brio Brace to Beset Book Fair," and "Roving Bands of Literates Plan to Descend on Book Fair Saturday." One popular feature was an auction ("something for nodding") conducted by literary scholar Paul Zall and antiquarian bookseller Glen Dawson. The Friends had to give up the book fair after 1980, when the library was rebuilt, because the basement in which they had accumulated about twenty thousand books a year no longer existed. The Friends opened a bookstore within the library, and there they sell donated books year-round.

Madeline Hensley, the fourth City Librarian, served from 1967 to 1972. Under her leadership, the library continued its involvement in the community. One outreach program was the delivery of books to the aged and ill in four local rest homes. The library also arranged orientation classes for junior high school students and sponsored a work-experience program for high school students.

When the South Pasadena Lyceum opened a free reading room in 1889, Jennie Collier acted as volunteer librarian, and she and her sister, Margaret Collier Graham, served on the board. Eighty-three years later their grandniece, Mary Helen Collier Wayne, was appointed City Librarian. Organization and expansion of the library's local history collection owes much to Mary Helen Wayne. As coauthor of *We Three Came West*, based on letters of her two great-aunts and of her great-uncle Donald Graham (South Pasadena's first mayor), she brought to the library a special appreciation of the need to preserve documents and photographs for historic research.

By 1975 the library was obviously too small to care for a population which had increased by nine thousand since 1930, when the building was last enlarged. According to one news story, "a voracious, well-educated reading public" borrowed 260,000 books in 1975, and in one week 4,000 people went through the main door of the library. Shelf space, storage space, and seating space were all inadequate.

Fortunately, Los Angeles County decided in 1976 that the South Pasadena Community Redevelopment Agency could impound tax increments from Altos de Monterey to finance construction of public facilities—among them a remodeled or rebuilt library. The library board thought the community would be served best by a new building in a new location, but the city council advocated renovation and expansion of the existing structure.

Rebuilding the library, which was declared a Cultural Heritage Landmark in 1972, called for a sensitive design to preserve as much as possible of the original structure and to integrate the new building with the old. The firm chosen to do the work— Powell, Morgridge, Richards & Coghlan—had historic ties with the library. Norman Foote Marsh designed the six-room building that opened in Library Park in 1908. His firm—by then Marsh, Smith & Powell—designed the additions made in 1930, and

Herbert Powell served as consultant for the remodeling begun in 1981. Powell was semiretired at the time, and his partner Howard Morgridge served as liaison with the library and as principal architect of the building.

South Pasadena architect Raymond Girvigian worked with Morgridge as a cultural heritage consultant. He was especially concerned about preserving the library facade, the loggias, and the Merrell Gage sculptures. In 1982— coincidentally, the same year the library was finished—the California Historical Society honored Girvigian for twenty-five years of civic and professional work to save and restore landmarks, including the State Capitol in Sacramento. In 1985 he became chairman of the State Historical Advisory Board.

Mary Helen Wayne retired as city librarian in June 1978. Plans for remodeling the library were now well under way, and tribute was paid to her skillful direction of the building program. The library board also praised her for expanding services to the community and for developing an unusually effective staff.

Jean Jones, the new city librarian, faced two contradictory challenges: guiding the building program to a successful conclusion, and at the same time adapting to severe budget cuts. California voters had just passed Proposition 13, which sharply reduced property taxes. The resulting loss in local tax revenues had a devastating effect on the library. The staff was reduced from twenty-six employees to nine, of whom only five were full-time, and the number of professional librarians went from eight to three. "The most unkindest cut of all," said one scholarly patron when the library reduced the time it was open from fifty-eight hours a week to a mere nineteen. Sixteen hundred people signed a petition asking the city council to increase the library budget. Calling the cuts totally unacceptable, patrons rallied to the defense of the library. In the words of one aroused citizen, "To maintain our public library is essential if we want to continue the quality of life we have been known for."

The city has since increased the budget, though not to its former level. The financial support of the Friends makes possible special services and programs the library could not otherwise afford. In addition, volunteer workers perform myriad tasks, from mending books to taking inventory, and give an overburdened staff more time for such specialized work as answering reference questions.

In January 1981, after five years of discussion and debate, the work of rebuilding the library finally began. During the sixteen months of construction, the library served its patrons from temporary quarters. Office work was carried on in two primary units of the old El Centro School— buildings that lacked even such amenities as indoor plumbing. The children's department moved into a trailer on the old school grounds, and other departments moved into what had been the El Centro auditorium.

Volunteers spent more than 1,100 hours packing and unpacking more than 85,000 books for the move across the street, or into storage, then back to the new library when it was completed. At the time of the two moves, the Friends of the Library sold items no longer needed by the library—such as old shelving, prints, and adding machines—and raised about $17,000 for new furniture and supplies.

South Pasadenans held the old library building in affectionate regard; so they were pleased to learn that much of the exterior would be preserved, and that arches, columns, and finials copied from the old structure would be repeated in the new.

In 1981 work began on rebuilding and enlarging the library. *Courtesy of South Pasadena Public Library.*

Preparing for the reopening of the library in 1982, Leo Politi retouches murals he painted for the children's department in 1957. *Photograph by Cassy Cohen.*

Patrons were especially happy that what had been the main reading room, with its handsome vaulted ceiling and painted beams, would be kept for use as a community room.

A two-story atrium has replaced the old rotunda, but the framework of the old skylight is still in use. It now holds a stained-glass inset whose colorful design suggests an orange tree. Some of the old library furniture also continues in use. The Friends raised money to repair and refinish the library's oak tables and chairs—most of them half a century old, and a few dating back to 1908. Local craftsman Brad Bryce transformed the venerable circulation desk, using the oak to build exhibition cases.

The new building contains 24,500 square feet and is almost six times larger than the original Carnegie library. Construction was financed by $1.9 million in CRA tax increments. New furniture and equipment were paid for with money raised in the community by the Friends of the Library. The Friends also appealed for contributions to pay for the skylight and the stained-glass panels at the library entrance. The two fund-raising drives, and two moving day sales sponsored by the Friends, brought in more than $55,000. The Rotary Club raised another $6,000 to benefit the children's department and to provide comfortable chairs in the reading area.

Through all the planning for the new library, Henry J. ("Duke") Wheeler was president of the library board. He spearheaded the drive for a new library, served as liaison with the city council, and inspired the fund-raising efforts of the Rotary Club. Librarian Jean Jones has said, "I don't think the library would be standing today if it weren't for Duke Wheeler."

More than two thousand people toured the new library on July 31, 1982, and enjoyed festivities that ranged from mime and rhyme to Dixieland jazz. One special guest was Leo Politi, who autographed copies of his books. For months Politi had been a kind of artist-in-residence at the library, adding color and a few lively creatures to the paintings he had made for the children's department in 1957.

The library's new display cases held two exhibits—one with photographs tracing the history of the library, the other with memorabilia of the Cawston Ostrich Farm. The ostrich has become an unofficial mascot of the library. It appears on the tote bags sold by the Friends and also on receipts given in the bookstore. A Steiff ostrich, seven feet tall, stands in the children's department, which held a name-the-ostrich contest during the opening day festivities. Two youngsters tied for first place with their prize-winning suggestion of Awston the Ostrich.

For more than a century South Pasadenans have demonstrated their interest in books and their support of libraries. In 1886 townspeople organized a club "to bring old and young together in social communion and for improvement in literary and musical lines." In the same month that South Pasadenans voted to incorporate, they discussed the need for a library, calling it a source of knowledge and pleasure. Dedicated booklovers opened a reading room and lending library in 1889 and maintained it for six years with volunteer help and voluntary contributions. When these proved insufficient, South Pasadenans took the extraordinary step of asking the city to raise their taxes and finance a public library. Since its beginning in 1895, the South Pasadena Public Library has grown from one room and a collection of a few hundred books to what has been called the city's proudest institution, a focal point of culture, art, and education.

In 1982 South Pasadena dedicated its new public library. *Photograph by Larry Frost; courtesy of Morgridge & Associates.*

CHRONOLOGY

1886

South Pasadenans organize a Social and Literary Society, with Leo Longley as president and O. R. Dougherty as editor of its paper, the *South Pasadena Crescent*.

1889

The South Pasadena Lyceum is founded and opens a free reading room. Leo Longley serves as president, Margaret Collier Graham as vice-president, and Jennie Collier as volunteer librarian.

1895

On September 10 the city council adopts Resolution 48 establishing a free public library and reading room. Nellie Keith is appointed first city librarian, and the library opens on November 4 in one room of the Graham and Mohr Building on Center Street.

1897

John Sharp publishes a brief history of the library and a catalog of the 720 bound books on the shelves.

1906

The Carnegie Corporation gives the city $10,000 for a library building, and the city provides a site at Diamond Avenue and Center Street.

1907

Architect Norman Foote Marsh designs a six-room library building, and the cornerstone is laid on September 28.

1908

South Pasadena's Carnegie Library opens on February 17 at the northwest corner of Library Park.

1910

Andrew Carnegie visits the library and expresses pleasure in the building.

1917

The Carnegie Corporation gives six thousand dollars for an addition to the library. During World War I, the new auditorium becomes a meeting room for the Red Cross and the Council of Defense.

1918

A flu epidemic closes the library and other public buildings for eight weeks between October and December.

1926

The library opens a children's room with more than three thousand books on the shelves.

The library has always been a popular background for photographs. It is shown here before the building was moved to the center of the property in 1930. *Photograph by H. J. Kenny; courtesy of Huntington Library.*

1930

The library is moved to the center of Library Park, remodeled, and enlarged.

Nellie Keith retires after thirty-five years as city librarian and is succeeded by Georgia A. Diehl.

1933

During the Great Depression, people who have not used the library before discover its resources.

Grants from the WPA and other relief agencies enable the library to hire extra workers in the years between 1933 and 1939.

1942

The library coordinates the local Victory Book Campaign to gather books for people in the service.

1943

To help patrons conserve gasoline, the library delivers books to neighborhood centers.

1944

Libraries in South Pasadena, Alhambra, and Los Angeles agree to reciprocal borrowing privileges.

1945

The library celebrates its fiftieth year as a tax-supported institution.

1946

Mary Murdoch succeeds Georgia A. Diehl as city librarian. The library dedicates the Georgia A. Diehl Room for Young People.

1947

The library sponsors the first Golden Age Club on the West Coast.

1950

The Friends of the South Pasadena Public Library organizes and elects Georgia A. Diehl as president.

1963

The Friends hold their first annual book sale to benefit the library.

1965

South Pasadena becomes one of five charter members in the San Gabriel Valley Library System, forerunner of the Metropolitan Cooperative Library System.

1967

Madeline Hensley succeeds Mary Murdoch as city librarian.

1970

The library wins a publicity award from the American Library Association "for an excellent presentation of a small library's energetic and imaginative program to involve all segments of the community."

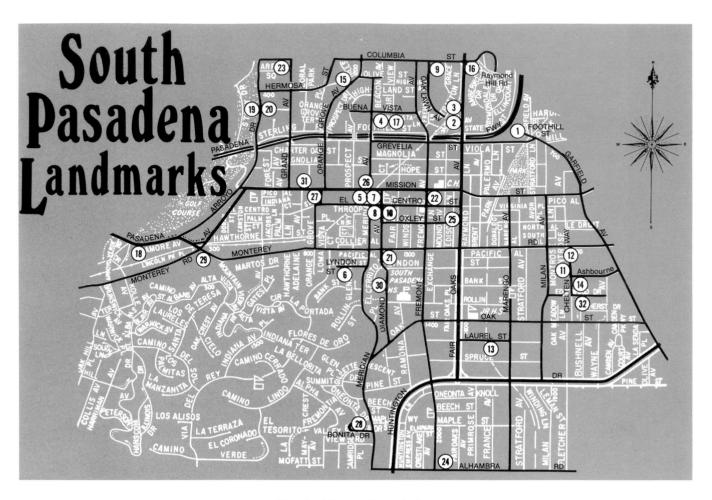

Map by Miriam Campbell.

1. Adobe Flores
2. Oaklawn Bridge and Waiting Station
3. War Memorial Building
4. Garfield House
5. Meridian Iron Works
6. Wynyate
7. Watering Trough and Wayside Station
8. South Pasadena Bank Building
9. Oaklawn Portals
10. South Pasadena Public Library
11. Miltimore House
12. Chelten Way and Ashbourne Drive
13. Clokey Oak
14. Ashbourne-Chelten Oak
15. Porter House
16. Raymond Hill Waiting Station

17. Howard Longley House
18. Cawston Ostrich Farm Site
19. Cathedral Oak Monument
20. Garfias Adobe Site
21. Leo Longley House
22. Grace Brethren Church
23. Tanner-Behr House
24. Morrison House
25. Rialto Theatre
26. Mission Hotel
27. Baranger Studios
28. Grokowsky House
29. Vivekananda House
30. School Administration Building
31. Lewis-Markey Building
32. Eddie House and Memorial Park

XIV

SOUTH PASADENA CULTURAL HERITAGE LANDMARKS

1. THE ADOBE FLORES, 1804 Foothill Street. Private residence.

The oldest building in South Pasadena, the adobe was built around 1845 by Manuel Garfias, who two years earlier had received a grant to Rancho San Pasqual. For one night in 1847 the adobe served as headquarters of the Mexican general José María Flores. When Clara Eliot Noyes bought the house in 1919, she named it Adobe Flores in honor of the general. The adobe is on the National Register of Historic Places.

2. OAKLAWN BRIDGE AND WAITING STATION, corner of Fair Oaks and Oaklawn avenues.

A bridge spanning two railways was built in 1906 from the Oaklawn tract to Fair Oaks Avenue. At the same time a waiting station, which also served Oaklawn residents, was built on Fair Oaks near a Pacific Electric trolley stop. Arroyo boulders form the base of the shelter, and projecting beams support the tile roof. Charles and Henry Greene designed the waiting station and the reinforced concrete bridge. Both structures are on the National Register of Historic Places. The pylon at the east end of the bridge (the only bridge the Greenes ever designed) is an official survey marker for the San Bernardino Base Line.

3. WAR MEMORIAL BUILDING, 435 Fair Oaks Avenue.

Norman Foote Marsh designed this building in 1921, both as a war memorial and as a meeting hall for American Legion Post No. 140. Marshal Ferdinand Foch laid the cornerstone of the building, and General John J. Pershing planted a redwood on the grounds. A collection of posters from World War I is displayed in the large meeting room.

4. GARFIELD HOUSE, 1001 Buena Vista Street. Private residence.

In 1904 Charles and Henry Greene designed a Craftsman bungalow for Lucretia Garfield, the widow of President James A. Garfield. The house is a two-story gabled structure—a form writers have compared to the Swiss chalet. "The reason why the beams project from the gables," Charles Greene told Mrs. Garfield, "is because they cast such beautiful shadows on the sides of the house in this bright atmosphere." The Garfield House is on the National Register of Historic Places.

The Oaklawn Portals mark the entrance to a tract whose homes are noted for their architecture. *Photograph by Tom M. Apostol.*

5. MERIDIAN IRON WORKS, 913 Meridian Avenue.

This simple redwood structure is the oldest commercial building in South Pasadena. Opened around 1887 as a grocery store, it has served also as ticket office, telegraph station, bicycle shop, chapel, and foundry. The city now owns the building, which is used as a historical museum.

6. WYNYATE, 851 Lyndon Street. Private residence.

A three-story redwood mansion in Queen Anne style, Wynyate is a splendid symbol of the boom of the eighties. The house was built in 1887 by Donald M. Graham (South Pasadena's first mayor) and his wife, author Margaret Collier Graham (the first South Pasadenan to be listed in *Who's Who in America*). John Muir planted the lemon eucalyptus that still flourishes on the grounds. Wynyate is on the National Register of Historic Places.

7. WATERING TROUGH AND WAYSIDE STATION, Meridian Avenue between Mission and El Centro streets.

Located near the busy center of town, the wayside station was a pleasant stopping place for people driving carriages and wagons between Los Angeles and Pasadena. Norman Foote Marsh designed the boulder structure, commissioned by the Woman's Improvement Association as a gift to the city, and erected in 1906.

8. SOUTH PASADENA BANK BUILDING, 1019 El Centro Street.

Erected in 1904, this was the second brick building in the city, and the first bank. The city had its offices in the building from 1908 to 1914. The old bank now is used for studios and offices.

9. OAKLAWN PORTALS, Oaklawn Avenue and Columbia Street.

Wrought-iron gates, with Arroyo boulder piers and a roof of Ludovici green tile, mark the entrance to Oaklawn. Charles and Henry Greene, who designed the portals in 1905, also designed the stone and redwood fence that partially encloses the tract. The portals and original fence are on the National Register of Historic Places.

10. SOUTH PASADENA PUBLIC LIBRARY, 1115 El Centro Street (Community Room entrance).

South Pasadena's Carnegie library, designed in 1908 by Norman Foote Marsh, was remodeled and enlarged in 1930 by Marsh, Smith & Powell. For the exterior, sculptor Merrell Gage made six stone panels representing literature of the past. A frieze along the top of the building displays the names of writers who have contributed to California literature. The building was again enlarged and remodeled in 1982, at which time the architects were Powell, Morgridge, Richards & Coghlan. The new library, which is entered at 1100 Oxley Street, has preserved the 1930 facade and the beamed and vaulted room that used to be the main reading room.

South Pasadena Cultural Heritage Landmarks

285

11. MILTIMORE HOUSE, Chelten Way. Private residence.

Architect Irving Gill designed this two-story cubic-form house in 1911 for Mrs. Paul Miltimore. Gill's plans included what he liked to call a green room—in this case a wistaria-covered pergola. The major surviving example in Southern California of Gill's residential work, the Miltimore house is on the National Register of Historic Places.

12. CHELTEN WAY AND ASHBOURNE DRIVE.

Caroline and Richard J. Dobbins visited the Raymond Hotel in 1886 and looked out on an oak-covered parcel where they decided to build a home. When Caroline Dobbins subdivided the property in 1907, she left most of the old oaks standing. A few still grow in the middle of Chelten Way and Ashbourne Drive, two private streets in the Ellerslie Park tract.

13. CLOKEY OAK (*Quercus lobata x engelmannii*), 1635 Laurel Street. Private property.

There are a number of rare hybrid oaks in South Pasadena—a cross between the evergreen Engelmann Oak and the deciduous Valley Oak. This specimen was named for Ira W. Clokey, a specialist in plant studies, who once lived at the Laurel Street address. His collection of 1,100 books and his extensive herbarium form the nucleus of the Clokey Botanical Library at Caltech.

14. ASHBOURNE-CHELTEN HYBRID OAK TREE

This handsome old oak survived until 1981, when it became diseased and had to be removed.

15. ANDREW O. PORTER HOUSE, 215 Orange Grove Avenue. Private residence.

In 1874 Andrew O. Porter selected a homesite south of Columbia Street at what was then the south end of Orange Grove Avenue. He planted an orchard, and in 1875—at a cost of $3,000—he built a frame cottage with filigree decoration. When Orange Grove Avenue was extended, the Porter house was moved a short distance to its present location.

16. RAYMOND HILL WAITING STATION, Fair Oaks Avenue and Raymond Hill Road.

Soon after the Pacific Electric began trolley car service through South Pasadena, the Raymond Hotel built a waiting station for guests who rode the Big Red Cars. The shelter is a cobblestone structure with shingled roof. Built in 1903, it was restored in 1978.

17. HOWARD LONGLEY HOUSE, 1005 Buena Vista Street. Private residence.

One of the oldest Greene and Greene houses still standing was designed in 1897 for Howard Longley, then mayor of South Pasadena. Eclectic in style, the house shows an Oriental influence in roof line and finials. The Longley house—now owned by the California Department of Transportation—is on the National Register of Historic Places.

The Miltimore House exemplifies architect Irving Gill's credo that "we should build our house simple, plain and substantial as a boulder, then leave the ornamentation of it to Nature." *Photograph by Robert E. Tryon.*

A motorcade pauses by the Cawston Ostrich Farm around 1904. This view is looking north on Sycamore Avenue toward the Arroyo Seco. *Courtesy of South Pasadena Public Library.*

The Tanner-Behr House, wrote a contemporary critic, reproduces the restrained charm of the Italian villa of the better class. *Photograph by Ralph Tillema; courtesy of South Pasadena Cultural Heritage Commission.*

18. Cawston Ostrich Farm Site.

South Pasadena's most famous tourist attraction opened in 1896 on a plot bounded by Sycamore Avenue, Pasadena Avenue, and the Santa Fe railroad tracks. The ostrich farm prospered for a quarter of a century; then its fortunes gradually declined. In 1934 it was sold at auction to satisfy a tax claim, and in 1935 it closed.

19. Cathedral Oak Monument, Arroyo Drive south of Hermosa Street.

According to legend, Father Juan Crespí held Easter mass in 1770 beneath a magnificent old oak on the west bank of the Arroyo. A simple cross set in a foundation of Arroyo boulders marks the site of the Cathedral Oak. Landscape architect Ruth Shellhorn Keeser designed the monument, which was commissioned in 1952 by the Oneonta Park Chapter of the Daughters of the American Revolution.

20. Manuel Garfias Adobe Site, 424-430 Arroyo Drive. Private property.

In 1852 Manuel Garfias built an imposing ranch house just east of the Cathedral Oak and near a spring in the Arroyo. Only a few sycamores and peppers, which may be offshoots of earlier trees, suggest the site of the old adobe, which by 1880 had crumbled into ruins.

21. Leo and Ada J. Longley House, 1103 Monterey Road. Private residence.

In 1888 Ada and Leo Longley built a two-story frame house that is notable for its many Carpenter Gothic details. Both the Woman Suffrage Committee for South Pasadena (1896) and the Woman's Improvement Association (1899) were organized in the Longley House.

22. Grace Brethren Church, 920 Fremont Avenue.

This building originally was part of the Pasadena Presbyterian church, a massive Victorian structure built in 1887. The Sunday School wing of the Pasadena church was moved to South Pasadena in 1907, reconstructed, and given a Mission Revival facade. Although extensively remodeled, the church retains its art-glass windows and the old pews with ornamental wood carving.

23. Tanner-Behr House, 225 Grand Avenue. Private residence.

Reginald D. Johnson designed this stucco mansion in 1916 as a winter home for Dr. John S. Tanner of Chicago. A Florentine palazzo served as inspiration for the house. A subsequent owner named it Villa Arno—a reference to Italy, as well as to her husband, Arno Behr.

24. Lloyd E. Morrison House, 1414 Alhambra Road. Private residence.

Architects Charles and Henry Greene formally dissolved their partnership in 1922, after Charles moved to Carmel. Henry Greene continued to practice in Southern California, and in 1925 he designed a small frame cottage for engineer Lloyd E. Morrison. The house has been considerably altered, but it preserves such Craftsman touches as carved beams on the porch and under the eaves.

This building was erected in 1904 as South Pasadena's first bank. The little shop at the right once served as a chapel. *Photograph by H. J. Kenny; courtesy of Huntington Library.*

Thornton Fitzhugh designed this two-story brick building in 1908 for A. R. Graham. It is located on Mission Street, in South Pasadena's Historic Business District. *Photograph by H. J. Kenny; courtesy of Huntington Library.*

25. RIALTO THEATRE, 1019 Fair Oaks Avenue.

L. A. Smith, who designed the Rialto in 1925, was the architect for some fifteen other theaters in the Los Angeles area at about the same time. The original facade of the Rialto has been altered, but the interior is essentially unchanged, and the theater has an intact scenery loft. The Rialto is on the National Register of Historic Places.

26. MISSION HOTEL, 950-966 Mission Street.

The Mission Hotel opened in 1923 in a two-story brick building planned for shops on the first floor, lodgings on the second. It advertised "New, modern, all outside rooms. Near streetcars and restaurants. Rate $6 to $7 per week." The old hotel building is in South Pasadena's Historic Business District.

27. BARANGER STUDIOS, 729 Mission Street.

G. A. Howard designed the Baranger Studios in 1925. The building has a firebrick exterior, leaded glass windows, turreted roof, and cast-stone Gothic detailing. For many years the studios housed the business of A. E. Baranger and Hazel June Baranger, who designed and built animated window displays.

28. GROKOWSKY HOUSE, 816 Bonita Drive. Private residence.

The California Department of Transportation owns the stucco house that Rudolph Schindler designed in 1928 for David N. Grokowsky. The house is representative of Schindler's de Stijl period, and is the only example of his work in South Pasadena.

29. VIVEKANANDA HOUSE, 309 Monterey Road. Private residence.

This Victorian cottage has cross-gable roof, ornamental stickwork, and sunburst designs. Historians believe the house was built in the 1880s for John P. Early, one of the first mayors of South Pasadena. Swami Vivekananda, founder of India's largest monastic order, was a guest at the cottage in 1900. The Vedanta Society of Southern California acquired the house in 1955 and dedicated it as a shrine in 1985.

30. SCHOOL ADMINISTRATION BUILDING, 1327 Diamond Avenue.

The Georgian-style building designed by Norman Foote Marsh in 1925 was taken down in 1984. The paneling and wooden benches were saved for use in the new administration center on El Centro Street.

31. LEWIS-MARKEY BUILDING, 634-636 Mission Street.

In 1928 Anna and Ormand Lewis built a shop whose English Gothic architecture was an appropriate setting for their antique business. The building has arched mullioned windows and a clinker brick exterior. The present owner, Thomas Markey, has restored the building and added a patio garden.

South Pasadena Cultural Heritage Landmarks

32. Eddie House and Eddie Memorial Park, 2017 Edgewood Drive.

In 1910 Arthur C. Eddie built a Greek Revival house on an oak-studded estate at Chelten Way and Edgewood Drive. His daughter, Ellen Mary Eddie, left the estate to the city in 1934 in memory of her family. The house and park serve as a meeting place for many groups in the community.

South Pasadena Historic Business District.

Most of the city's old commercial buildings are on Mission Street, between Fairview Avenue and a point just west of the Santa Fe tracks. These buildings date from 1906 to 1924 and are still in use today. Also located in the Historic Business District are the old El Centro School and five structures individually designated as landmarks: the Meridian Iron Works, the South Pasadena Bank building, the Mission Hotel, the watering trough and wayside station, and the public library. The Historic Business District is on the National Register of Historic Places.

The Vivekananda House is both a Cultural Heritage Landmark and a Vedanta shrine. *Photograph by Tom M. Apostol*

292

The Woman's Improvement Association raised the money (more than three hundred dollars) to build a drinking fountain and watering trough on Meridian Avenue. *Courtesy of South Pasadena Public Library.*

Donald M. Graham was the first mayor of South Pasadena. He was also one of the subdividers of Rancho La Laguna, which was renamed Elsinore at his wife's suggestion. *Courtesy of Huntington Library.*

MAYORS OF SOUTH PASADENA

South Pasadena has a five-member city council responsible for setting policy and passing legislation. A city manager, appointed by the council, is responsible for administration. Council members are elected at large, on a non-partisan basis, for overlapping terms of four years. One council member serves as mayor, or presiding officer.

1888-1889	Donald M. Graham	1940-1943	Andrew O. Porter
1889-1890	George W. Wilson	1943-1944	Edward C. Petersen
1890-1892	Leo A. Longley	1944-1946	Charles F. Hutchins
1892-1893	Edward Gardner	1946-1948	Walter A. Garmshausen
1893-1894	John P. Early	1948-1950	Edward C. Petersen
1894-1898	Frank Howard Longley	1950-1956	Joseph C. Partsch
1898-1900	George W. Wilson	1956-1960	Roy L. Anderson
1900-1902	Samuel M. Woodbridge	1960-1964	Joseph C. Partsch
1902-1904	Ernest H. Lockwood	1964-1966	Burton E. Jones
1904-1905	Joseph B. Soper	1966-1968	Lila Cox
1905-1906	Orin W. Orcutt	1968-1972	William C. Harker
1906-1908	Richard W. Pridham	1972-1974	John L. Sullivan
1909 Jan.-May	Charles N. Taylor	1974-1976	Fletcher H. Swan
1909 May-Sept.	Jonathan S. Dodge	1976-1977	William C. Harker
		1977-1978	AlvaLee Arnold
1909-1910	Charles B. Boothe	1978-1979	Fletcher H. Swan
1910-1912	George W. Adams	1979-1980	Ted R. Shaw
1912-1915	Ernest V. Sutton	1980-1981	Michael B. Montgomery
1915-1916	Warren N. Carter	1981-1982	Samuel G. Knowles
1916-1917	Jonathan S. Dodge	1982-1983	Ted R. Shaw
1917-1922	Edward T. Grua	1983-1984	AlvaLee Arnold
1922-1926	Philip F. Dodson	1984-1985	Ted R. Shaw
1926-1934	Burton A. Garlinghouse	1985-1986	Samuel G. Knowles
1934-1940	John C. Jacobs	1986-1987	Lee D. Prentiss

The Oaklawn Waiting Station, designed by Charles and Henry Greene, is on the National Register of Historic Places. The shelter was built for the convenience of nearby residents who used the Pacific Electric trolley cars. *Drawing by Vance Gerry.*

SELECTED BIBLIOGRAPHY

BOOKS, PAMPHLETS, AND ARTICLES

Angelino, Marie. "Nelbert Chouinard." *American Artist* 32 (May 1968): 28-32.

Apostol, Jane. "Horatio Nelson Rust: Abolitionist, Archaeologist, Indian Agent." *California History* 58 (1979/80): 304-315.

Apostol, Jane. "Margaret Collier Graham: First Lady of the Foothills." *Southern California Quarterly* 58 (1981): 348-373.

apRoberts, James P. "Roy Knabenshue, 1876-1960: King of the Air." *Southern California Quarterly* 54 (1972): 31-53.

Bell, Howard T. *Genesis of a Town—South Pasadena, California. A Preliminary Study of the Origin and Development of South Pasadena's Historic Business District*, 1976.

Bell, Howard T. *A Survey of Public and Private Archives in Los Angeles County Dealing with the History of South Pasadena*, 1976.

California State Library Foundation. *The Mystique of Printing: A Half Century of Books designed by Ward Ritchie*. 1984.

Carpenter, Thomas D. *Pasadena: Resort Hotels and Paradise*. Pasadena: Castle Green Times, 1984.

Cawston, Edwin, and Fox, Charles E. *Ostriches and Ostrich Farming in California*. Los Angeles: Bentley & Sutton, [1887].

Chaput, Donald. "Horatio Nelson Rust and the Agent-as-Collector Dilemma." *Southern California Quarterly* 64 (1982): 281-295.

Clark, Alta. *Stories of South Pasadena's Yesterdays*. South Pasadena: South Pasadena Unified School District, 1963.

Cleland, Robert Glass. *The Cattle on a Thousand Hills: Southern California, 1850-1880*. San Marino: The Huntington Library, 1951.

Cleland, Robert Glass. *El Molino Viejo*. Ward Ritchie Press, 1950.

Crocker, Donald W. *Within the Vale of Annandale. A Picture History of Southwestern Pasadena and Vicinity*. Pasadena, 1968.

Crump, Spencer. *Ride the Big Red Cars: How Trolleys Helped Build Southern California.* Corona del Mar: Trans-Anglo Books, 1952.

Dakin, Susanna Bryant. *A Scotch Paisano in Old Los Angeles: Hugo Reid's Life in California, 1832-1852, Derived from His Correspondence.* Berkeley: University of California Press, 1939.

Dewar, John. "As I Remember Moviemaking." *Terra* 9 (Fall 1970): 16-17.

Dumke, Glenn S. *The Boom of the Eighties in Southern California.* San Marino: Huntington Library, 1944.

Farnsworth, R. W. C. *A Southern California Paradise.* Pasadena, 1883.

Gebhard, David, and Winter, Robert. *Architecture in Los Angeles: A Compleat Guide.* Salt Lake City: Gibbs M. Smith, 1985.

Goodwin, H. Marshall, Jr. "The Arroyo Seco: From Dry Gulch to Freeway." *Southern California Quarterly* 47 (1965): 73-102.

[Hill, Laurance.] *On Old Rancho San Pascual: The Story of South Pasadena.* 1922. Reprint. [Los Angeles]: Security Pacific National Bank, 1986.

Holder, Charles Frederick. *All About Pasadena and Its Vicinity: Its Climate, Missions, Trails and Canons, Fruits, Flowers and Game.* Boston: Lee and Shepard, 1889.

Johnston, Bernice Eastman. *California's Gabrielino Indians.* Los Angeles: Southwest Museum, 1962.

Lata, Robert Anthony. *Multiple Family Dwellings in South Pasadena: A Historical Survey of Spatial Distribution and Occupant Characteristics.* Master's thesis, California State University, Los Angeles, 1976.

McCloskey, Jane. *6 Horses and 10 Head: Two Hundred Years on the Rancho San Pasqual, 1770-1970.* Pasadena: Boys' Club of Pasadena, 1971.

Netz, Joseph. "The Great Los Angeles Real Estate Boom of 1887." *Annual Publications of the Historical Society of Southern California* 10 (1915): 54-68.

Oaklawn. A Suburb De Luxe. Reprint. Pasadena: Oaklawn Press, 1978.

Page, Henry Markham. *Pasadena: Its Early Years.* Los Angeles: Lorrin L. Morrison, 1978.

Pasadena Community Book. (Ralph Arnold Edition). Pasadena: A. F. Cawston, 1955.

Peterson, Robert H. *Altadena's Golden Years.* Alhambra: Sinclair, 1976.

Pineda, Manuel, and Caswell, Perry E. *Pasadena Area History.* Pasadena: Historical Publishing Co., 1972.

Powell, Gertrude Clark. *The Quiet Side of Europe.* Los Angeles, 1959.

Powell, Lawrence Clark. *Fortune & Friendship; An Autobiography*. New York and London: R. R. Bowker, 1968.

Powell, Lawrence Clark. *From the Heartland: Profiles of People and Places of the Southwest and Beyond*. Flagstaff: Northland Press, 1976.

Raitt, Helen, and Wayne, Mary Helen, eds. *We Three Came West: A True Chronicle*. San Diego: Tofua Press, 1974.

Raymond, Arthur E. *A Gentleman of the Old School: Walter Raymond and the Raymond Hotel*. Pasadena: Pasadena Historical Society, 1982.

Raymond, Arthur E. (Interview conducted by Ruth Powell.) Pasadena: Pasadena Oral History Project, 1982.

Reid, Hiram A. *History of Pasadena*. Pasadena: Pasadena History Co., 1895.

Reid, Hugo. *The Indians of Los Angeles County*. Edited and annotated by Robert F. Heizer. Los Angeles: Southwest Museum, 1968.

Ritchie, Ward. *A Concise Account of Ward Ritchie, His Printing & His Books*. Compiled by David W. Davies. Los Angeles: Dawson's Book Shop, 1984.

Ritchie, Ward. *Printing and Publishing in Southern California*. (Interview conducted by Elizabeth I. Dixon.) Los Angeles: University of California, 1969.

Robinson, W. W. *The Indians of Los Angeles: Story of the Liquidation of a People*. Los Angeles: Glen Dawson, 1952.

Robinson, W. W. *Land in California: The Story of Mission Lands, Ranchos, Squatters, Mining Claims, Railroad Grants, Land Scrip, Homesteads*. Berkeley: University of California Press, 1948.

Robinson, W. W. "Pasadena's First Owner, As Disclosed by The Expediente for The Rancho San Pasqual." *Southern California Quarterly* 19 (1937): 132-140.

Robinson, W. W. *Ranchos Become Cities*. Pasadena: San Pasqual Press, 1939.

Robinson, W. W. "The Story of Rancho San Pasqual." *Southern California Quarterly* 37 (1955): 347-353.

Rosenberg, Betty, comp. *Checklist of the Published Writings of Lawrence Clark Powell*. Los Angeles: University of California, 1966.

Scheid, Ann. *Pasadena: Crown of the Valley. An Illustrated History*. Northridge: Windsor Publications, 1986.

Seims, Charles. *Trolley Days in Pasadena*. San Marino: Golden West Books, 1982.

Sherwood, Midge. *Days of Vintage, Years of Vision*. San Marino: Orizaba Publications, 1982.

Sorenson, Conner. "Apostle of the Cacti [Minerva Hamilton Hoyt]: The Society Matron as Environmental Activist." *Southern California Quarterly* 58 (1976): 407-430.

South Pasadena, California. Los Angeles: Baumgardt, [1905].

[South Pasadena Public Library.] *Catalogue and Finding List of the South Pasadena Library, To which is added A Short History of the Library*. [South Pasadena: John Sharp, 1897.]

SP 75. South Pasadena's Diamond Jubilee Souvenir Publication. South Pasadena: Liljenwall and Shane, 1963.

Stoney, Frank C. *South Pasadena: A Short History*. South Pasadena, 1970.

Sutton, Ernest V. *A Life Worth Living*. Pasadena: Trail's End, 1948.

Swan, Sally, ed. *The South Pasadena Public Library: A History, 1895 to 1982*. [Pasadena]: 1982.

Talking About Pasadena: Selections from Oral Histories. [Pasadena]: Pasadena Oral History Project, 1986.

Thompson, Edward Grant. *The History and Development of South Pasadena to 1917*. Master's thesis, University of Southern California, 1938.

Walker, Franklin. *A Literary History of Southern California*. Berkeley and Los Angeles: University of California, 1950.

Ward, David Allen. *A Historic Analysis of South Pasadena's Commercial and Residential Development from 1877 through 1977*. Master's thesis, California State University, Los Angeles, 1978.

Wilson, Benjamin Davis. *The Indians of Southern California in 1852: The B. D. Wilson Report and a Selection of Contemporary Comment*. San Marino: Huntington Library, 1952.

Wilson, Carol Green. *California Yankee: William R. Staats—Business Pioneer*. Claremont: Saunders Press, 1946.

Wilson, Florence Slocum. *Windows on Early California*. 1971.

Wood, John A. *Auto-Biography of Rev. J. A. Wood*. Chicago and Boston: Christian Witness, 1904.

Wood, John W. *Pasadena, California, Historical and Personal. A Complete History of the Organization of the Indiana Colony*. 1917.

Wood, Raymund. "Juan Crespí, the Man Who Named Los Angeles." *Southern California Quarterly* 53 (1971): 199-234.

Newspapers

Federated News, 1918-1921, 1924-1927.

Foothill Review, 1928-1938.

South Pasadena Bell, April 6, 1888, and September 21, 1888.

South Pasadena Courier, 1917-1924.

South Pasadena Journal, 1963-1986.

South Pasadena Record, 1908-1919.

South Pasadena Review, 1939-1986.

South Pasadenan, 1893-1908

INDEX

304

SOUTH PASADENA: A CENTENNIAL HISTORY
WAS DESIGNED BY WARD RITCHIE
TYPESET BY TYPE WORKS
PRINTED BY TYPECRAFT
AND BOUND BY
STAUFFER EDITION BINDING COMPANY